MW00933335

AROUND THE WORLD

IN 70 YEARS

MY CUBAN-AMERICAN JOURNEY

FRANCISCO "PACO" SABIN

outskirtspress
DENVER, COLORADO

The opinions expressed in this manuscript are solely the opinions of the author and do not represent the opinions or thoughts of the publisher. The author has represented and warranted full ownership and/or legal right to publish all the materials in this book.

Around the World in 70 Years
My Cuban-American Journey
All Rights Reserved.
Copyright © 2012 Francisco "Paco" Sabin
v4.0

Cover Photo © 2012 JupiterImages Corporation. All rights reserved - used with permission.

This book may not be reproduced, transmitted, or stored in whole or in part by any means, including graphic, electronic, or mechanical without the express written consent of the publisher except in the case of brief quotations embodied in critical articles and reviews.

Outskirts Press, Inc.
http://www.outskirtspress.com

ISBN: 978-1-4327-8177-4

Outskirts Press and the "OP" logo are trademarks belonging to Outskirts Press, Inc.

PRINTED IN THE UNITED STATES OF AMERICA

AROUND THE WORLD

IN 70 YEARS

A Alfred y Ofelia

Con afecto y

admiración.

Paco y Yuchy

Mayo 2014

DEDICATION

- To Lucky, my muse, first mate, and life partner
- To our children and grandchildren:
    Yvonne, Guy, Alexandra, and Isabella Claveloux
    Alina, Kurt, Sophia, and Andrew Swanson
    Frank, Minerva, Lucas, and Emma Sabin
- To our future generations: remember your heritage
- To our parents, for teaching us to overcome life's challenges and live fully
- To my half-brother Dr. Jorge Oteiza, wife Lala, and nieces Drs. Esther Oteiza and Elizabeth Oteiza-Steinberg
- To Tía Bibiana and Tío Darcio Sanmartin, who shared much of our lives
- To friends around the world, who enrich our journey

Contents

LETTER TO MY CHILDREN 1

MY BIRTH AND FAMILY 7

MEMORIES OF MY HOMES.............................. 21

HAVANA, CUBA: GOLDEN CHILDHOOD YEARS—
1940-1959 23

17 ENTRE 14 Y 16, VEDADO: 1940-1947 23

F y 15, VEDADO: 1947-1949 25

F ENTRE 13 Y 15, VEDADO: 1949-1951........................... 27

88 ENTRE 9 Y 11, AMPLIACIÓN DE ALMENDARES:
1952-1955.. 30

EDIFICIO POTIN, PASEO Y LINEA, VEDADO:
1956-1959.. 33

BOSTON, MASSACHUSETTS 53

MYLES STANDISH HALL—1959-1960 53

272 MALBOROUGH DRIVE: 1960-1961 55

857 BEACON STREET: 1961-1962 59

WILMINGTON, DELAWARE 62

MONROE PARK APARTMENTS: 1962-1968..................... 62

2506 CAYUGA ROAD, DARTMOUTH WOODS:
1968-1969.. 70

MARYLAND: 1969-1971 .... **73**

    895 AZALEA DRIVE, ROCKVILLE AND 7117
    ROSLYN AVENUE, GAITHESBURG 73

GENEVA, SWITZERLAND: 1971-1974 .... **76**

    19, CHEMİN DES CHATAIGNIERS, CHAMBESY 76

SAN JOSE, CALIFORNIA: 1974-1977 .... **87**

    7034 SHEARWATER DRIVE, ALMADEN VALLEY 87

WESTPORT, CONNECTICUT: 1977-1984 .... **92**

    13 ENO LANE 92

**SANTO DOMINGO, DOMINICAN REPUBLIC:
1984-1986** **102**

    LA TALANQUERA.. 102

GORGONZOLA, MILAN, ITALY: 1984-1986 .... **106**

    13 VIA PIEMONTE.. 106

NEW HAMPSHIRE **119**

    4 COLD SPRING ROAD, DURHAM: 1986—1996 120

    153 OLD HEDDING ROAD, MELLING GLENN,
    EPPING: 1996-PRESENT 127

**MIAMI, FLORIDA: CUBAN-AMERICAN SNOW BIRDS:
LATE 1990s TO PRESENT** **136**

TRAVEL MEMORIES **149**

UNITED STATES AND CANADA **156**

LATIN AMERICA AND THE CARIBBEAN **158**

WESTERN EUROPE **170**

EASTERN EUROPE—2010 199

ASIA AND FAR EAST 204

TURKEY—2011 210

TUNISIA, NORTH AFRICA—1972 215

PEARLS OF WISDOM 217

YESTERDAY, TODAY, TOMORROW 225

GLOSSARY.. 241

LETTER TO MY CHILDREN

Dear Yvonne, Alina and Frank:

You have repeatedly asked: "Would you please write your autobiography for us and your grandchildren? You were refugees from Cuba, are the first Americans in our family, overcame many setbacks, and have led amazing lives. Tell us also the main lessons you have learned." I have worked on my memoir intermittently for several years, and decided to finish it as I turned 70 to celebrate our 50th wedding anniversary. My main objective is to leave our family and future generations a legacy that will help them benefit from my experience.

History is one of my passions, and I would have loved to have inherited a similar document from my ancestors, particularly my paternal grandfather Don Pancho. He emigrated from Galicia in the late 19th century and made a fortune that enabled my family and me to enjoy a privileged life in the mythical pre Castro Cuba. I have also heard that every Cuban-American should write a book about their experiences, and many are in fact writing about their years in Castro's despicable jails, their escapes, impact of exile on their identity, and their rise to the top of their professions. I was fortunate to live intensely *en la Cuba de ayer*, and have priceless memories of these years of my golden childhood.

Frank Sinatra's *"That's Life"* is my favorite song, and I like to think it is an apt metaphor for my journey: *"I've been up and down and over and out; and I know one thing: Each time I found myself flat on my face, I picked myself up and got back in the race."* I have had more than my fair share of ups and downs; fortunately, the downs enabled me to appreciate and enjoy the many ups in my path. I have had a peripatetic life: I have lived in 22 homes in 13 cities in 5 countries, and have visited 40 countries. Your mother and I hope to continue traveling, sailing, and pursuing other interests as long as we live.

I arrived in America at 18 in 1959 to study at Boston University, and my family came in 1961 after losing hope that Castro would be overthrown. We left for political reasons and worked hard to regain the good life we lost. More recent arrivals only experienced hardships in Cuba, and were motivated to leave an oppressive regime and to pursue a brighter future. Many risked their lives to escape, and I have seen in amazement the crafts some used to cross the shark infested Gulf of Mexico. The Cuban diaspora deprived the island of its most educated, talented, and enterprising citizens.

After graduating from B.U. in 1962, I went to work for E. I. Du Pont de Nemours in Wilmington, Delaware. Because of my immigration status, I received only one job offer; that was all I needed to launch my corporate career in financial management. After my first day at work, I met a group of fellow Cuban-Americans that had worked for Du Pont in Cuba. Among them was your mother, Lucila Gardiner Ulmo, a beautiful refugee with a prophetic nickname: "Lucky." Cupid struck, and I gained a partner to face life's challenges and raise a family. Five months after our encounter, we tied the knot and our lives merged; we have literally sailed the oceans of the world, faced storms, enjoyed many sunrises, and are inseparable.

I got an M.B.A. at night at the University of Delaware in 1969, and soon after joined General Electric in Bethesda, Maryland, which opened opportunities to realize our dreams. The next three decades took us far away from Cuba, as we literally went around the world with G.E.: Geneva, Switzerland; San José, California; Westport, Connecticut; Milan, Italy; and Durham and Epping, New Hampshire. We are fortunate to have lived in exciting places, and believe you benefited from exceptional learning experiences which are helping you raise your own families.

In 1995, I retired at 55 under G.E.'s Special Early Retirement Option, five years earlier than when my father had his first job. I was lucky to receive a pension and medical benefits, have lots of mileage left in my odometer, and the leisure to pursue many interests. We continue to live in New Hampshire and are snowbirds in Miami, a city with the largest Cuban population after Havana. It is the ideal location to pursue our passion for all things Cuban.

In taking 70 years to go around the world, I did not set any speed records but enjoyed great adventures and met many interesting people. Frank McCourt, whose *Angela's Ashes* was the all-time bestselling autobiography, said only memoirs based on a miserable childhood are worth writing about, and critics frequently deride books on happiness. I agree that tragedy is often the source of great literature, but I emphatically disagree that misery is the only worthy subject. I believe the world has enough pain and suffering that an occasional reprieve should be welcomed.

In my memoir, I will tell you about my birth and small immediate family; reminisce about my life in each of my 22 homes; write of personal experiences from selected trips around the world; give you my pearls of wisdom; and ponder about yesterday, today, and tomorrow.

Love, Dad

Cuban Origins

(Clockwise from Top Left)

1. Paternal grandparents Don Pancho and Josefa Sabín
2. Maternal grandmother Eladia Díaz with me
3. Father Francisco and mother Esther with brother Jorge Oteiza
4. Paquito, three years old
5. Paquito, three months old
6. Don Pancho's funeral, Colón Cementery

MY BIRTH AND FAMILY

I WAS BORN on a beautiful island far away from the horrors of World War II. My immediate family was small, consisting of my parents and a half-brother. I believe Cuba was not an ordinary country, and my family was definitively not the average Pérez family. I inherited good health, boundless energy, love of adventure, and the ability to connect with strangers from my mother; I got my intellectual curiosity and eclectic range of interests from my father. My wealthy and eccentric parents doted on me: I was their *consentido, el hijo de la vejez.* My parents married late, had me in their late thirties, and raised me as an only child: I was dad's only son and my half-brother Jorge Oteiza is 14 years older.

Paquito's Birth

On September 1, 1939 Hitler's Panzer tanks backed by 1.7 million German solders invaded Poland—a key event in launching World War II. On September 27, Poland surrendered; one year and one day after, on September 28, 1940, I was born in Havana's *Clínica Miramar.* 1940 was one of the most tumultuous years in world history, as the mightiest nations were quickly preparing for all-out war. The Japanese entered Indochina, and in October the British lost 103 ships to German U-Boats. In sum, humanity was at the brink of destruction.

Where and when you are born, and who your parents are, go a long way to determine a baby's happiness. In Cuba, they say that a rich baby *nació con una cuchara de plata;* in America, they say the baby was born with a silver spoon, and I believe every country has a similar saying. At a time when millions around the world were suffering torture or dying in battle you could say that Fortune was generous with this baby, who was named Francisco José Wenceslao Sabín Hennríquez and nicknamed "Paquito."

My mother's milk was not quite grade "A" so she hired a *criandera*, a woman with big breasts and abundant milk. During my early childhood, mother overfed me as Cuban mothers tend to do to show their boundless love for their precious children. Actually, I believe a desire to overfeed family and friends are common in Mediterranean cultures. Our years in Italy were full of gastronomic marathons with our Italian friends lasting hours and consuming countless calories.

I was named Francisco after my father and grandfather. My mother gave me my second name after a Saint of her devotion and for my father's third name. Wenceslao was the Catholic Saint celebrated on the date of my birth. Sabín was, of course, my father's last name. Henríquez was my mother's maiden name, and I find it curious that mothers' names were preserved in a society dominated by a majority of chauvinist males. When I came to America, I started to drop names and finally kept my first and last; I also dropped the accent in Sabin. I kept the nickname Paquito until my father died in 1974 when I assumed his nickname: "Paco." My grandchildren call me *Abo,* an abbreviation for *abuelo* first used by our oldest granddaughter Alexandra. In our 2011 visit to Turkey, my granddaughters Alex and Izzy gave me a Turkish nickname: Ab Kabab.

We named our son Frank, as we adapted to the predominantly Anglo-Saxon culture of our adoptive country. Another three decades later, we celebrated the birth of Frank's son, who was named Lucas after I reassured the parents that I would probably survive the shock. Lucas was a popular name for boys born in 2003, and at the end my grandson was named Lucas Francisco Sabin.

But let's return to my birth. My mother was six months pregnant when she joined my father and brother Jorge in a two-week cruise aboard the *Corona*, dad's 28 foot Chris Craft he had purchased from one of Cuba's most popular comic actors: *el gallego Piñeiro*. These marine adventures may account for my innate passion for the sea and boats. The *Corona* frequently headed west, and anchored in places like Bahía Honda and Mariel, where years later Jorge attended the Navy's officers school. In 1979, it was the exit port from which 125,000 Cubans left to seek refuge in the United States; this exodus is known as the Mariel boat lift. Occasionally, they headed east and went as far as Cayo Coco off the Province of Camagüey. My father employed a *marinero* named Fermín, who had an intimate knowledge of Cuba's north coast; he was an expert navigator, mechanic, and cook. World War II brought many restrictions, and it became almost impossible to get fuel so dad sold the boat which I wish he had kept. Many years later, *Palu III,* my third boat and first cruiser, was a fiberglass version of the *Corona.*

Mother was assisted by her well-known obstetrician, Julito Ortiz Pérez. She was proud of having a beautiful baby in her late 30s, particularly since the baby was a boy and her first and only son with my dad, her second husband. Similar to many Chinese parents, she had a strong preference to give birth to a baby boy, liked to proclaim that she had three sons and no daughters, and was disappointed to eventually discover that male sperm determines a baby's sex. I have two daughters and four granddaughters, and can attest to my mother's foolishness, rooted no doubt in the historic assumption of male supremacy, which is now fading.

I was a big baby, and according to my half-brother Jorge, I weighed around nine pounds; the way my mother talked, you would have thought I was at least thirteen. According to her, visitors would say: "Esther, Paquito *parece que ya está criado,"* or the baby looks much older. She was afraid that women who wanted to kiss baby Paquito might pass on germs, so she got a gold button with the inscription *No Me Beses*—don't kiss me.

Father Paco—August 21, 1905-October 2, 1974

Dad, Francisco Maximiliano José Sabín Romero, was the only son of Francisco Sabín Tejeiro, Don Pancho, and Josefa Romero Santiesteban; both were from El Ferrol, Galicia, Spain's poor northwestern corner north of Portugal. It is known for its rough weather and stubborn hardworking people that migrated to the Americas in search of a better life. In 1986, we visited Galicia and concluded that areas of our adoptive New England have much in common in terms of the terrain and the character of the people; they both have long winters, fog, dangerous coastlines, and some of the world's best seafood.

In Cuba, *gallegos* were credited with two major creations: *alpargatas,* for the inexpensive canvas shoes they wore on arrival, and *mulatas,* for their frequent liaisons with black women which produced exceptionally beautiful women. Many owned grocery stores, were part of the national folklore, and were immortalized in a popular *cha cha cha* called *El Bodeguero.* Don Pancho came to Cuba in the late 19th century. He prospered, became a successful *bodeguero,* and invested the profits from his businesses into real estate; by the early 1930s, his annual rental income exceeded $50,000—a considerable income particularly in the middle of the world depression. Because of his success, he did not join other compatriots in *blanquear* the black population: he "imported" a well-educated *gallega,* my grandmother Josefa.

According to dad, Don Pancho attended the last *fusilamiento* to take place in the 1890s, when Cuba was still a colony of Spain. For some reason, a Spanish officer dropped his sword, a panic ensued, and he had to run for his life. The next public execution occurred in 1959 after Castro assumed power; many were shot while the crowd yelled: *"Paredón, paredón."* *Bohemia* and other Cuban magazines published many graphic photos approving these executions as justified and thoroughly documented the crimes of the Batista dictatorship. The editors of these magazines soon had to flee or were jailed. I hope the crimes of the Castro regime will be equally documented some day in the future; they will probably require an entire library, as Batista's regime lasted seven years while the Castros stole the country for fifty-three years and counting.

Like many Spaniards in Cuba, Don Pancho had a strong animosity against the United States. One reason was probably the American intervention in the war of 1898. Don Pancho would have been shocked to know that his son and grandson ended as refugees in America.

Don Pancho was an important man in Cuba and became Secretary of the *Centro Gallego*. In the best immigrant tradition, he brought a few relatives from Galicia and helped them settle in Cuba. He died in 1937 from a heart attack when my father was 32 years old; as you will note from the picture of his funeral, it was an elaborate ceremony befitting his high position.

Dad was stricken with polio when he was a young child, which left him partially handicapped for life. He was lucky to survive this terrible illness and eventually was able to walk with some difficulty. His physical limitations made it impossible to participate in sports and led to a passion for reading and intellectual interests: literature, history, art, languages, and music. I recently learned that his private tutor was a multi-lingual White Russian who probably helped develop his intellect. He had a wonderful memory, and could recite pages of poems by José Martí and Rubén Darío, two of his favorite poets. His knowledge was particularly strong in Spanish literature, and was an expert on the *Generación del 98* literary works. He was fluent in four languages, had frequent contacts with Cuba's intelligentsia, and studied law to please his father. He also earned a Ph.D. in humanities, studied in Spain and Portugal, was highly respected in Cuba's intellectual circles, and frequently gave conferences on a broad range of literary subjects.

As a young man, he had a close friend with common Galician roots: Juan Marinello, who later became President of Cuba's Communist Party. Raúl Roa, later Castro's Foreign Minister, was a close friend during his University years. Dad was very Conservative, ferociously anti-Communist, and believed that the least Government is always the best. The Spanish Civil War generated heated passions in Cuba, and General Franco was one of his heroes; he would say, "El Gallego may be short, but has big *cojones*."

Dad's library contained around 30,000 of the world's greatest books which he frequently read in their original language. Upon leaving Cuba, this library was moved at night book by book to Jorge's next-door neighbor by using a children's slide; they were afraid to attract attention with the neighborhood *chivatos*. After coming to America, he again started buying books, a large number of which I inherited and are now in my own library. Dad was a man of modest demeanor, a great sense of humor, and a stoic personal philosophy that only needed a book to be happy. Our granddaughter Sophia loves to read, always has a book in her hands, and reminds me of my father.

He faced a second personal tragedy when his mother died when he was a teenager. Perhaps as partial compensation for the two blows he endured in his youth, he inherited a fortune from *Tío* Antonio, Don Pancho's brother, who had also come from Galicia. *Tío* Antonio never married and left dad several properties worth then around $100,000, making him financially independent at a young age. Don Pancho died in 1937, and for the second time dad inherited many properties which were worth then around half a million dollars. These inheritances enabled him never to work in Cuba. Remarkably, his vast knowledge allowed dad to reinvent himself as a college professor after fleeing Cuba in 1961; I will cover these refugee experiences later.

I remember only three of dad's relatives. One was a bachelor whom I think was dad's nephew. We visited him two or three times over the years, and he offered us sherry in his humble apartment. The second was Catalina Valle Sabín, an old widow with three children; I talked to the youngest, Pepín, after fifty years. The third was another of Don Pancho's nieces who married Naval. He had been a *botero*, or jitney taxi driver. Later, he entered the construction business, made a fortune, and never changed his simple life style with one major exception: he visited Galicia every year and returned with a shipment of Spain's best preserves and cheeses. I vividly remember the delicious snacks he offered when we visited: *chorizo, jamón Serrano, lomo embutido,* and *queso manchego.*

Mother Esther—March 7, 1903—September 28, 1996

Esther Henríquez Díaz descended from an old Cuban family with roots in the Western town of Consolación del Sur, in Pinar del Río. Her mother, Eladia Díaz Armenteros, married Dr. Agustín Alvarez and had five children: Agustín, Aurelio, Emilia, Lalita and María. I only met the last two, as the others had died before I was born. Dr. Agustín died of tuberculosis, leaving Eladia to struggle to support her large family. She opened a small school with daughter Emilia who was a Pharmacist; she died of influenza in 1917. Eladia remarried, and her second husband, Agustín Henríquez, was a first cousin of her first husband. They only had one daughter, my mother Esther. Unfortunately, her father also died of tuberculosis, leaving Eladia a widow for the second time and Esther fatherlesss at eight.

Agustín Alvarez Díaz, her much older half-brother, treated mother like a loving and generous father. Agustín became a building contractor and was a close friend of Gerardo Machado. Machado was a General in Cuba's War of Independence and President from 1925 to 1933. Agustín was heavily involved in the construction of Cuba's Carretera Central, the road that traverses Cuba from east to west, and became a millionaire. Coincidentally, Lucky's grandfather Andrés Ulmo, a civil engineer, worked with Agustín on this project.

Agustín courted Margarita Skull, a divorced high society woman. In order to marry her, Agustín lobbied in Congress to pass the law that allowed divorce in Cuba for the first time. He was successful and they subsequently married. They entertained lavishly and frequently hired famous artists to perform at their parties, including the legendary singer *Bola de Nieve*. Agustín went frequently to the Union Club, a favorite meeting place for politicians and business leaders who liked to play high stakes poker. Agustín lost $100,000 in one night, a huge sum even today.

They had a son nicknamed Michín who often went frolicking with my half-brother Jorge. He eventually married Blanquita Cohen, a beauty who years earlier had been elected Miss Dominican

Republic. Rafael Leonidas Trujillo was the brutal dictator of the Dominican Republic, and his brother, nicknamed *El Negro,* wanted to force the young woman to be his mistress. Blanquita's family sent her to Cuba where Michín met her. He had a habit of marrying girls of less than virginal standards, and fell for the beautiful *Dominicana.* I remember visiting Michín and Blanquita at their small farm at El Cotorro, near the famous nightclub Sans Souci, which Agustín owned in the 1930s.

Agustín built a palace in Miramar's Primera Avenida, but he never lived there since he developed throat cancer and died in his early fifties probably caused by his heavy smoking. My parents took me to this house to roller skate; I still remember the enormous bar in the first floor and the high iron fence around the palace. This mansion was located near the biggest theater in Cuba, the *Teatro Blanquita;* the legendary Senator Alfredo Hornedo named it after his mistress, the famous artist Blanquita Amaro. As a child, I ice-skated frequently at that theater, and years later I went to see a production of Paris' Folies Bergère. I concluded that had Columbus seen such a collection of perfectly shaped bare breasts, he would not have named Cuba "the most beautiful thing human eyes ever saw." I am certain that the primitive Taíno Indians were no match for this group of French *mademoiselles.*

My mother's first husband was Ricardo Oteiza, a profligate lawyer whose family owned one of the fanciest stores in Havana, *La Galería.* It was located at Galiano and San Rafael, covered an entire block, and later became *El Encanto* after the Oteizas sold it to the Solís family. They had two boys, Jorge and Ricardito, who died at age thirteen of peritonitis after appendicitis surgery before the discovery of antibiotics. When he was stricken in 1938, they were in a cruise in the *Corona.* Ricardo never contributed to the support of his two sons. Mother divorced Ricardo under the law her half-brother Agustín had championed to marry Margarita, and he supported Esther and her two children lavishly for years. She had a chauffeured automobile, a Chinese cook, and a beach house in Baracoa. Friends gathered at this beach house, and two of her friends got in an argument and shot each other, although none were killed.

Machado stayed in power beyond his elected term and was eventually deposed. Agustín rented a house for Esther's family in El Vedado, it was ransacked, and their dog was thrown to his death from the second floor. Agustín fled to Miami with Machado and returned to Havana months later; Machado died in Miami.

A neighbor introduced my mother to my father, Paco. He was wonderstruck when he met her; she was a tall and striking woman of commanding presence who could also be a charmer. My grandfather Don Pancho also fell under my mother's spell; by this time, he suffered from Alzheimer's and wanted to disinherit his son and leave his fortune to Esther. Agustín gave Paco a warm welcome, particularly after he saw a list of the properties owned by my grandfather, and the hope that he would not have to keep supporting his half-sister and her family.

Half-Brother Jorge—1927

When mother Esther divorced, Jorge was 6 and Ricardito 8 years old. By the time Ricardito was in 5th grade and Jorge in 3rd, she enrolled them at the Jesuit *Colegio Belén* as borders. Fidel Castro was a classmate and fellow boarder for five years; his younger brother Raúl also went to *Belén* two or three years later. According to Jorge, Fidel tried hard to ingratiate himself with the Jesuit brothers, carrying basketballs and eager to help with their requests. In one occasion, Jorge did a particularly nasty trick to a teacher's automobile, and Fidel disclosed the culprit's identity; Fidel was a tattletale, *a chota,* a venial sin compared to those to come in later years.

Jorge left *Belén* at 16, and in 1943 was admitted to Cuba's Naval Academy at the now famous port of Mariel. Mother had to give a special approval because the minimum age for joining the navy was 18. Jorge passed challenging exams to be admitted; 1,253 applied for 50 openings, half as Navigators and half as Machinists. He obtained first place and chose to follow the Navigators program. At the time, World War II was raging, and the Cuban Navy was primarily involved in looking for German submarines. The cadets frequently circumnavigated the island, an experience I envy. The navy ships, small as they were, also visited ports in Mexico, Venezuela, and the Caribbean.

My brother was tall and handsome, owned a big Harley Davidson, and wore the beautiful uniform of a Navy cadet. He was involved in numerous amorous affairs. On one occasion, while riding in his motorcycle in Pinar del Rio with one of his lovers, a thunderstorm struck; he sought refuge in a relative's nearby home, claiming he had recently married. They left the next day. Mom was shocked and upset when the relative called to congratulate her for the enchanting daughter-in-law.

When he was close to graduating from the Naval Academy in 1945, Jorge decided that he no longer desired to pursue a military career and wanted to study medicine. Under these circumstances, it was almost impossible to get an honorary discharge unless you had the right *padrino*. Jorge's real *padrino* was Dr. Arturo Aballí, an old family friend and legendary pediatrician; the University of Havana's Medical School bears his name. Dr. Aballí was the physician of Batista's children; Batista was then Cuba's legally elected President, and Jorge's wish was granted. Years later, Aballí was my pediatrician; I still remember the fine lion statues in his reception room, and the small soaps he gave me as gifts.

Jorge finished three years of high school in three months, which was possible due to the fine education he had at the Naval Academy; in Cuba you could study *a la libre*, meaning one could take the required exams at one of the official *Institutos* without taking classes. He entered medical school in 1945, while Fidel was a law student at the time. They both were leaders at the *F.E.U.*, *Federación de Estudiantes Universitarios*.

F.E.U. operated as an autonomous organization akin to the Vatican: it had its own President, State Department, and University police. The merging of politics and academics proved ruinous to

Cuba, as the University—which was practically free—had too many professional students who stayed for years without even wanting to graduate. The *F.E.U.'s* President was a politically powerful man who controlled many jobs and influenced Cuban politics. This position was held by Manolo Castro (no relation to Fidel) who was popular and reelected many times. Fidel went on to plot his assassination with a close buddy, Gustavo Ortíz Fáez, to kill Manolo; they both aspired to become president but could not do so as long as Manolo was alive. They plotted to meet Manolo at a *vidriera,* in front of *El Cinecito* in Barrio Colón, a red-light district where Manolo had a girlfriend. Fidel was supposed to kill Manolo, but somehow convinced Ortíz Fáez to shoot while Fidel talked to Manolo. It befits Fidel's character that Manolo was shot in the back, *en la nuca.* Ortíz Fáez went to jail for thirty years; Fidel walked out free, was never elected *F.E.U.* President, and went on to steal the entire country. I recently met a friend of Manolo Castro's son, who told this same story that few people know.

Jorge was appointed *Pagador del Ministerio de Salubridad* by his uncle Alberto Oteiza, who became Health Minister as soon as Carlos Prío Socarrás was elected President in 1948; he was a distinguished physician and Prío's lifetime friend. Jorge developed a close relationship with the entire Prío family through his uncle. On March 10, 1952, Fulgencio Batista launched *a coup d'état* that forever disrupted Cuba's democratic process and created the climate that permitted Castro's emergence. Alberto called Jorge at 2:00 A.M. to immediately come to his home for an important favor: take Prío's immediate family to seek political asylum. They jammed into Jorge's Chevrolet: First Lady Mary Tarrero, her two daughters, Prío's sister Yeyé and husband Cotubanaba Enríquez, who was a Senator for Oriente Province. They crossed the Almendares tunnel, proceeded vía Calzada, and reached the Guatemalan embassy in El Vedado. A Miami newspaper erroneously reported that Prío's family had been taken to the embassy by Alberto's son-in-law, Alberto González Recio, who was asphyxiated in a truck taking Bay of Pigs prisoners to jail.

Jorge went on to finish medical school, practiced at several hospitals, and developed a successful private practice as an allergist. I will describe later how I benefited from Jorge's relationship with Fidel Castro and Ché Guevara.

MEMORIES OF MY HOMES

HAVANA, CUBA: GOLDEN CHILDHOOD YEARS—1940-1959

SINCE MY BIRTH, I was destined to constantly move. During my eighteen years in Havana, we traveled often and lived in five different homes, which was unusual as most Cuban families spent their entire lives in one or two houses. Three generations also frequently lived in the same house. I believe our moves primarily reflect my mother oscillating between desiring big houses with lots of servants, to wanting a simpler life with less help. I will focus on the fascinating city of my birth, memories of each of my five homes, and family tales and anecdotes of my earliest childhood.

17 ENTRE 14 Y 16, VEDADO: 1940-1947

MY FATHER OWNED a big house in *el Vedado*, a section of Havana, with a long driveway on the left, a large covered porch in the front, followed by dad's library and living room, a hall connecting many rooms, and finally a dining room and kitchen at the end. I remember that a family of mice took residence behind the library's sliding doors, and to evict them was a challenge. It had a separate house for the servants: two cleaning ladies, a cook, and a gardener. In addition, two nannies were needed to keep up with me as apparently I was a very active child; their names were Ofelia and Armantina. I vaguely remember them feeding me in the front porch and taking me to a nearby park where I could play with other toddlers while they socialized with other nannies.

A chauffeur named Celso had worked for my grandfather for many years and drove a large black Packard. In the 1930s, the Spanish Civil War generated heated emotions in Cuba; Celso ardently favored the Republic while my father strongly backed Franco.

♪♪♪♪

Our pet was a German shepherd bitch named Norca. She had a litter with seven adorable puppies. Unfortunately, my parents decided to put them all up for adoption. Norca was gentle and loved to play with me but she was protective of her territory. Once she bit a Chinese *afilador de tijeras en las nalgas,* and he started to yell insults in his native language. Scissor sharpeners were common among the many Chinese who settled in Cuba in the late 1940s fleeing Communism.

♪♪♪♪

In 1944 a major hurricane hit Havana: we lost power, lit candles, and put protective boards on windows. Most Cubans refer to this storm as the big *ciclón*, which caused great damage on the island. Most children view storms as a great adventure, and I vaguely remember having a blast during this cyclone. Lucky also remembers that this storm blew a big cage with several canaries from her backyard, and they found it later several blocks away with all the canaries still alive inside.

♪♪♪♪

The Holy Week procession at the nearby Church of El Carmelo, also called *El Derrumbe* because it was falling apart, was reminiscent of the famous Seville Holy Week festivities. Jesus' crucifix was placed in a platform and carried around the park in front of the church by four men. All Saints were covered in purple cloths until Good Friday. The ceremony took approximately one to two hours. All radio stations played only *música sacra* on most days of the Holy Week, especially on Thursday and Good Friday.

F Y 15, VEDADO: 1947-1949

This large apartment was in front of *Baldor* School's pre-kindergarten where I enrolled. I have forgotten about my classmates except for one: José Basulto, who in exile went on to head *Hermanos al Rescate*, a group of patriots that helped Cuban rafters fleeing the island; they were attacked by Castros' MIGs on February 24, 1996, shooting down and killing four pilots, and creating an international incident. Basulto's nickname was Gugú, and I remember that his nanny came to school every day with a thermos in the shape of a bear.

꩜꩜꩜

El Día de los Reyes Magos, the Three Wise King Men, came on the 6th of January, or the Epiphany. In Cuba, most children received toys from them "if they had behaved well." Since my behavior was always impeccable, I was rewarded with many gifts. I still remember some of the gifts: a music box and a beautiful red Ferrari which ran after winding it. Santa Claus, an American tradition, bypassed my home.

꩜꩜꩜

A family that lived a block away from our apartment ran a *quincalla*, a small convenience store with selected grocery items and miscellaneous goods in a large room facing the street. In the back, the enterprising owners ran a *teatrico*: they owned one of the first black and white TV sets in Cuba, a Dumont some seventeen inches wide, set up chairs and benches in the form of a homespun theater, and charged five cents admission to watch the few available programs.

I occasionally went to this *teatrico* and still remember some of the shows. Gaspar Pumarejo was a TV pioneer and the programs he produced were very popular. One of my favorite was Germán Pinelli's *El Palo Encebado* in which young couples struggled to get the prize of a furnished house if the groom was able to climb a greasy pole. Pinelli was a popular character and encouraged the grooms to climb by yelling *Arriba! Arriba!* Most of the grooms failed to reach the top. Pinelli's grandson is now a singer and member of the Miami group *"Los Tres de la Habana."*

Other popular shows were *Gabi, Fofó y Miliki,* which consisted of three excellent musicians dressed as clowns; *El Show de Dick y Biondi,* two talented Argentine comic actors that settled in Cuba; *La Corte Suprema de Trespatines y Nananina,* a funny show where a judge had to render judgment in a court; *Mamacusa Alambrito, la del alma grande y el cuerpo chiquito;* and *El Negrito Garrido y el Gallego Piñeiro.* Reruns of these legendary shows are frequently shown in Miami's Cuban TV channels and in Google.

ᴧᴧᴧ

In the summer of 1948 we went to South America; I will cover related memories later. While we were away, my grandmother Eladia moved in with one of my mother's half-sisters. Upon our return, Eladia returned to our home without the valuable jewelry she had acquired as gifts from her son Agustín. This led to a family breakup, and we had no further relations with these relatives until after we fled Cuba; some sixty years after the family rift, I again met one of my cousins, Chín, and her husband, Dr. Víctor Ubieta. In Cuba, my parents and Jorge had been close to the Ubietas.

Grandmother Eladia died in her mid 80s, in November 1948. To spare me from all the funeral arrangements, our servant Armantina offered to take me for a few days to her family's home in a small hamlet in *Pinar del Rio,* Cuba's westernmost province where the world's best tobacco is produced. This crop requires a lot of artisanal effort and is kept under a *mosquitero* to avoid insects and birds from damaging the leaves.

My mother agreed, and Armantina and I were off, boarding a train for a three-hour ride. She lived in a *bohío,* with no electricity, a *palmiche* roof, and dirt floors that were kept immaculately clean. Armantina was a black woman, and when we arrived I was surrounded by perhaps twenty *negritos* who initially looked at me with great curiosity. At first, I was somewhat apprehensive, but soon we established a friendly relation. The whole family dotted on me as if I were a prince, and let me play with an array of goats, horses, and chickens. We bathed in a river which is one of the pleasures of *guajiritos*, a word used by *Habaneros* to describe anyone living outside Havana.

I believe my mother's acceptance of Armantina's kind offer says a lot about her character; this experience was quite an adventure. It also shows less racism among most Cubans. I cannot imagine that a Southern Belle in the United States in 1948 would have ever accepted a similar offer from one of her black servants. In my lifetime, I never saw segregated bathrooms or buses, as I saw for the first time in my 1948 visit to the U.S.

My half-brother Jorge married Igdalia "Lala" Perera, shortly after my grandmother's death in December 1948, and came to live with us moving to her room. They had one daughter, Esthercita.

F ENTRE 13 Y 15, VEDADO: 1949-1951

WE MOVED TO another big house which my father rented from noted architect Morales's widow. It had two floors, many bedrooms and servant quarters, separate rooms for the laundry, and three garages. During these years, I went to Baldor's elementary school which was located one block away in a big complex of buildings facing *Avenida de los Presidentes*. My kindergarten teacher was *Señorita* Ada Sánchez, and I became very attached to her. I remember neither the names of othert teachers nor my classmates. I recall the *actos cívicos* that were held every Friday, when students of all grades were gathered to listen to the national hymn and swear allegiance to the flag.

Baldor held elaborate year-end ceremonies at the Auditorium Theater, in front of the popular restaurant *El Carmelo*. During these ceremonies, the students received many medals for their grades in each subject, including good behavior: gold for first, silver for second, and consolation medals for lesser accomplishments. I went home covered with many gold medals. In Miami, they have an annual

Cuba Nostalgia Fair where they sell many items rescued from *la Cuba de ayer*. I found a Baldor *memoria* of the late 1940s where I appeared as 1ˢᵗ in my class. They wanted $20 for the yearbook, and I decided not to buy it.

I sold soap and small trinkets to my family and servants would get upset if they refused to buy them. This convinced my parents that I was a reincarnation of my grandfather Don Pancho, and that I was destined for a brilliant future in the commercial world as an entrepreneur.

An incident during this period is a preamble to my lifelong love for adventure. Maricusita, our cook's 13-year-old granddaughter, was visiting us. I convinced her to take a trip with me. I had a few *pesos* and decided to start taking *guaguas*, as buses were called in Cuba; they are now called *camellos*. Each ride was just five *centavos*, and we went in and out of several *guaguas* and decided to go for a walk in an unknown area—the slum called *el barrio de Llega y Pón*. We were attacked by a gang and I was hit by a rock. Maricusita started yelling: "*Policía, policía, por Dios nos matan, auxilio, socorro.*" The Police came to our rescue, made us get in the patrol car, and drove us to the Police Station; they called my parents to pick us up. They were very angry, and punished me by cutting my allowance for two weeks. Poor Maricusita was sent immediately to her mother's house in *Remanganagua*.

During the afternoons, I was an avid radio listener and generally went to the kitchen to hear some of my favorite programs before dinner. They included: *Los Tres Villalobos, Leonardo Moncada, Tamacún* and *El Derecho de Nacer,* the classic Cuban soap opera about a baby abandoned at *la Beneficencia* who grew up to be a gorgeous woman, and finally married the *señorito* of the house where she worked as a domestic. These radio programs relied on the listeners' imagination and were more thrilling than the movie *Avatar* in creating action images.

⁔⁔⁔

I was 10 years old when my parents found a stray Boston terrier when they were returning from a Pro-Arte concert at the Auditorium. When an ad in the *Diario de la Marina* elicited no responses, we kept him as our pet and named him Bobby. Bobby was a perfect gentleman and was always well behaved. Eventually, we decided Bobby needed a girlfriend and accepted as a gift from Jorge's fellow medical student, Leonel Plasencia, a young Boston terrier bitch we named Patsy. Patsy immediately proceeded to corrupt Bobby and drive him to unimaginable levels of canine erotic pleasures. We soon had a litter with four beautiful puppies; we gave three away, and kept one we named Jackie. When we lived in Westport, Connecticut we bought a Boston terrier, named him Black Jack, and I will tell you more about him later.

⁔⁔⁔

My parents had two close friends who lived in a guesthouse down the block, Adolfina and her husband, *el Gallego Feal*. I visited this house frequently, particularly since the owners had an attractive daughter named *Chabela*, with whom I enjoyed playing and who was three years older. In the garden they kept a monkey, who must have been a male, as he disliked seeing me play with *Chabela*. One day I came within reach of his chain, he attacked me, and bit my leg with animal force. I left bleeding and crying, but fortunately the monkey had no rabies—he was just afflicted by a case of understandable jealousy.

One of Adolfina's brothers took me to hunt a few times near *Batabanó* in the *Ciénaga de Zapata*. We would board a boat with an outboard motor, and go in the many canals shooting at birds and *jutías* from the boat. I borrowed a caliber 22 rifle and imagined I was hunting in Africa in search of big cats.

Ignacio was our chauffer during these years. He was a pleasant man who frequently took me on adventures. We would go hunting to *La Quinta de los Molinos*. I owned several pellet air and BB rifles, also called *rifles de municiones*. Ignacio frequently brought one of his many nephews to be my playmate, and we would walk for hours to kill a few poor little birds. I also played *pelota* with his nephews who were excellent baseball players. I was always selected to be the captain; I confess that ownership of the equipment rather than athletic ability was the reason for their selection.

88 ENTRE 9 Y 11, AMPLIACIÓN DE ALMENDARES: 1952-1955

MY PARENTS BUILT this fine house and hired the Architect César Guerra, who had built Cuba's Capitol where a big diamond marks the beginning of the Carretera Central. They bought an extra lot where they planted banana and orange trees, and had chickens and a goat named *Cabrón*. Jorge and Lala built a separate house, and their property abutted our lots. The house was located near the Monte Barreto, a large space of several acres that ended in the Quinta Avenida. I frequently went hunting for birds and lizards in this area with Quimbo and his friend Pepe, the son of a taxi driver and a *lavandera*. Pepe's dad had been smashed against his car when standing outside the driver's door; to this date, I am very careful when I need to go near a car when there is traffic.

Our next-door neighbor was a few years older than me but very nice and amicable. I frequently played poker with him and his friends. You may think they wanted to take advantage of me, but I had a knack for the game and was able to keep up with my older friends.

During these years, I attended Ruston Academy, and, briefly, the Havana Military Academy where I was a student on March 10, 1952—the date when Fulgencio Batista gave the *coup d'état* that forever ended democracy in Cuba. From the Havana Military, I gained a dislike for military life and love for horses, as I started riding at the Biltmore Yacht Club during this period. *Comandante* Cosío was the riding instructor, and the horses assigned to the classes were ready by the time the school bus arrived at the *picadero*. As soon as the bus stopped, the children rushed to the barn of their favorite horse. After I gained proficiency and learned to jump, I loved to ride a horse named *Boa* which was a good jumper but had bad habits: he enjoyed standing in his two hind legs and throwing his rider to the floor if possible.

After a few months, I enrolled in the *Club Hípico Nacional (C.H.N.)*, initially located in Havana's Palatino area developed by the same *Senador* Hornedo that owned the *Teatro Blanquita*, as I previously mentioned. To get to the Club, we had to drive around a fountain popularly called *el bidet de Paulina* in reference to Cuba's First Lady during the Grau administration in the late 1940's. Aureliano Solís was the riding instructor, a retired cavalry officer who had previously specialized in *dressage* at the Miramar Riding Club. By the 1950s, he had suffered riding accidents, could not ride, and gave his riding instructions standing in the center of the rink. Solís was a lifetime bachelor, and a gentle soul afflicted by alcohol addiction, although he never showed up drunk.

C.H.N. eventually moved to the grounds of the *Feria Ganadera* in Rancho Boyeros near the José Martí airport. Once a year, mayor agricultural fairs were held on these grounds, with important cattle and show jumping events. My first horse, named *Filete,* was a mediocre jumper. In our first horse show in Tarará, we were eliminated when he refused to jump the first relatively small obstacle three times. We paid $40 a month to board the horse, a relatively insignificant amount in today's world; back then, a doctor working for a hospital made approximately $150 per month and a servant $40. After two years, we bought my second horse, *Copey,* bred by Carlos del Valle in his extensive farms near the town of Sancti Spiritus, a well preserved city from the time of the sugar trade founded in 1514.

Two close friends from the C.H.N., Eduardo y Segundo García, also owned large farms in *El Jíbaro* near Sancti Spiritus: primarily cattle, rice, and sugar cane farms covering thousands of acres. They invited me several times to visit their farms; *El Jíbaro* felt like an old west town. Horses were the main means of transportation for the *guajiros,* and they tied the horses to poles in front of the houses. We would ride for many hours from farm to farm, bathe in the rivers grabbing the tails of the horses pulling us, play in the irrigation system of the rice farms, and hunt for *jutías,* a cousin of rats that were a culinary delicacy. Their stepfather was a doctor named Lorenzo de Armas who was very nice to me; he drove a Jeep through the dirt roads connecting the farms, and often had to drive through *fanguisales* shifting into four-wheel drive to avoid getting stuck. I will never forget these adventures. The Garcías owned a big chauffeured black Cadillac, a *cola de pato* that made us feel wealthy; the tailfin era of styling started in the 1950s, the style spread worldwide: it was the golden epoch of American autodesign. General Motors designer chief, Harley Earl, is generally credited for the Cadillac tailfin, and he was inspired by the look of World War II fighter aircraft.

I participated in horse shows riding *Copey* in Sancti Spiritus and other *pueblos del interior,* as all towns outside Havana were called. I also rode the horses of other friends when they were unable to go to these events. One of these horses, named *Pelito de Oro,* had a peculiar way of breaking into a slow canter. These agricultural fairs were a good excuse to party for days, consume many *Polar* and *Hatuey* beers and mojitos, and dance with pretty *señoritas.* In one of these fairs, I dressed as Richard Lion Heart; at another, as Sancho Panza and rode a burro.

We frequently had daylong excursions. One of our favorite destinations was Rancho Luna, a famous country restaurant in a huge Cuban *bohío* where parties were frequently given, including Lucky's *quinceañera* party. It had an unforgettable chicken lemon recipe. Eulogio González was the leader of these wonderful excursions.

During my horseback riding years, I had my share of falls. The worst occurred when I was relaxing at a slow walk. My horse slipped, we stumbled, ended on the ground, and my horse's hoof grazed my head. I started to bleed profusely and was taken to the nearest emergency room. An x-ray showed that my skull was not fractured; I was very lucky.

I always enjoyed going to horse races, and in Cuba accompanied the Juelle family to the farm where they raised some of Cuba's best race horses. One of them was named *Chévere Inc,* and I saw him win races at Oriental Park, Havana's racetrack. Years ago, I read in a newspaper that the owner of a horse that ran in the Kentucky Derby was a Cuban-American named Juelle, probably a relative of my friends in Havana. Horses have been one of my lifetime passions, and will tell you later about some of my equestrian adventures after leaving Cuba.

After three years, my parents sold this house and invested the proceeds in building a rental property in a lot owned by my father in Calle Corrales, in Habana Vieja. We moved to a new apartment in Edificio Potín, in Vedado.

EDIFICIO POTIN, PASEO Y LINEA, VEDADO: 1956-1959

I LIVED MY last three years in Cuba in this well located apartment, on the seventh floor of a new building, and with wonderful ocean views. The famous restaurant Potín was located on the first floor. Fidel Castro frequently ate at this restaurant after he assumed power in 1959. I enrolled in St. George's School for the 3rd year of *bachillerato,* and had classes in the afternoon from approximately 1:30 to 6:00 P.M. Every morning at 8:30 A.M., my private teacher, Dr. Francisco Prieto, came to help me understand the mysteries of physics, chemistry, and mathematics. Dr. Prieto was a character; he was slightly obese, had a passion for watches, and wore an immaculately ironed *guayabera de hilo.* He was a professor at the *Instituto de la Habana*, and an excellent teacher.

As soon as I finished my classes, my parents and I drove to the

Habana Yacht Club (H.Y.C.) Early on during my youth I visited the yacht club frequently; during my last three years in Cuba, I went almost every morning before school classes started in the afternoon. It was a large part of my teenager years; I will describe some of the good times I had at the yacht club, including parties I attended during this time, and my last seven months in Cuba after Castro's reign started on January 1, 1959.

A Google search for the H.Y.C. provides pictures and interesting information of the place that was like a second home to me. It lists the world's oldest yacht clubs:

- The Flotilla of the Nova *is* the oldest, and was founded in Russia in 1778.
- The Narragansett Boat Club (N.B.C.) in Rhode Island, the oldest in America, was founded in 1886; in the 1970s, we frequently visited this club during our cruises aboard *Palu III*, *Dulcinea,* and *Freyja*.
- The H.Y.C. was founded in 1885, one year earlier than the N.B.C.

This search also refers to a newspaper article describing the 1928 regatta, crediting Commodore Poso, for directing them aboard a large yacht owned by the H.Y.C. According to the article, "The races were run in the outside course, laid out off the Malecón, with the start and finish in full view from shore, which for all events was lined with spectators. The hospitality of the Cubans was extraordinary. The beautiful yacht club, facing the blue waters of the Gulf of Mexico, was the headquarters of the yachtsmen." In the early 1990s, we were sailing Down East and participated in festivities planned by the Cruising Club of America at the Wooden Boat quarters in Brooklin, Maine; at the library I pulled a brochure at random, and it was the H.Y.C.'s 1928 regatta program.

In another Google entry I found the following write-up: "The H.Y.C., near the golden beaches of Marianao, once the jurisdiction of tyrants and businessmen, and artists of international renown, is today a dignified but dilapidated residence for the ghosts of pre-revolutionary Cuba. You can almost hear the sun drenched daughters of tycoons giggling by the pool, taste the fresh mint of endless pitchers of mojitos and see the world's most extravagant yachts in the harbor." I believe the writer captured some of the flavor of the good old days, but his reference to tyrants is absurd. In fact, Gerardo Machado and Fulgencio Batista were the two only dictators in Cuba's history as an independent republic before Castro. Neither of these gentlemen were H.Y.C. members; Batista repeatedly tried but failed to gain membership which had been closed for decades.

According to a H.Y.C. story, the battleship Maine's officers were at the H.Y.C. when the ship exploded in Havana Harbor on February 15, 1898 which led to the Spanish American War. On April 16, the U.S. Congress adopted the Joint Resolution for war with Spain; on April 21, U.S. President William McKinley ordered a blockade of Cuba. For years, I kept my 28-foot Sabre sloop *Dulcinea* and dinghy *Sancho Panza* in the Portland, Maine harbor; in a cliff a few hundred feet above my mooring there is a statue commemorating the Maine's explosion including part of the battleship.

Winston Churchill was among the dignitaries that visited the H.Y.C. He went to Cuba for the first time in 1895, when he was just 21. He eventually wrote that that his main purpose had been "adventure for the sake of adventure," and devoted long passages to the Cuban patriots. He reportedly credited his time in Cuba for developing a passion for fine cigars, rum, and *siestas*.

In 1946, immediately after he lost the elections and had to step down as Prime Minister, he stayed at the *Hotel Nacional* with his wife Clementine. Although he was 71, he disappeared for several hours and eventually it became known that he had escaped to enjoy the beauty of the women of Havana in an exclusive and secluded house of ill repute. Before his departure, he was invited to the Presidential Palace by Cuban President, Ramón Grau San Martín, and went to the terrace to observe a crowd that had come hoping to see him; he declared in perfect Spanish: *"Que viva la perla de las Antillas."* Just before leaving, he said: "If I did not have to meet Harry Truman, I would have stayed another month."

The fiercely passionate redheaded Maureen O'Hara, who often worked with the legendary director John Ford and actor John Wayne, was among the Hollywood stars to visit; she starred in *Our Man in Havana*. Errol Flynn, known for his swashbuckler roles and flamboyant lifestyle, once anchored his yacht *Zaca* in the harbor, and went ashore with the beautiful Italian actress Gia Scala topless. In those long gone days this sight caused quite a stir. Flynn and Gia eventually returned to Flynn's yacht to the dissapointment of the few men enjoying the scene.

On the eastern side of the H.Y.C was *La Concha*, a public beach attracting lots of working class families and bachelorettes. We frequently visited in one of the club's wooden boats, rowing over from the H.Y.C. and beaching them, which we pulled into on the sandy shore, and then went looking for girls. La Concha had a high diving platform supported by four concrete piers with a very large and tall bottle of *"Terry Malla Dorada"*, a popular brand of brandy consumed by Cubans of that era from which daring young men would dive or jump into the waters below from a height of about 20 feet.

The western neighbors of the H.Y.C. were the *Círculo Militar* from which land had been purchased for future projects; the *Casino Español*, popular primarily among Spanish merchants; and the *Club Náutico* at the end of the harbor.

The clubhouse was a fine four-floor palace; a model of the original wood building which burnt down in the 19th century was in a room at the right of the entrance. The first floor included two bars, a restaurant area, a large swimming pool built in the early 1950s, and the ladies changing quarters; the changing area for children was in a separate building. The second floor included a big ballroom and bar, and the men's quarter had a massage room, showers and lockers, several rooms and a large porch facing the ocean where we occasionally played poker. I remember getting massages from a black masseuse who used to do the same job for professional baseball players at the *Marianao (Los Tigres Amarillos* — The Yellow Tigers), one of the four winter baseball teams; the others were the *Habana (Los Leones Rojos* — The Red Lions), *Almendares (Los Alacranes Azules* — The Blue Scorpions), and *Cienfuegos (Los Elefantes Verdes* — The Green Elephants). I went to a few of these games, was a fan of *los Leones Rojos del Habana*, and saw a number of legendary *peloteros*, including Minnie Miñoso, Edmundo Amorós, Camilo Pascual, Pedro Ramos, Fermín Guerra and Jim Bunning—who went on to be a U.S. Senator. Lucky saw Ted Williams at an exhibition game.

The H.Y.C. grounds included baseball, basketball, and clay tennis courts. Perico Cardoso was the coach, and he later became a devoted member of the Communist Party. I participated in these sports without great distinction. In baseball, I played the outfield, and remember one hit that came my way; I extended my glove and somehow caught the ball to the applause of the few parents watching the game. We frequently went bowling, and the pins were set manually by young ragamuffins for tips. The building had four bowling lanes and to its side an indoor four wall squash court.

The large area in the back of the main building leading to the beach area included grounds with gardens and almond trees. This beach area was partly enclosed and protected from the open sea by two concrete docks extending like arms some two hundred feet into the ocean. During the summer months, wooden platforms were used to tie row boats for the members, and on the other side to gain access to the racing lanes and diving boards; both concrete docks (10 feet above) allowed ample room for walking and stairs allowing you to swim in the ocean surrounded by safety buoys. Delicious sandwiches, ham croquettes, and refreshments were sold at an open and roofed stand just short of the westernmost concrete dock.

I owned a small Elgin outboard bought at the Havana Sears and frequently set it up in one of the row boats, and went for long rides—when the engine cooperated. I carried a jug of gasoline and went close to shore as far as the Biltmore Yacht Club. The H.Y.C. also maintained a fleet of sailboats, called *barcos escuela*, which in the summer were moored in the harbor. They were sturdy wooden boats, excellent to learn to sail, and I often went sailing for hours. A huge houseboat was moored in front of *La Concha* in the summer, offering live music and snacks. You could swim to the houseboat from an area of shallow water, a kind of sandbar aptly named *el bajito;* more frequently, we would take a rowboat and tie it to the houseboat.

We used to go outside the club grounds in the direction to of *La Universidad de Villa Nueva*. The main purpose was to buy candy at the nearby kiosk; my favorite was a coconut concoction called *mojón de negro*. Other offerings included *pastelitos de guayaba* and *merenguitos*. I also went a few times to the greyhound racetrack located near the club, and to the nearby Coney Island inaugurated in the early 1950s. I enjoyed *la montaña Rusa, los carros locos,* and many other rides. When Coney Island opened, you had to wait your turn in a long line, but in later years its popularity faded and the park decayed rapidly.

At the H.Y.C., I frequently listened to conversations between some of dad's friends that were among Cuba's intellectual luminaries, including Jorge Mañach, José María Chacón y Calvo, and the painter Felipe Cosío del Pomar. Although I was a teenager, I had a taste for literature and the arts, and felt privileged to join these groups as a silent participant. I fondly remember the poet Gustavo Godoy, who looked like a poet, thin, tall, and with flowing hair; he played the violin and was the grandfather of my friend Alicita Godoy. I met Alicita again many years later when her husband and my father were professors at Towson State College in Maryland. Sometimes we gave Chacón a ride home to his home in *el Vedado*. He had been Cuba's highly respected cultural attaché in Madrid before the Civil War, at a time when many members of the *Generación del 98*, the famous group of Spain's literary giants, philosophers, and writers, were still very active. Chacón was descendant of one of Cuba's most aristocratic families, *los Marqueses de Casa Bayona*.

The club employed a number of *marineros* that maintained the fleet and the grounds. Jaime was one of them, and he taught generations of children to swim; he was fat, jolly, and a great *cuentista*. Tingo was another *marinero* with whom I interfaced frequently. He was a superb fisherman, accompanied me when I reserved one of the fishing boats, and had everything ready by the time I arrived. *Lancha uno* and *lancha dos* were approximately 22-foot open boats with a single inboard gas engine; the larger boat was named el *Albacora* and had a 24-foot LOA. When I wanted to go fishing, I reserved one of these boats; *Tingo* would buy or catch *carnada* (bait) by throwing a big *tarralla* (catch net). I would bring a fishing pole puchased in Miami.

I arrived at around 7:00 A.M. and went aboard. *Tingo* started the engine, untied the boat, and gave me the helm. I have never been an avid fisherman, but I have always enjoyed the ocean early in the morning with the sea breeze and sun in my face; those who have enjoyed this salty experience understand the thrill it provides, and I have always maintained my passion for the marine life. We would first do some *pesca del alto*, which involved letting the boat drift and dropping a *chambel*, or heavy wire with several fishing hooks and a heavy weight or *plomada,* to a depth of some 60 to 80 feet. *Tingo* checked the line every few minutes to see if we had caught fish; when he thought the time was right, he started to pull the line—which took a few minutes particularly if we had caught more than one fish. As the *chambel* got within a few feet you could see the fish through the crystalline water: generally, one or two big *pargos, chernas,* and occasionally a small shark.

After *Tingo* made certain that I was happy with our catch, we would start *curricaneando* (trolling), which to me was a lot more exciting. One time we went over *un pez dama*, a type of whale, and I could see the enormous animal below the hull of our relatively small boat. In two separate occasions we caught a blue marlin, and I still remember these thrilling experiences. One weighed 90 pounds and the other 110 pounds. After the marlin bit the hook and started its amazing jumping frolics at a distance, *Tingo* made certain that it was properly hooked and would not escape before passing the fishing rod to me to fight the monster—which took a major effort. Finally, he would use a *bichero (gaff)* to pull the marlin into our boat. He took great precautions to avoid being hurt as these animals have a *pico* that is like a dagger. We would then hoist the appropriate flag to show we had caught a marlin as passing yachts waived with a touch of envy. In other occasions, we caught lesser fish: a shark or a *peto,* which was prized to make *escabeche.*

Between *La Concha* and the H.Y.C. there was a *cayito,* a small key. I was around 15 years old when it was used as the location to film a commercial. Curious with the commotion going on at the *cayito,* I grabbed a rowboat and landed nearby. To my surprise, the commercial involved three gorgeous *sirenas* or mermaids: a blond *sirena,* a *mulata,* and a *China Cubana.* I was delighted to admire such feminine beauties so close to me. When I was asked to help move *la sirena mulata* my heart pounded with excitement, and I remembered a poem written by my father's friend Agustín Acosta, who was named *Poeta Nacional* by the Cuban Congress in 1955:

> *"No es delito suyo la blancura,*
> *pero que importa,*
> *si la mulata*
> *va derramando miel*
> *por la cintura."*

I do not want to ruin this beautiful ode to the Cuban *mulatas* with a literal translation. According to the poem, what does it matter that she is not white, since the *mulata,* in Celia Cruz' words, is *Azúcar.* My *cayito* experience remains as one of my youth's joyful moments. I think the commercial was about *el meneíto* you get from drinking a *Cerveza Polar* or *Hatuey: "Si no tiene meneíto, cerito,"* or perhaps it was advertising *Café Pilón: "Rico hasta el último buchito."* In admiring a beautiful woman, Cubans would say a *piropo,* something like *"Mami, que linda estás."* I believe this Cuban expression aptly applies to my three mermaids, as the three were equally beautiful.

Winters were particularly delightful. In crisp days, the sun was bright and a gentle breeze kept you cool and invigorated, the club was practically empty, and you felt as if you owned it. In a few occasions, sharks or *cazones* were detected under the docks. Sometimes a fisherman would come by to offer freshly caught *pargos, langostas,* or calamares. My mother was a customer, and prepared exquisite dishes in the evening, such as *calamares en su tinta* or *langosta enchilada.*

The yacht club closed on Mondays as part of an agreement to resolve a labor dispute in the mid-1950s; I accompanied my parents to *La Habana Vieja* on these days. My father always visited *la Librería Martí,* where he was a very good customer, and a meeting place for his intellectual friends. I think the bookstore was located in or near *Calle Muralla* where my mother shopped for fabrics at stores owned primarily by Jewish merchants.

In Cuba there were approximately 16,000 Jews. Most Cubans incorrectly called them *Polacos,* and many started their commercial lives as peddlers. Some came from Poland, a fascinating country we visited in 2010 which is predominantly Catholic. Many came from Turkey and war-torn Europe trying to escape the Nazi nightmare. There were also American Jews, Sephardic Jews who spoke Ladino, and Ashkenazic Jews who spoke Yiddish. Although there were many differences among Cuba's Jews, most of them were highly intelligent, enterprising and hard-working people who fled soon after the Revolution; this was another loss to the island of a highly desirable segment of Cuba's population who needed freedom above all, and who were forced once more to leave their new country.

We always went to *El Encanto,* in Galiano and San Rafael, which was called *la esquina del pecado* because of the beautiful women that walked by. It was Havana's equivalent to Saks Fifth Avenue. We took home a box of delicious éclairs we bought at Woolworth's *Ten Cents* store, which was a great place to shop. During these excursions, we frequently saw the legendary *Caballero de París,* a very popular street character in Havana; he was a well-educated man who suffered from psychological disorders, and became part of Cuban folklore. He was immortalized by Cuba's great singer Barbarito Diez in a *danzón*. We also occasionally ran across *Me Voy*, a black *pregonero* announcing his departure and selling memorable Cuban desserts; he walked miles carrying two big boxes of sweets that sold for a few *kilitos*.

I attended many *quinceañera* parties, from elaborate expensive affairs to simple *guateques;* I owned a tuxedo and a dinner jacket for my busy social schedule. Some were held at one of the Big Five clubs: the *H.Y.C., the Biltmore Y.C., Vedado Tennis Club, Country Club, and El Casino Español.* Parties included open bar, and entertainment by legendary artists, including Benny Moré, Celia Cruz, *La Sonora Matancera,* Fajardo *y sus Estrellas,* and *el Trío Matamoros.*

After these parties ended, we frequently went to casinos at the *Tropicana, Hotel Nacional, Capri,* or the *Riviera* to play Black-Jack, and check the action. We often made a *vaca* to pull our resources and have enough to try our luck. From there, we ventured into the Red Light districts, which was a rite of passage among upper and middle class teenagers. I remember visiting *Casa Marina, Casa Luisa, el Mambo Club* and other popular brothels; they were very democratic establishments that attracted Cuban men of all classes, in addition to American sailors. I also visited the legendary *Teatro Shanghai,* where raw burlesque shows were the main attraction, and frequently went to bed at four or five in the morning. A few times we went sailing at the H.Y.C. after a long night out.

Many of these brothels had a statue at the entrance of the most popular Saints or versions of the Virgin Mary, which in Cuba's *Santería* religion had been fused with African Gods and syncretized. *La Virgen de la Caridad del Cobre,* Cuba's patron Saint, turns into *Ochún;* she is the goddess of love, honey, and all sweet things. One of the avocations is *Yemayá,* owner of the upper levels of the Oceans. Scholars and anthropologists have studied the Afro influence on religion, which has always fascinated me. I believe *Ochún* and *Yemayá* came to my rescue more than once when I faced foul weather and pea-soup fog in my cruising adventures. *Santería* has been Cuba's predominant cult for a long time, and deeply impacted music and the arts; the practice increased in popularity after Castro came to power. As a teenager, I boarded a colorful small vessel that carried passengers for a few *centavos* to Regla during the celebration of the Virgin's day. The parties centered on *Santería* practices, including hundreds of people *arroyando* and dancing to the beat of drums in processions through the town's streets.

Celia Cruz, Cuba's greatest Afro-Cuban singer and idol, sang a tribute to alternative medicine, *El Yerberito*. The song vividly describes the many herbs this street vendor carries which will cure every conceivable illness. Cubans facing bad luck blame it to having a *mal de ojo* and go for a *despojo,* or actions by a *Santero* to get rid of bad spirits. These practices accompanied some Cubans when they moved to Miami. We went to see Celia at one of her last concerts in Miami's South Beach.

⁖⁖⁖

Antonio "Tony" Maceo was a close friend among my St. George's School classmates. We frequently studied together for exams at my apartment or at his house, and I developed a warm relationship with both of his parents. He bears the name of his famous great-grandfather, Major General Antonio Maceo y Grajales, *El Titán de Bronze,* the Bronze Titan. On October 10, 1868, Carlos Manuel de Céspedes' *Grito de Yara* started Cuba's Ten Years War against Spain; two weeks later, Maceo, together with his father and brothers, joined the war as privates and quickly rose to eventually become Major General because of his bravery and ability to outmaneuver the Spanish Army. His mother, Mariana Grajales, also joined the family in the *manigua* to support the *mambises,* as Cuban rebels were known in the 19th century; she went into history as Cuba's *madre de la patria,* mother of the nation. Maceo participated in more than 500 battles, and gained the recognition and admiration of the great Dominican strategist

Máximo Gómez. The first major war in Cuba's history ended in 1878 with the Pact of Zanjón.

Cuba's War of Independence started in 1895 with Gómez as General in Chief and Maceo as second in command. Starting from Mangos de Baragua, Maceo and Gómez led two columns and advanced more than 1,000 kilometers towards the west in 96 days. Maceo favored accepting weapons from foreign countries but opposed the U.S. intervention. On December 7, 1986, he was trying to reach Gómez near Punta Brava accompanied only by Gómez' son, Panchito, and a small escort; they were detected by a strong Spanish column which opened fire, and Maceo was hit with two shots, one in the chest and another that broke his jaw and penetrated his skull. Panchito tried to protect the body, and was shot and killed with machete strikes, leaving both bodies abandoned not knowing the identity of the fallen. Gómez, Maceo, and Martí are the three main leaders of Cuba's independence.

In Cuba's corrupt system, many with lesser credentials became wealthy *haciendo patria,* as Cubans ironically referred to politicians who benefited from their claims to their war contributions. Maceo's dad earned a living as a physician and never benefited from his illustrious name. This admirable honesty was rare in Cuba's history as a republic.

Tony's father, Dr. Antonio Maceo, was one of the three civilian leaders of the Cuban Revolutionary Council, with Drs. Manuel Antonio de Varona and José Miró Cardona. Tony was at one of the training camps directed by the C.I.A. in Central America to launch the ill-fated Bay of Pigs invasion in April 1961; a few other friends also participated. I have kept Tony's May 15, 1961 letter describing how he was reported killed in the invasion and miraculously avoided death or prison.

ノノノレ

I took private painting lessons from María Pepa Lamarque who lived near our apartment. I learned a lot of basic techniques about this art which has always been one of my passions. María Pepa graduated from Havana's prestigious San Alejandro Academy of Fine Arts, founded in 1818. The Academy was the incubator of Cuba's most famous painters including Wifredo Lam, René Portocarrero, and Amelia Peláez. One of María Pepa's paintings was for sale at a recent Cuba Nostalgia fair; the price was $4,000, and I wish I could have bought it.

I look for the work of Cuban artists in museums around the world. Miami's Art Museum recently had an excellent exhibit of Lam, Cuba's most important painter. He was born in 1902, and died in Paris in 1982. He was influenced by Picasso and Matisse, and his most famous masterpiece, *The Jungle,* which he painted in 1943, is now at New York's Museum of Modern Art (M.O.M.A.). His paintings command many zeroes at auction houses in the world's art capitals.

We also saw a particularly interesting exhibit of another important Cuban artist at the M.O.M.A.: the fascinating work of Ana Mendieta, who left Cuba in 1962 with Operation Peter Pan. She became an important figure of the "earth-body" art, used her naked body to explore and connect with Earth, and created the female silhouette using nature as both her canvas and her medium. She died from a suspicious fall from the 34th floor of her Greenwich Village apartment after an argument with her husband. Her work was influenced by her interest in *Santería* and her connection to Cuba. Her work is also exhibited at Connecticut College Art Museum, where our granddaughter Alexandra attends.

))))

On February 23, 1958, the legendary Argentine Formula One car driver José Manuel Fangio was reputedly kidnapped and released by rebels when he was preparing to participate in the Grand Prix of Havana. During the race, one of the cars driven by Polito Cifuentes went off the racecourse injuring many people. I was in an apartment building directly in front of where the accident occurred. Amazingly, you can see a video of the accident by doing a Google search under "Disaster at Cuban Grand Prix after Fangio's kidnapping."

♪♪♪

Columbus was the first European to set foot in Cuba five centuries ago. The native Taíno Indians had a habit to smoke tobacco leaves, and the newcomers were quickly seduced by this habit which over time has killed countless millions of people around the globe. I became addicted and started to enjoy a good cigar when I was fifteen. Cuba is home to the world's best cigars, and I paid 25 *centavos* for a fine *H. Upman Número Uno* that today sells for $25 or more, and the quality is not even the same. During my years in Geneva, I occasionally visited the Davidoff cigar store which sold fine Cuban cigars to magnates around the world. Years after the Revolution, Dino Davidoff started to buy the choicest cigars in the Dominican Republic, as tobacco is an artisanal production that is almost an art form; he concluded that Cuba no longer produced the best cigars. In my case, I was also a cigarette and pipe smoker. Fortunately, I finally quit 12 years ago after many unsuccessful attempts. I was the only smoker in our family, which helped me overcome my addiction but still believe that a fine cigar is one of life's great pleasures.

♪♪♪

The Revolution was gaining ground in the fall of 1958, and my parents were increasingly concerned about the security risks, with frequent bombs in Havana and Batista's police adopting increasingly harsh repressive measures. Under these circumstances, they decided to keep me away as much as possible. During a one-week school vacation, I came alone to Miami, and took a Greyhound bus to New York. It made a million stops along the way, and I swore I would never again travel by bus.

At this time of the year, the Big Apple is particularly delightful. I went to two performances at the old Metropolitan Opera House before it moved to Lincoln Center; I saw Giuseppe Verdi's *Aida* and *La Traviata*, and I gained a lifelong love for opera. I walked alone for miles in Chinatown, Broadway, Fifth Avenue, and crossed the Brooklyn Bridge. Reluctantly, I had to take the bus back.

ﮩﮩﮩ

After partying with our H.Y.C. friends on December 31, 1958, we went to sleep at Alberto Blanco's home at *Calle 14,* near *Quinta Avenida* in Miramar. At approximately 3:00 A.M. Alberto's dad got a call from Carlos Piedra, Chief Justice of Cuba's Supreme Court. He announced that Batista had fled, Cuba had no government, and suggested meeting with prominent Cuban leaders to exchange ideas. *Bohemia,* Cuba's preeminent magazine, wrongly accused this group of wanting to benefit from the circumstances. Castro instituted censorship later and confiscated *Bohemia.* On August 12, 1969 Miguel Angel Quevedo, *Bohemia's* Director, wrote a letter accepting his guilt before committing suicide; the letter lists the countless mistakes by Cubans over many years that resulted in the total disaster of Castro's Revolution.

It is impossible to find the right words to describe the excitement most Cubans felt during the first weeks of 1959. Castro's triumphantly came from *Santiago de Cuba* dressed in olive fatigues and sporting a beard. Everyone wanted to welcome the *barbudos* that had overthrown the hated dictator Batista, expected to enjoy a democratic regime, and a return to the Constitution of 1940. Everything was orchestrated for maximum effect. For example, in one of Castro's interminable speeches a pigeon flew to his shoulder and this was portrayed as an omen of love and peace. The *fusilamiento* of prominent *esbirros* of the Batista regime was welcome by most during this honeymoon period with the Revolution. Soon after, Castro's true intentions started to surface: free press was abolished; the slightest criticism was met with severe reprisals; opponents began to be jailed; President Urrutia, nicknamed *cuchara* because of his total inability to have any decision making authority, was fired; the so called Urban Reform effectively confiscated private property in the cities; and land "reform" was in process for farm lands. The Government adopted an adversarial relationship with the U.S. and increasingly aligned with the Soviet Union.

Like many thousands of Cubans, we became alarmed at the direction Castro was taking. In February, we went to Miami to sell our car which we had bought before going to Mexico in 1958 and had Florida license plates. We boarded the ferry to Key West, sold the car for $3,500, and opened a bank account with this money.

We also decided that I should apply to Boston University to start classes after I graduated from *bachillerato* from St. George's School that summer. We selected that university because we liked Boston, and someone had indicated that it had a good business school. I stand back in awe in comparing my college selection process with the major effort my children and oldest granddaughter went through to pick their colleges. Every day new developments brought increasing consternation and fear about our future; we were delighted when B.U.'s admittance letter arrived.

El Diario de la Marina, Cuba's oldest newspaper, was the first to write in opposition of the arbitrary and dictatorial measures the Government was announcing daily starting in early 1959. Distinguished journalists Francisco Ichaso and Gastón Baquero, and the Jesuit Father José Rubino wrote increasingly critical articles against the regime in a column named Vulcano. The regime instructed the newspaper union to add *coletillas* to any critical articles. This was the beginning of the end of free press in Cuba, which symbolically ended by bringing a casket of the *Diario de la Marina* down the stairs of the University of Havana in May, 1960; concurrently, the paper was intervened by the Government and ended its long and distinguished life.

࿔࿔࿔

In August 1959, after finishing *bachillerato* and just a few days before leaving for Boston, I spent a few days at Alberto Blanco's Varadero apartment. We were a large group, and some stayed at the apartment of his uncle Carlos, a career diplomat and Cuba's Ambassador to the United Nations for many years. Pedro Hernández and I borrowed

Tony Viñals' brand new yellow Corvette and tested how fast it could go at the nearby Vía Blanca. I drove first, headed for *Cárdenas,* and reached a speed of some 120 miles per hour. After fifteen minutes, we switched and Pedro took his turn at the wheel. When he was close to exceeding the speed I had reached, we heard a siren from a *caballito* as police motorcycles were called. Pedro was jailed, and took the intervention of one of his dad's friend to get his release. I will always lovingly remember Pedro's mother, Mercedes Menocal, with whom I enjoyed a warm relationship from my early childhood; she used to say: "Paquito, you are a *sibarita"* for my interest in the arts, travel, and fine things in life.

One day, I went with another friend to the Intercontinental Hotel to play Black Jack. The dealer helped us by suggesting when to draw and when to stand put, and we made a few hundred dollars—a considerable sum in those days. With the proceeds we rented an I-Zeta, an egg-like two-seat vehicle you entered through the front door. The next day we returned to the Casino in hope of making another killing; instead, we lost almost all our money and had to return the I-Zeta to recover our deposit and have some money left.

Another night someone said, "Hey, guys, lets drive to *Cárdenas* and check out the *putas."* Everyone liked the suggestion, and off we went. In retrospect, we faced serious dangers that night from driving at a high speed after having a few *mojitos;* I do not remember who the driver was, but he probably was as drunk as the rest of us. After a ride of approximately one hour we arrived at the brothel. After the living room at the entrance, some eight rooms had walls facing a long hall; the walls did not extend to the ceiling and left some two feet open. After socializing with "the girls" and enjoying a Benny Moré tune blasting in the background, somebody started yelling *"Socorro. Socorro. Llamen a los bomberos. Policía."* Apparently, a lighted cigarette butt thrown by one of my friends landed on a mattress, causing a fire. In the turmoil, we managed to escape before the arrival of the firemen and the police. The experience was sobering, and we returned to Varadero grateful to have avoided jail or death by fire.

Castro's propaganda machine portrayed the abolition of prostitution as one of the Revolution's objectives, certainly an admirable and humane goal. Unfortunately, the last half-century has made prostitution even more widespread as one of the few avenues to survive for many Cubans. Countless women now work as *jineteras* and earn a living by enticing foreign tourists of all sexual preferences. Male prostitutes were previously practically nonexistent; they are now called *pingueros* in homosexual relations, or *jineteros* in heterosexual encounters. Many of these prostitutes are professionals unable to earn a living. A few lucky ones manage to entice older men, particularly Spanish or Italian, into marriage and eternal bliss outside their tropical "paradise." We have met some of these women in Europe; from a rational viewpoint, some may prefer this escape to leave the island in creaky rafts to face likely death as a shark's meal.

As property owners, we were labeled enemies of the Revolution, called *gusanos* or vermin, and felt physically threatened. The urban "reform" announced in March effectively confiscated all private property: *nos dejaron como el gallo de Morón, sin plumas y cacarendo.* Like most Cubans, we believed in the myth that a Communist regime 90 miles from the United States would not last. With the Bay of Pigs fiasco in March 1961, John F. Kennedy reneged on his promise of air cover, and the Cubans that bravely tried to free their country were killed or imprisoned. A short time later the Russians placed nuclear weapons in Cuba. As part of the deal to avoid a nuclear holocaust—which Castro actually favored—Kennedy agreed to protect Castro from any future attempts by Cuban-Americans to free their homeland. My family lost any hope to overthrow Castro, had a clear early vision of the future, and left in 1961. Fortunately, when I was ejected from my "Garden of Eden" and arrived in the United States as a refugee, I brought some advantages with me including language skills, ambition, and energy.

I was a party animal during those golden days of my irresponsible youth and cherish my teenager hell-raising memories. Some of these experiences were dangerous, and I hope my grandchildren have better common sense. They need to understand that these were simpler by-gone days.

Very soon I replaced Havana's tropical warmth with Boston's artic winters as a penniless refugee. I moderated my frolicking and was fortunate to start my new life as a student at B.U. For years, I played the haunting anthem which poetically expresses the feeling of most Cuban-American exiles:

Cuando salí de Cuba	When I left Cuba
dejé mi vida, dejé mi amor.	I left my life, I left my love.
Cuando salí de Cuba	When I left Cuba
dejé enterrado mi corazón.	I left my broken heart burried.

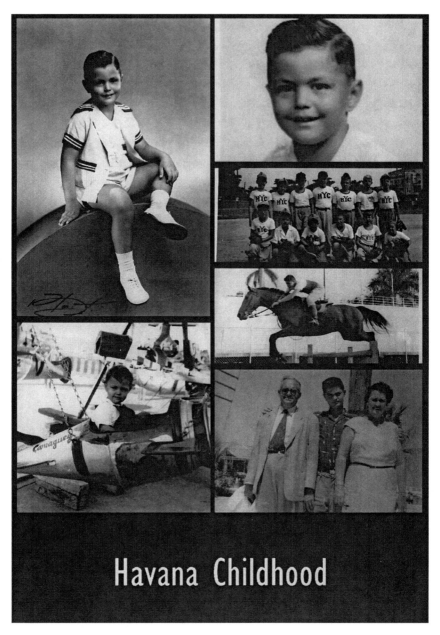

Havana Childhood

(Clockwise from Top Left)

1. Paquito, five years old, in a sailor suit
2. Paquito smiling, six years old
3. Paquito's H.Y.C. baseball team
4. Paquito jumping on his show horse *Copey*
5. Father Paco, Paquito, and mother Esther at the H.Y.C.
6. Paquito in airplane named *Camagüey* at amusement park

BOSTON, MASSACHUSETTS

MYLES STANDISH HALL—1959-1960

I ARRIVED IN Boston in August 1959 worried about the survival of my country and my family. On the other hand, striking on your own for the first time in a cosmopolitan city like Boston, which I had visited as a tourist in better times, was exhiliarating. I got a small individual room at Myles Standish Hall, Boston University's dormitory that accommodates hundreds of male students during the school year; it is located on Bay State Road, in Kenmore Square, and five blocks from the main university building. I enrolled in a course for international students, and we had intensive English classes in the morning. The students came from around the world, and I had never interacted with so many nationalities. In the afternoon, we went on field trips to the many tourist and historical sites around Boston; I remember an interesting visit to a chocolate factory.

We had plenty of free time, and we were introduced to an American institution called mixers, or dances that were intended to facilitate meeting other students. I could dance reasonably well which help me meet girls. Several kind American families also hosted the foreign students to their homes during weekends and holidays. Boston suffered from a heat wave that summer that made Havana's summer feel cool in comparison.

I stayed in my small room at the beginning of the fall semester when thousands of students descended on campus; there were two other adjoining double rooms. My other roommates were from a wide variety of backgrounds: two were at B.U. on full athletic scholarships, a Canadian ice hockey player built like a wall, and a football player from Maine; the two athletes were Catholics. The others two roommates were Jewish, a Canadian playboy from Montreal, and a Conservative Jew from New Jersey so fair that looked almost like an albino. The student from New Jersey was very religious, prayed tied up, bragged about knowing the singer Connie Francis, and invited me to his home in New York for Thanksgiving.

The whole process of registering for classes was chaotic, and I enrolled in courses required for the business administration curriculum. Since B.U. is a large city school, some freshman classes were attended by close to 100 students in large classrooms where the professor gave speeches from a podium. I took careful notes and studied hard; I was aware that I was on my own for the rest of my life and had to take advantage of the opportunity I had received.

⁂

Things in Cuba went from bad to worse. It was becoming increasingly difficult for my father to send me dollars. Fortunately, he got approval to pay for my tuition, room and board. Money for extracurricular activities was limited, but I still managed to get dates. My Cuban accent was an asset, and college students do not have to spend much to have fun. My friends were Americans, Cubans, Puerto Ricans, Colombians, Brazilians, and Venezuelans.

Christmas of 1959, was one of my life's saddest moments as my parents made me stay in Boston when almost all other students returned home. I had a feeling of loneliness and despair that I will remember as long as I live. A White Christmas is a festive experience under normal circumstances as snow enhances the season's unique atmosphere. For me, it reinforced the feeling of being far away from a home and family I thought I might never see again. At eighteen, these are strong feelings, but I understand my parents did not let me go back to Havana because of their forebodings and panic about possible consequences. As it was, I think I learned from this experience to be self-reliant, but I am happy that my grandchildren's college experience will be less dramatic. I also needed to finish college as soon as possible to start earning a living and took very heavy loads in two summers to graduate in less than three years.

272 MALBOROUGH DRIVE: 1960-1961

AFTER FINISHING SUMMER school in 1960, I flew to Miami to meet my parents for a brief vacation, and we stayed in an efficiency apartment in Miami Beach. A hurricane made us move to a hotel in downtown Miami where I met Modesto "Mitch" Maidique. We used to play Ping-Pong years earlier at Ruston Academy's old building in Vedado; he was studying Electrical Engineering at M.I.T. We renewed our friendship, and he offered me a vacant room in the apartment he shared with Robert Goldschmidt, another M.I.T. student. I also bought a one-third ownership of a 1952 Ford that still had some life left. This was the beginning of our long and close friendship.

The apartment was part of a beautiful brown stone building that many years later would reach a valuation of millions. It had a number of tenants. A gay man lived in an apartment in the basement, and had decorated it beautifully. An old lady named Mrs. Gufstatson lived in the 1st floor. We lived in the 2nd floor; another M.I.T. student and his girlfriend lived in the 3rd floor, and a Boston College Social Work Graduate student lived in the 4th floor. The building was located directly across M.I.T., near the Charles River, and some two miles from B.U.

Boston is an exciting city for a student, where you have opportunities to meet smart and attractive girls. Bob had disadvantages to find nice dates, including coming from Wichita, Kansas, definitely not a glamorous location for Bostonians. Striking out depressed Bob, and he began to play the horn to lift up his spirits. We decided to take action. He had to practice in front of a mirror on how to look at girls and walk and talk with panache, and should not disclose his place of origin. We gave him a choice: say he was from New Orleans or San Francisco. After days of practice, we walked to a mixer and identified a tall and healthy looking girl for Bob to apply our lessons. Her name was Margaretta, and turned out to be Sweden's junior shot put champion; she cured Bob from depression.

Parking was scarce in Boston even in those years, and we got a parking ticket almost every day. Once a month, one of us would go to the police to settle our account. It was cheaper to pay the fine than to pay for a legal parking place. We also had a big phone bill that had a number of errors, and I was selected to resolve the questions. I established a very cordial phone conversation with a young female telephone company employee that helped with the problems; at the end of the call, I suggested having a date. She turned out to be quite attractive, and both Mitch and Bob were impressed.

One day Bob's parents came to visit, and invited Modesto and me to Chinatown for dinner. Two days earlier our car broke down and had to be junked. On the way to the restaurant, we found out that the taxi driver was selling a 1952 Ford convertible for $100. We thought this was a godsend opportunity, gave him $50 to bind the sale, and went later in the day to pick up the car. Modesto was driving down Storrow Drive, when suddenly we noticed a clicking noise. We thought going faster might cure the problem, and sure enough, the noise disappeared. Just as we were rejoicing from being so smart, I looked to my right and saw one of our wheels, running next to us as fast as we were going. We crashed and thankfully were not injured. We left the car in Storrow Drive, called the taxi driver to come and pick up the wreck, and told him the car was a "lemon." We lost our $50 deposit.

By mid-1960, we started to worry about how to pay for my sophomore year at B.U. It was by then almost impossible to obtain approval to exchange *pesos* for dollars to pay for college. I asked B.U. to give me an invoice detailing tuition and living expenses to try to obtain Central Bank approval. My brother Jorge had become a prominent allergist well-known by Fidel Castro from their days as fellow boarders at *Colegio Belén* and student leaders at the University of Havana. After assuming power, he referred Ché Guevara, President of Cuba's Central Bank, to Jorge for the treatment of his asthma. Every time Ché came to Jorge's office, his bodyguards and security forces accompanied him and closed traffic for many blocks. Jorge asked Ché repeatedly to approve Boston University's invoice, and assured him that I could not wait to finish my studies to return to Cuba and help the Revolution. At his third request, Ché finally signed the approval for the necessary remittance; it paid most of my sophomore year's college expenses.

In early April 1961, Cuban-Americans knew that events were soon to happen that would determine Cuba's future for decades to come. Many of my friends had joined the forces that would soon unleash an invasion of the island under C.I.A. sponsorship and pressure was mounting to join the action. Finally, I wrote my parents on April 17 that I was planning to quit B.U. and join the invasion. The effort frizzled quickly when Kennedy decided against using American air power, one of the conditions to have any chance of success. I was concerned that my letter would be opened by the Castro Government in Cuba which would compromise my family. Somehow, I succeeded to have the Post Office return the letter to me. The Bay of Pigs fiasco made it clear that Cuba was lost forever; my only chance for a good life depended in completing my studies at B.U. and giving up any patriotic dreams. It also convinced my family members that they had to flee Cuba for their lives and foresaw a long and increasingly brutal regime. They actually underestimated both the duration and the cruelty of Castro's reign.

My parents and 10-year-old niece Esthercita arrived in Miami in June as refugees. They moved to the most economic efficiency they could find in South Beach's Ocean Drive, an area that then was not chic as it is today. Dad was a highly educated lawyer in Cuba, never practiced law, had no teaching record, was physically frail, and never worked a day in his life before coming to America. Under his circumstances, no career counselor would take him as a contingency client. He found a minimum wage job at a movie theater as an usher and started looking for a teaching job. He sent his resume to a teachers' clearing house and soon after received an offer to teach at Mt. Saint Scholastica College—a Catholic women's college in Atchison, Kansas.

They landed in Atchison in late August just before the start of class-es. His salary was $5,000 a year, and he was assigned an extraordinary load: over 20 hours of classes covering Spanish, French, Italian, and Portuguese, plus literature courses. I think dad was the college's en-tire Romance Language Department; he established excellent relations with the students who voted him the most esteemed professor. Although the nuns were obviously exploiting him, the job opened opportunities to procure future teaching positions in the future. He used to say that to work for Catholic nuns was a cruel and unusual punishment.

Soon after their arrival in Atchison, mom and dad bought a used Plymouth for a few hundred dollars, one of the ugliest cars Detroit ever built. My mother, who had not driven in years after she had a panic attack while driving, learned again how to drive; she became the main chauffer, and drove repeatedly cross-country. I flew from Boston to Kansas for the Christmas holidays and remember skidding on a road with a thin layer of ice. I lost control of the car and started spinning around. My parents were terrified and thought their lives would end in the Midwest.

My father received an offer in the summer of 1962 to teach at Montana State University, in Missoula, Montana. At M.S.U., he taught Spanish culture, received excellent reviews, and was offered to stay as Associate Professor. Concerns about Montana's harsh winters made him decide to move to Texas, where he accepted an offer at a Negro college, Jarvis Christian College, located in Hawkings, near Dallas. He taught there successfully for years.

He applied for a new teaching position at Towson State College, in Towson, Maryland to be closer to the family, since I was working in Wilmington and Jorge in Maryland. I picked him up at the Baltimore airport to interview with the Chairman of the Languages Department, a Spaniard with strong academic credentials. The Chairman appreci-ated dad's unique qualifications and offered him the job immediately. Dad rented the Chairman's home while he was in a sabbatical and taught at Towson State until he retired years later due to poor health. They moved to Georgia, where Jorge lived.

After my parents left in 1961, Jorge stayed in Cuba. He was carefully watched as a prominent doctor and Ché Guevara's personal physician; he had to invent a story to leave Cuba on October 8, 1961. He tried to get help from Fidel's mistress, the powerful Celia Sánchez, whom he knew well; she told him: "Jorge, *tu eres un gusano, y lo que quieres es irte.*" As a devoted revolutionary, she refused to help him get the necessary approvals. Somehow, he claimed his daughter had been take hostage, had to rescue her, and was fortunate to have been allowed to leave. He and Lala settled near Atchison, and he went to work in the emergency room of a big hospital located in St. Joseph, Missouri.

As a well-trained doctor in his early thirties, Jorge was able to get a job immediately, passed the exam that allowed foreign medical doctors to practice, later passed the Board, and completed residency requirements. He practiced in Wilmington, Delaware; Maryland, Georgia; and Lake City, Florida. Esthercita, who is also my godchild, earned her Ph. D., and went on to a career in education in Ocala, Florida. A second daughter, Elizabeth, was born in Wilmington, Delaware, and is now an ophthalmologist specialized in retina surgery in West Palm Beach, Florida. Elizabeth and her husband Seth Steinberg, a gastroenterologist, have three children; in 2009 she converted to her husband's Jewish religion.

857 BEACON STREET: 1961-1962

IN THE SUMMER of 1961, Modesto, Bob and I moved to a newer and nicer apartment at 857 Beacon Street, near Kenmore Square within walking distance to B.U. Modesto and Bob went on to very successful careers. Both obtained their Ph.D.'s at M.I.T., accumulated many patents, and became wealthy businessmen. Modesto found Analog Devices, taught at M.I.T. and Harvard Universities, and was Florida International University's President from 1986 to 2009. Bob started high technology companies and obtained many patents for his electrical inventions.

A few months before my graduation, in the spring of 1962, I started my search for my first career job. I was uncertain what professional direction to take but looked for a job in finance or international business. I went to many campus interviews and sent letters to executives attending financial management events. Students with lesser qualifications were getting multiple offers; I was not getting a single one since I was a Cuban citizen with a student visa that allowed three six-month training periods after graduation. Other foreign students were hired with the idea of returning to their countries of origin after their training was finished. International companies eagerly sought these graduates of American universities but none wanted to hire a Cuban as Castro had already expropriated their subsidiaries in the island.

I was already planning to head for New York City without a job offer when I received a letter from the E.I. Du Pont de Nemours and Company inviting me to visit Wilmington, Delaware for a day of interviews. I looked in a map where Wilmington was located, traveled by train, stayed at the Du Pont Hotel, and was interviewed by three or four managers. I had lunch at the fine Du Pont restaurant with a graduate student from Cornell University, an Employee Relations Manager, and the senior finance manager to whom I had addressed my letter. By the end of the day, I had a job offer of $500 a month, a good starting salary in 1962, and a one-year training program that involved rotational assignments in several finance departments. I still remember that day as one of the happiest in my life, as prospects of unemployment were looming. I had a good job to launch my career with a fine company.

B.U. & Cupid

(Clockwise from Top Left)
1. Paquito studying at B.U., Boston, Massachusets
2. Lucky and Paco aboard *Dulcinea*
3. Paquito landing in Havana, Cuba
4. Paquito and Lucky newlyweds, Wilmington, Delaware
5. Lucky and Paco promoting their financial workshops
6. Lucky at her Du Pont office, Wilmington, Delaware

WILMINGTON, DELAWARE

MONROE PARK APARTMENTS: 1962-1968

IN MAY, I took a train to Wilmington to start work at Du Pont. Dimitri Zafiroglu, a Greek from Cyprus who had just earned a Master's degree in Chemical Engineering from Cornell, was in the same train and also heading to work for Du Pont. We became friends and decided to get a two-bedroom apartment at Monroe Park, which had a large number of these apartments in clusters of four per building; later I found out that several Cuban-Americans lived in these apartments. After a few days at the Y.M.C.A., Dimitri and I bought some furniture and moved to our apartment; he was very tall and had to order a custom-built long bed.

I also bought my first automobile: a beautiful mid 1950s Oldsmobile 98 convertible. It was painted white and light blue, had leather seats, and every imaginable extra. I enjoyed it for a short time until it started making my life miserable. First, the previous owner received a record number of parking tickets which were mailed to me as the registered owner. Second, it had many mechanical problems, needing new brakes, transmission, and shock absorbers. I soon traded it for a white Ford Falcon, with no character and no problems, which unfortunately later on caught fire.

My first job was in Accounts Receivables. As one of some fifty clerks, I had to apply cash receipts against invoices which were in the form of I.B.M. cards. We also had to write simple letters for minor delinquencies and resolve multiple reconciliation problems. It was a big production job and a good experience for a first job.

Cupid Strikes

During my first day at work I met Ramonín Florez, a *gallego* brought to Cuba by his uncle, the owner of the famous restaurant *El Carmelo* in El Vedado; it was located across the American Dominican

Academy, Lucky's High School. Ramonín has been one of my best friends ever since and our daughter Alina's godfather.

After work, Ramonín and I walked over to the street under the crossing bridge between the Du Pont and the Nemours buildings where several Cubans met for their rides home. They had worked for Du Pont's Cuban affiliate and came to Wilmington soon after Castro confiscated the company in December 1960. Armed *milicianos* came to take possession, which was an unforgettable frightening experience. Humberto "Burt" Villa was the General Manager, who acted as godfather of Du Pont's Cuban employees; he helped them resettle and find employment with the parent company, E.I. Du Pont de Nemours, in Wilmington and in South American affiliates. Villa was a leader admired by everyone; he had been a track start during his University of Havana student days. Eventually, he moved to Venezuela where he was the General Manager for many years.

Although it was summer, I wore one of the two Brooks Brothers' dark suits I had bought to be properly attired for work; I held my big umbrella in my right hand, on a sunny day. That's how I met Lucila Gardiner Ulmo, *un pollo* soon to be my wife; her prophetic nickname was "Lucky." She claims I looked like a dork; I think I looked hot and irresistible. Lucky worked in the International Department and I in the Treasurer's Department, and I quickly conquered her heart.

We started dating immediately and frequently had lunch at Woolworth's; they had a banana split special: you popped a balloon, and paid the price written in a small piece of paper inside from 1 to 39 cents. We shared the banana split, which was the beginning of our habit to share most of our meals. I soon gave up my plans for a long and active bachelor life, and we tied the knot almost six months after our first meeting.

My father was teaching at Jarvis Christian College in Hawkins, Texas when I called to announce our fateful decision; I have kept and translated parts of the letter he wrote on November 9, 1962: "Dear Paquito, when we were starting to answer your November 3rd letter, we received your phone call and the news of your decision to marry

Lucky. We were not surprised, since we thought you were close to the most frequent and honorable of surrenders, despite your heroic resistance. We are very happy since you needed a partner like her. She is a kind woman who loves you, is smart, intelligent, and pretty. Lucky is a highly symbolic name. When we met her, we knew your surrender was going to be imminent. We hope God will give Lucky and you all the happiness you both deserve."

Before our wedding, we got two memorable and reassuring visits. First, Modesto Maidique came to visit me from Boston, met Lucky, and told me he would marry her if I changed my mind; Lucky says she would not have fallen for our good friend as she was in love with me. Second, Raúl Barreneche, Lucky's neighbor in *La Víbora*, told me: *"Paco, te llevas la crema, y espera a que conozcas a tu suegra, Zunilda."* I frequently remember these words, and how accurate they turned out to be.

Our wedding reception on November 30, 1962 cost less than $200, and was held at the Monroe Park apartment of our friends Amalia and Guilllermo Bosch; she was one of the Cuban-Americans who had worked for Du Pont in Cuba. None of our parents were in Wilmington; Bibiana, Lucky's sister, was the only relative present. We headed to an idyllic resort in the Pocono Mountains for our honeymoon, but soon after drove to the Big Apple for more excitement. We came back to our own apartment in Monroe Park where many of our friends already lived. Sister Bibiana moved with us. Our first daughter, Yvonne, was born here. At that time, I was not allowed to go to the hospital's delivery room to witness her birth.

Our wedding was dictated by our hearts and not by careful planning and analysis. Weddings of the rich and famous cost a fortune; despite our humble beginnings, we are particularly proud of the family we formed and the fifty years of marital bliss we are celebrating, despite the challenges we faced. We are still best friends, lovers, and soul mates. Almost two decades ago, she inspired me to write the following poem for her birthday—which she still keeps:

Although years keep passing
like the Lamprey River in spring,
despite a minor rebellion
here and there, now and then,
my love grows on like the grass in spring.
With beavers and snappers we share
our daily life and inspirations;
I feel it coming, I feel it coming,
new adventures are coming.
But the greatest of them all,
our loving partnership,
shall always be the greatest
adventure of them all!

Lucky's Family

Bibiana left Cuba when she was 16, and joined her older sister Lucky in Delaware; she was mistakenly flown to Wilmington, North Carolina, and had to take a second flight to Wilmington, Delaware. Bibiana started her junior year of high school at the Ursulines Academy, a Catholic school ran by nuns in town. We became like her parents.

My father-in-law, Carlos Gardiner Andricaín, was an esteemed Criminal Defense Lawyer in Havana. He studied High School in Boston and received his law degree from the University of Havana. His father Charles, born In St. Paul, Minnesotta, was an American executive with Scottish and Basque ancestors. Charles traveled widely abroad on business, and Lucky has several letters he wrote from Buenos Aires and other foreign capitals when he was courting Carlos' mother. His family was related to the wealthy Gardiners who owned Gardiner's Island in Long Island and were settlers of East Hampton. During our annual reunion of New Hampshire friends in June, we visit their impressive mausoleum in East Hampton's cementery.

Carlos' mother, América Andricaín Torres, was member of a distinguished Cuban family from Matanzas; she and her sisters were

sent as youngsters to study in the U.S. She met Charles while studying in New York, married, and became a widow two years after her
wedding. Charles died of a heart attack in his early forties. América
remarried three years later; her second husband was José Manuel
Carbonell, a noted diplomat and former president of the Cuban
Academy of Arts and Letters. As a child, he had lived in Tampa, where
his father was actively involved in Cuba's independence movement;
he personally met Cuba's Apostle José Martí. My father knew José
Manuel from Cuba's intellectual circles, and I was honored to meet
this distinguished Cuban in Miami shortly before his death.

Carlos felt threatened in the Courts for his outspoken opposition
to actions taken by the Revolution, resigned his job, and applied to
leave the country. He had to come to the U.S. through Mexico, where
he stayed with his half-sister, Lydia Carbonell Andricaín; she had married a Mexican, and settled in Mexico City. Lydia's father, José Manuel,
had been Cuba's ambassador to Mexico many years earlier. After finally getting the necessary papers, Carlos joined us in Wilmington and
moved to Philadelphia later. He worked as a translator, and with other
Cubans in a bakery; he also worked in the wine cellars of the Bellevue
Strafford Hotel when they had a scare about Legionnaires Disease.

Mothers-in-law have a fearful reputation; mine was simply the
best as Raúl had already told me. Zunilda Luisa Ulmo Oliva, Zuni
for short, was called *abuela* by her grandchildren and *nonita* by her
great-grandchildren. She had many admirers; everyone she met soon
liked and respected her. She was not a tall woman which is evidence
of the wisdom of an old French proverb: *"Le meilleur parfume se
trouve dans une petite bouteille,"* the best perfumes come in small
bottles. I like to say I won the Power Ball with Lucky and a second
lottery with Zuni.

Zuni's paternal ancestors were physicians who immigrated to
Cuba from Germany and France, and settled in Matanzas, *la Atena
de Cuba,* or Cuba's Athens. Her father, Andrés Ulmo Caraballo, was a
civil engineer loved and respected by all, and liked to dance *el danzón,* Cuba's typical beautiful dance. Her mother, Lucila Oliva y Raya,

was a schoolteacher in Matanzas, and related to the distinguished Montejo Mexican family. She died of tuberculosis in her early thirties, leaving three young children: Zuni, Andresito, and Lydia. Zuni was raised in Havana by her maternal aunt, Alicia Oliva Raya de Alfonso.

Luciana "Nena" Ulmo, Zuni's aunt, married a German agricultural engineer, Kurt Hannebeck, who was General Manager of *Henequenera Jarcia de Matanzas*. Their house was in *La Cumbre*, a hill visible from the bay; he was arrested several times during Word War II as the police thought he was signaling German submarines. Santiaguito Rey, a noted politician, repeatedly helped obtain his release.

Zuni stayed in Cuba to take care of her father Andrés, who Lucky loved as I hope and believe my grandchildren love me, while he was suffering from prostate cancer. After he died, she also left Cuba through Mexico, where she also stayed with Carlo's half-sister Lydia Carbonell while processing her papers. As soon as she arrived in Wilmington, she started looking for work to support her family, and found a job as a seamstress at one of Philadelphia's best stores, John Wanamaker's. She had never worked in Cuba and had only a basic knowledge of sewing. She was hired to make alterations at the store's *haute couture* department, where dresses sold for a minimum of several hundred dollars in the mid 1965s—equivalent to thousands in today's world. Zuni, Carlos and Bibiana immediately moved to an apartment in the City Line area of Philadelphia.

Zuni acquired sufficient language skills to communicate effectively and integrate with her coworkers, and a few became part of her extended family. She had to endure harsh winter conditions and had to take the train to work early in the morning. She was diagnosed with ovarian cancer shortly after starting to work at Wanamaker's; took only one month off for an operation and radiation treatments. These were tough times for the entire family. I will always marvel at how she recovered, returned to work, and went on to have a full and long life. Zuni's actions at that time were a miracle.

She worked for Wanamaker's for over 14 years, and, despite Union efforts, was laid off just six months before she would have qualified for a modest pension. I believe there are no words to justify this despicable action. She had to cope with Carlos when he was stricken with Alzheimer's; Zuni also suffered with her sister and brother, who stayed back in Cuba and depended on her remittances to survive. Her innate diplomatic and survival skills were formidable; I believe Zuni could tame lions if thrown in the middle of a jungle. A devout Catholic, she faced life with grace, courage, and optimism. She had a great sense of humor and was always ready for adventure; our entire family was enriched by our close and loving relationship with a truly exceptional human being. As you can tell, I admired Zuni greatly and loved her deeply.

Our parents, like many other Cubans, struggled to start anew late in life. None of the members of our family complained about their fate or expressed the slightest question about the wisdom of their decision to leave Cuba. Losing one's nationality, profession, financial means, roots, and culture are some of life's most traumatic experiences, particularly if you are in your late fifties. I marvel how our family, like so many other Cuban families, managed to successfully make this difficult transition.

♪♪♪♫

During my years in Wilmington, I had two of my life's most profound experiences, the birth of our daughters Yvonne Lourdes on April 20, 1965, and Alina Bibiana on May 18, 1968. My feelings for them are best expressed by one of my favorite old Spanish songs, entitled *Mi Niña Bonita*:

> *Yo creo que a todos los hombres*
> *les debe pasar lo mismo que cuando*
> *van a ser padres quisieran tener un niño.*
> *Luego les nace una niña*
> *sufren un decepción y después la quieren tanto*
> *que hasta cambian de opinión.*

The English translation of these lines ruins the profound impact of this song to fatherhood: a father who wishes to have a son and later loves the daughter so much. In addition to my two daughters, I have been blessed to have four beautiful granddaughters, and learned to appreciate my special loving relationship with them many years ago. We were equally fortunate when Frank Charles Andrew came along on October 22, 1973, while residing in Geneva, and with our two grandsons Andrew and Lucas. Fatherhood was a key passage in my life, and I cannot imagine my life without my family.

❧❧❧❧

Immediately after my arrival in Wilmington, I was accepted at the University of Delaware's Evening M.B.A. program. In the fall of 1962, I started driving to Newark at night to take one course which I later accelerated to two courses.

My career at Du Pont continued to progress at a steady pace, and I received several raises and promotions. I rotated to other sections and eventually was assigned to the Foreign Economic Section, where I learned about banking, foreign exchange, and international economics. One of the members of the staff was a fellow Cuban, John Finlay, a few years older than me, who had managed Ireneé Du Pont's estate in Varadero estate, in the province of Matanzas; his famous uncle, Carlos Finlay, discovered that mosquitos were what caused yellow fever during the construction of the Panama Canal.

During these years, we alternated each Sunday between driving to visit my parents in Towson and the Gardiners in Philadelphia. I had a challenging job, Graduate School, and growing family responsibilities; but Lucky and I felt it was our duty to look out for our four parents. We are proud that we always tried to help them as much as we could in their painful resettlement from a privileged life in Cuba to starting all over again with old age fast approaching. We did our share of heavy lifting in our twenties but feel our efforts have been richly rewarded and feel no regrets.

𝄢𝄢𝄢

I answered a newspaper ad for a riding instructor, and got the part-time job, which paid practically nothing but allowed me to ride for free. The owner of the stables wanted to expand my responsibilities and asked me to correct the bad habits of a horse that flipped backward when a rider tried to mount. I declined the offer, and suggested he should put an ad for a cowboy.

2506 CAYUGA ROAD, DARTMOUTH WOODS: 1968-1969

WE WERE VERY happy with the ownership of our first house which made us feel we lived in a palace. It had three bedrooms, two bathrooms, dining, living, and family rooms, a garage, and was located in a wooded lot on approximately one third of an acre. We had our second daughter, Alina, while living in this house in Wilmington.

The racetrack for trotters was near our house and, after 10:00 P.M. when entrance was half price, we could go to see the last two races. The babysitter was more expensive that the entrance. One night, when trying to read the boards showing the odds of each horse, I discovered I could not see well and needed to have prescription glasses.

𝄢𝄢𝄢

Eventually, I was transferred to the Foreign Affiliates Section where I was responsible to coordinate financial matters of selected South American affiliates. In seven years at Du Pont I had made reasonable progress, but I was ambitious and anxiously waiting to finish my M.B.A. to pursue new career opportunities. The title of my Master's thesis was "The Pound Sterling: Dilemmas of Adjustment Instruments." Dr. Lazlo Zsoldos, a Hungarian economist and a very nice human being, was my advisor and the sole reader of my work, apart from Lucky who was my typist and proofreader. He passed away at a young age, and I hope my thesis did not contribute to his premature demise. I still have thee copies in case anybody in the family develops insomnia.

In May 1969, I received my degree dressed in full academic regalia for the graduation ceremony with Yvonne watching her father's proud acceptance. Immediately, I started to look for job opportunities outside Du Pont. In August, I answered a Wall Street Journal ad from the General Electric Company looking for an International Business Specialist in their Information Services Department in Bethesda, Maryland. I interviewed for the job, indicating I wanted a 20% raise and a commitment to be transferred overseas if I performed well. Soon after, the hiring manger offered me the position, including the raise and indicating that opportunities for foreign assignments were excellent, but he could not make a commitment. The offer was good enough for me and asked that it be confirmed in writing.

I went to my Du Pont management and asked for a similar offer. They offered to include me in their bonus plan but could not promise an international position. I told them I understood but I would try my luck with General Electric. I wanted to leave in friendly terms and agreed to remain one more month before moving to Bethesda. During this month, I also obtained my U.S. citizenship at an emotional ceremony. I still get teary eyes when I hear the stirring Star Spangled Banner. A large number of my Du Pont associates gave me a farewell party with speeches predicting many accomplishments for years to come.

ﮞﮞﮞ

My seven years in Wilmington were very productive, but my greatest accomplishment was to conquer the heart of a wonderful *Cubana*. During the past half century, Lucky has greatly contributed to my happiness, so I would like to finish this section with Ignacio Piñeiro's classic ode *a las Cubanas*. It applies to many of her attributes, and cannot be adequately translated:

Las hay buenas de almas puras
otras que malas son
pero las de mi tierra
se salen del montón.

Si no subyugan sus ojos divinos
y con amor le borran
todo su pesar,
esas no son Cubanas.

La Cubana es la perla del edén,
La Cubana es bonita y baila bien.

MARYLAND: 1969-1971

895 AZALEA DRIVE, ROCKVILLE AND 7117 ROSLYN AVENUE, GAITHESBURG

FOUR LETTERS CAPTURE the essence of my first two years with G.E. in Maryland: W-O-R-K. We rented a townhouse in Rockville, approximately 30 minutes away from my office in Bethesda; although it was a nice unit, it did not compare with the house we had owned for just one year in Wilmington, Delaware. We had made some profit from the sale of our home and did not want the risk of buying a house until I gained some confidence about my job prospects. At age 29 and after 7 years with Du Pont, I thought this was the moment to realize my dreams; I wanted to freedom to look for a new job if things did not work out at G.E. This was the moment to be single-mindedly focused on my career.

G.E.'s computer time-sharing business comprised one Division with four departments. Information Services Department (I.S.D.) was responsible for sales and marketing. International Information Services Department (I.I.S.D.) was G.E.'s smallest Department, and handled international sales of computer time-sharing packages to licensees abroad; my boss, Ed Bescherer, was I.I.S.D.'s Manager-Finance. Information Networks Department (I.N.D.) was in charge of computer hardware and software; Howard Teaford, the Manager-Finance, hired me years later to work for him in the International Group, in New York. Ed was very smart and had been an auditor like almost all G.E. financial employees with management potential. He had an excellent mind for mathematics and had only two professionals and a secretary. As soon as I arrived, Ed started to test me; he gave me financial models to complete which were extremely tricky; I worked very hard and was the first to arrive at the office and the last one to leave.

Shortly after my arrival, the business was reorganized. The small department was merged with the bigger one, and my management assumed leadership of the larger business. I benefited from the reorganization and ended up doing the work my boss did before the restructuring. In addition, new technological advances dramatically changed the way we did business abroad. Computer power was now going to be transmitted through satellites which presented complex legal and financial questions. This gave me the opportunity to gain visibility with management. Within a year, I received a glowing performance appraisal and a good raise. We immediately started to look for a new house and bought one in Gaithersburg. It was very nice to own a house again.

⁓⁓⁓

Dogs have been one of my favorite friends; a few months after moving to Azalea Drive, I thought a pet would complement our family and started looking for one. From a logical viewpoint, this was the last thing we needed, as we were already spread thin with long work hours, and parenting and family responsibilities. Nevertheless, I ended up buying an adorable male Wire Hair Fox Terrier puppy with a long pedigree. We named him Bon Bon, and from the beginning he was a wonderful addition.

Bon Bon swallowed a small ball a few weeks after joining our family, and we had to rush him to a veterinary clinic to extract the round foreign object. The veterinarian and his staff examined the animal and carefully pondered alternative treatments. Finally, they concluded that the best way to keep our pet alive was to give him a powerful canine laxative. The treatment worked; when I got the bill I found out that the ball cost far more than what I had paid for him.

Bon Bon was very smart, and I enrolled him in obedience school. In the first class, the instructor emphasized that the first golden rule in obedience school was to show your pet that you are the boss. He sternly directed that we join a circle of marching dogs. As fate would have it, we found ourselves sandwiched between a Grand Dane and a Boxer. He refused to move and the instructor yelled: "Sir, please remember the golden rule. You need to establish your authority. That little dog is spoiled. Pull the leach hard!" I tried my best to follow the instructions and failed miserably. After this session, Bon Bon decided to punish me and ignored me for a whole week. He even refused to touch a juicy bone I brought him as a reward. I finally accepted his libertarian idiosyncrasies, eventually gained his pardon, and never returned to obedience school.

When we moved to Geneva, love almost killed Bon Bon; that story belongs later.

⁊⁊⁊

During the time we lived in Maryland, we continued to drive almost every weekend to visit my parents in Towson, outside Baltimore, where my dad was teaching, or to Philadelphia to visit my in-laws; they loved seeing their two granddaughters. We had become the center of our parents' lives and tried to do everything in our power to bring some sunshine to them.

Less than two years after joining G.E., my boss called me to his office; from his voice I could tell the meeting was going to be important. He said, "Frank, the Europe Area Division has an opening for a Financial Analyst in Geneva, Switzerland. I have agreed to let you interview for this job, but you should understand your odds are low as you will face strong competition from more experienced older candidates. You will be interviewed in New York by the hiring manager, Bob Overholtzer, who was the financial analyst of G.E.'s C.E.O., Reginald Jones, and is one of the company's fastest rising financial managers." We had hoped for a foreign assignment in South America in another year and had not dreamed of moving to Switzerland—it was too good to be true. We prayed to God to help me get this job.

The interview went well, and the job offer came soon after; we were elated. We also received an invitation to go house-hunting to Geneva, and afterwards to visit the European affiliates for budget and strategic reviews with the affiliates.

GENEVA, SWITZERLAND: 1971-1974

19, CHEMİN DES CHATAIGNIERS, CHAMBESY

GENEVA IS A glogal city, a financial center, and an important diplomacy center with numerous international organizations. After World War I, the city became the seat of the League of Nations. It is very attractive location because of its central location, geography, culture, and opportunities to live in the heart of Europe. It has a fascinating history, and played a key role in religious conflicts between Catholics and Prostestants. In sum, we felt we had died and gone heaven.

We arrived in Geneva on our house-hunting trip, stayed at the old and distinguished *Le Richmond Hotel*, and tasted the famous and well deserved Swiss reputation for impeccable hospitality. In our first night, as we entered the hotel's beautiful restaurant, two violinists played *La Guantamera,* Cuba's unofficial national anthem. We imagined the musicians knew we were Cuban-Americans and were playing this song just for us. We had a five-course dinner and still remember the delicious taste of the main course, a rack of lamb with puree of chestnuts. After dinner, I had a fine Havana cigar and was served coffee by a Turk with slippers that looked like Aladdin.

The next day, an elegantly dressed realtor picked us up at the hotel to show us a few possibilities for our next residence. I received the generous benefits of a Foreign Service Employee (F.S.E.). Under the housing factor, an F.S.E. paid rent and utilities amounting to only 15% of his salary, and the company paid the balance grossed up for local and U.S. taxes. In Geneva housing was stratospheric, and the F.S.E. had a built-in incentive to get the best and most expensive since effective the company was underwriting the rent.

After looking at several properties, we found a lovely chalet in Chambésy, an attractive small town a few kilometers from Geneva in the hills surrounding Lac Leman. It was close to the United Nations; the famous Rothchild family owned a mansion in the town. We had scenic views of Mont Blanc from our front porch and the Jura

Mountains from the back garden. Our *cave des vins* or wine cellar, an absolute necessity for any *maison* in the neighborhood, was bigger than our bedroom; it had a pebble floor to maintain the precise humidity of the wines. The kitchen and the refrigerator were very small in proportion to the rest of the house. The lease was several pages long, and listed every minute item, including every key and each little hole in every wall throughout all the rooms of the house.

We enrolled Yvonne in 1st grade at *le Lycée des Nations*, an English school in *Versoix*, and Alina at the United Nations kindergarten; she later also attended the *Lycée*. G.E. reimbursed expenses for these expensive private schools. I also received a cost of living allowance; a location premium for the hardships of living in Geneva and being deprived of peanut butter; and reimbursement for airfare to return once a year to our home base. When I accepted this job, the U.S. was still on the international monetary system established after the Second World War in Bretton Woods, New Hampshire, close to our present home. Under this system, the Federal Reserve bought and sold an ounce of gold for $35, and you got 4.32 Swiss Francs for a U.S. Dollar; today, the price of gold is close to $2,000 an ounce, and one dollar will not get you even one Swiss Franc. These factors enabled us to afford a good life during our three years in Switzerland.

Lucky returned to Gaithesburg after having accomplished the mission of her visit, and then I joined the Vice President and his staff for my first round of budget and strategic reviews. In 1971, Geneva was the headquarters of G.E.'s Area Division Europe (A.D.E.), where the Vice President and General Manager and his small staff lived; the General Managers of the International Group's affiliates also reported to the V.P. A corporate officer of a major American corporation is akin to a baron, and his staff is responsible to ensure everything goes without the slightest glitch.

Our host in Milan was Paolo Fresco, C.E.O. of the Italian affiliate Cogenel, and years later G.E.'s Vice Chairman; he looked like the Italian movie idol Marcelo Mastroiani, and visited Geneva frequently dressed in a fur coat. The business reviews entailed considerable work and went on the whole day; elaborate receptions were hosted for the group in the evening. I still remember that after the first day of meetings they reserved a private salon at *Savini's,* a fancy establishment in the *Gallería Vittorio Emmanuelle.* I suspect that one of my ancestors was *Signore Savini,* who enjoyed *la buona cucina Milanesa.* From Milan, we went to affiliate reviews in Madrid, Bilbao, and Lisbon in similar splendor.

I had to work hard and under pressure, but we enjoyed a significant improvement in our living standard; when I left Cuba in 1959, I would have never guessed that my future was going to be this bright. We were starting a new and exciting chapter in our lives.

We established friendly relations with all the neighbors, and gained fluency in French quickly. They were primarily Swiss professionals, a few foreign diplomats, and two English couples with children. We became close friends with the McNeills, a family from California with seven children that had lived in Europe for many years. Our next doors, the Gowens; we still visit them every time we are in Geneva; Bud became a naturalized Swiss citizen, married Mima, a charming Italian; he learned how to speak only rudimentary French despite having an important job and lived in Geneva for half a century. It reminds us of Cuban-Americans acquaintances in Miami that do not speak English despite having started significant businesses.

A few days after we moved to our house, Lucky found a suspicious looking hole in the back door. She asked Mima if she knew anything about it, and she confirmed our concerns that the house had been broken in, but did not want to scare us. We were very surprised, since burglaries are exceptional in Switzerland.

Soon after our arrival in Geneva in 1971, I traveled to Stuggart, Germany to get our new Mercedes Benz 220 D sedan which I had ordered through a dealer in Maryland for only $3,500. It was pale yellow, with tan leather seats. I felt I was in cloud nine driving my own Mercedes in Switzerland 12 years after leaving Cuba as a penniless refugee. This was another of my life's happiest moments, and I felt I had returned to a privileged life on my own efforts and good fortune. Only later, I discovered two flaws of my magnificent new machine. A diesel engine was too heavy and slow for the mountainous Alps and even the tiniest cars passed us with impunity. It also had manual shift which was new to Lucky; in learning, she strained the car's transmission and my nervous system. She drove me to pick up the bus at a nearby station; in the summer, I drove a bicycle to work which I recently donated to our church's white elephant sale.

We will never forget the first time we went to Gruyére, the hometown of the delicious Swiss cheese. We were driving uphill in the incomparable Swiss countryside when we had to wait for a large herd of cows to pass across the country road. We had never seen such beautiful and well cared animals, with black and white colors and enormous *oeuvres*. The best part was the heavenly ding-dong of the huge bells that hung from their necks echoing in the valley; the head cow wore the biggest bell. After they crossed in front of us, we headed for the location where the cheese is made and stored. Cheese is one of my life passions, and I love visiting artisanal cheese manufacturing establishments, particularly in Switzerland, France, Italy, and Holland. I love the fragrance of a carefully aged cheese.

♪♪♪

For most people that live around the Alps, downhill skiing is part of life during the winter. They begin skiing when they are toddlers, and continue to ski all their lives until their old age. When we moved to Geneva, I was impatient to try skiing and rented skis for Yvonne and me for the season. After the first snow storm, I headed for the nearby Jura Mountains. The ski lifts were still not operating as it was early in the season and there was not enough snow. I could not wait to take classes or wait for adequate conditions, jumped on my skis, set them in parallel, and went downhill without knowing even the basic snow plow technique. I was gaining more and more speed without being able to stop. I fell a few seconds later; fortunately, I did not break an arm or a leg.

Our first visit to Zermatt could never be duplicated. It had been snowing for days, and conditions were perfect. We parked our Mercedes a few kilometers away and boarded the train for the famous resort that allows no cars. Zermatt looked like a place out of a fairy tale, with snow covering the quaint chalets and fountains, horse carriages carrying tourists around, and bells ringing. I arranged to be accompanied by a ski instructor, and as we were going up the mountain, we could see a herd of antelopes in the distance. We skied all the way to Italy and back, had lots of *vin chaud*, and returned at the end of the day exhausted and exhiliarated. Yvonne and Alina took ski lessons. Unfortunately, Lucky did not ski; she was caring for Alina who was too young to ski, and for Frank as a toddler.

Yvonne and I frequently skied together, and she was able to keep up with me after taking just a few lessons. Ski slopes in France were frequently not clearly marked, and you had to be careful. On one occasion, we took the wrong turn and got lost. After a few minutes, we were not able to find the right path to return to the main slopes and had to go down the steep hill with many rocks and crevices. As time went by, Lucky started to get worried when we did not return on time to the base. As the lifts started to close, she alerted the attendants; they were getting ready to send a rescue team when Yvonne and I showed up exhausted with scratches and blood in our faces.

In another ski memory, I tore a ligament in my right leg in France's Jura Mountains. It forced me to fly for two months in a cast, which was very uncomfortable especially in long flights. At the time, Lucky was pregnant with our son Frank; she had to help me get dressed, and drive me around.

Monsieur Pierre Pará was our French language instructor. He emphasized that we should speak Parisian French and not Genevoise French which he deplored. He was a lifelong bachelor, tall and shy, and we became good friends. I went skiing with Pierre to nearby resorts in France, which were cheaper than in Switzerland and just as challenging; he was a fine skier, and he had to slow down so I could keep up with him. Thanks to his French lessons, we were able to communicate effectively very soon, but the children learned even faster with their Swiss playmates. Lucky practiced her French daily with neighbors and at the markets, while I spoke only English at work.

We made two life-long friends in Geneva, Sam and Barbara Egbert. Sam was the Division's Communications Director, had worked with Bull G.E. in Paris, and is an avid skier to this date. Barbara studied at the *Cordon Bleu* Cooking School in Paris, is a talented chef, and wrote a French cookbook. Once a week, Barbara gave a cooking class to the wives of G.E.'s other expatriates. She planned the menu to include multiple courses, including fabulous desserts. Lucky loved spending almost the whole day cooking and eating in their home in the border with France near *Divonne les Bains*.

The Egberts love cats and had several of them. They started to disappear one by one. After they lost the third cat, they inquired with their neighbor if they had seen them, and were shocked to learn that the French farmers across the Swiss border considered cat meat a rare delicacy. In fact, there is an old Spanish proverb saying *"Cuidado no te den gato por liebre."* When we eat rabbit, we always wonder whether we are actually having cat. In Switzerland, we accompanied the Egberts in many ski and culinary adventures. We still visit them occasionally at their White Mountains chalet and at their Maine summer home.

꒰꒰꒰ꋲ

Occasionally, I went to the Casino at *Divonne les Bains* where I enjoyed watching the action and playing Black Jack. At the time, this was the biggest Casino in France and competed with the more famous Monte Carlo Casino. One evening, I saw an older man placing enormous bets on each roulette round. The other gamblers placed their bets first, and finally the croupier placed the bets on behalf of this man—stacks of big rectangular each worth thousands of French Francs on many numbers. I was told he was a member of the famous Agnellis, owners of the Italian automobile company FIAT. He played so many numbers that he would hit the winning number frequently, but I believe that overall he was losing a fortune.

꩜꩜꩜

Our pet Bon Bon almost died for love in Geneva, which shows how important it is to keep a cool head in matters of the heart. An enticing bitch lived across the street, and Bon Bon looked at her admiringly from a distance. When she got in heat, he dug a tunnel under the two fences that separated the two houses. Unfortunately, the bitch had also attracted a big and ferocious Boxer that did not appreciate competition, and proceeded to mercilessly bit Bon Bon. A neighbor frantically yelled for Lucky: *"Madame, madame, votre chien es prochain de la mort!"* —-Lady, lady, your dog is being killed! Lucky grabbed a toy rifle she found in the garage and went on to bang the boxer on the head until he let go of our pet. Thank God, he did not attack Lucky. A neighbor took her and Bon Bon to a veterinary clinic to be sewed up, and he had to be fed intravenously for a few days. I think the Swiss love dogs as much as they love their children, and they typically behave much better than little brats—especially in restaurants. The incident caused consternation in the neighborhood, and the police came several times to ensure the owner of the attacking beast paid all expenses. They even suggested asking compensation for pain and suffering which we of course declined. Bon Bon eventually recovered and years later moved with us to California.

꩜꩜꩜

My parents came to visit us in the summer of 1972, during my father's summer vacation from his teaching job at Towson State College, Maryland. It was an extraordinary event for them to visit us in Geneva after years of exile and hardship in America. They went to Madrid and Paris before visiting us.

Lucky took my mom sightseeing and later went shopping downtown. They were admiring some jewelry and decided to go inside the store. When it was time to leave, Lucky asked my mother to get Alina. To their surprise, Alina was nowhere to be found. My mother started to have a panic attack, and the owner had to sit her down and give her a tranquilizer with water. She was gasping for air; Lucky almost fainted; the owner phoned the police. Meantime, Lucky started to imagine that Alina had been abducted or involved in an accident in the heavy downtown traffic. Lucky went to the nearby police station, was amazed to find Alina at age three sitting on a desk, speaking in fluent French, and telling the police her name, address, and phone number. The police escorted Alina and Lucky back to the jewelry store where my mother was still in a state of shock. Lucky swore that she would never get distracted and let go of Alina's hand in the future.

⁘⁘⁘

Lucky went to the doctor's office thinking she had a urinary track infection; the diagnosis was unexpected: "Surprise, madame, in Switzerland your malady is called pregnancy. You will return to America with a Swiss souvenir." She came immediately to my office to tell me the news; we were both very excited. My office was situated across the Rhone River with a superb view of the Lake Leman.

Our son, Frank Charles Andrew Sabin, was born on October 22, 1973, at the Clinic *Bois Gentil*, where Sophia Loren also delivered her children. Only the doctor and a midwife were in the delivery room; at Lucky's insistence, I was dragged into the scene for the second time in my life (I almost fainted when Alina was born), but this time there was no preparation as it is usually in the U.S. Swiss clinics ensure that fathers share this memorable experience with little fanfare. I didn't wear any green hygienic gown, which I had to wear in Alina's delivery room. The nurse gave Lucky the baby immediately after birth and walked with him in her arms to her room; she was not allowed to breast feed him for three days, which did not make sense, and stayed one week in the clinic. We repeatedly flew with baby Frank across the ocean which was thankfully a lot simpler back then. When he was only three-months old, the stewardess hung a crib from the ceiling of the airplane; we can't imagine that happening under current safety regulations.

٪٪٪٪

In early 1974, my boss enrolled me in G.E.'s famous institute in Crotonville, New York, for four weeks of intensive management training to prepare me for promotional opportunities, since he had ranked me as the only high potential employee in his staff. Because of the distance, I was not able to visit my family back in Geneva during all of this time. We kept the letters Yvonne and Alina wrote during my absence:

Yvonne, age nine: "Dear Daddy: I miss you a lot. Hurry home. I learned the times in one day. We are going to have a vaccination on Monday. We made two rag dolls. Frank found his feet. He is trying to eat them. He is very cute and big. Frank tried to bite Bon Bon. Carolina slept over on Friday night. From your lovable daughter. I love you. Love, Yvonne."

Alina, age six: "Dear Daddy: I like to go with you on trips. Please come home soon. I miss you a lot. Love, Alina."

٪٪٪٪

In my three years as E.B.D.'s Financial Analyst, I had the exceptional opportunity to have close exposure to three G.E. Vice-Presidents, a very high turnover of officers; they were Marshall Bartlett, Chris Kastner, and Dick Foxen. Intelligence was one trait they shared but each was totally different.

Marshall was a classy intellectual who enjoyed discussing a wide range of subjects with his staff of equally brainy people. One of my favorites was Bill Barron, the Legal Counsel; he was an excellent skier and had been a lawyer with the U.S. Legal Corps at the Nuremberg Trials after World War II. For lunch, I frequently joined Marshall and his staff for a leisurely repast; *les Armures*, a few blocks from the office, was one of the favorites. I developed a taste for *moules mariniere*, or one of their Swiss specialties like *fondue* or *raclette*, and washed them with *Fandan*, a tasty Swiss white wine. Many years later, we were having dinner at this restaurant, and, according to Lucky the famous Greek movie star Melina Mercouri flirted with me; her 1960 movie *Never on Sunday* had been an international sensation. She was a famous Greek actress, singer and politician.

Kastner was the second Division head. He was a brilliant operating manager who had returned to G.E. after running into problems years before with antitrust issues that temporarily derailed his meteoric corporate career. He had a talent to inspire and put everyone at ease and to quickly go to the heart of a business problem. He was the most impressive operating manager I met in my career.

Foxen lived in Brussels, and was intent in moving E.B.D. to that city. For months, he would fly back and forth to Geneva, where he conducted his business meetings. One rainy afternoon, I noticed the meetings were extending close to Foxen's flight time; knowing taxis were hard to get under these conditions, I suggested Lucky could pick us up at a bus stop, and we would then drive him to the airport. My suggestion was summarily dismissed, and at the last minute Foxen's secretary failed to get a taxi, as I had predicted. Lucky had to get into action and somehow get a sitter. I decided that the only way we might make Mr. Foxen's flight was to take a bus to a station in direction to the airport where Lucky would pick us up. I tried to punch two bus tickets in a machine downstairs from our office, but the machine was broken and a bus was approaching. We had to get in without paid tickets, and I prayed an inspector would not show up, fine us, and make Mr. Foxen miss his precious Friday flight to his Brussels home. My office associates thought the incident was hilarious; I failed to appreciate the humor.

G.E. had an unwritten rule that to stay in a fast career track you needed a promotion at least every three years. In addition, you were expected to move to wherever the best job opportunity would open up. I had joined G.E. with the expectation of expatriate assignments if I performed and had been lucky to get the ideal job in the ideal location after just two years. Although we were enjoying every day of our lives in Europe, we became increasingly aware of possible negative consequences on our children's development of moving from country to country every three years. We wanted our children to have feelings of nationality and belonging, and we had seen that children of permanent expatriates frequently struggled with identity issues. Since both Lucky and I were born and raised in Cuba, we were particularly concerned. In addition, competition for jobs at my relatively high level was intense, and internal candidates within a G.E. business had an advantage; it would have been extremely difficult to get a job back in the U.S. if we stayed in Europe for one or two more assignments.

Under these circumstances, I informed my management that we needed to return to the United States and would move to whatever location was necessary to get the best possible job. As luck and fate would have while attending a one month management training program in Crotonville, I was informed that G.E.'s International Nuclear Operation in San Jose, California had an opening for a Manager, Operations Planning and Analysis. I flew to San Jose, was offered the job, and we started planning for our move shortly after. We waved good bye to our European life style, started packing for our next intercontinental move, and said "California, here we come." During our three years in Switzerland, I traveled extensively on business and pleasure, and I cover our favorite memories of trips outside Switzerland later.

SAN JOSE, CALIFORNIA: 1974-1977

7034 SHEARWATER DRIVE, ALMADEN VALLEY

EVEN WITH THE major promotion I received, we had a difficult adjustment in re-entry. We lost our Foreign Service Employee allowances; we replaced our beautiful Mercedes with a Plymouth, one of the ugliest American cars ever built; international travel disappeared; our views of the Jura Mountains and the Mont Blanc were replaced with an old apple orchard; we traded the Rothchilds for young homeowners; our diet changed from *escargots* to peanut butter and jelly sandwiches; our children stopped improving the French language. On the positive side, the former apple orchard was actually pretty; the house had a three-car garage; we did a beautiful landscaping job, and learned how to install a sprinkler system and lay bricks; the children walked to Greystone Elementary and to a swim club, both only one block away; the weather was amazing: during our three years in San Jose, the sun shone almost every day and it rarely rained—too much of a good thing, as drought caused severe hardships in California's important agricultural sector. There were days we couldn't use the sprinkler system; lakes and reservoirs were very low. Lucky once again made custom lined draperies for our new house.

We had a number of unwelcomed guests. One day a garter snake came to visit and hid in our garage. I have always been afraid of snakes, even small ones. This one was about a foot and a half long, and our neighbor across the street came to my rescue. He managed to capture the snake, and adopted it saying it would be good for his garden. Another day, I went down to the crawling space in the basement and found a family of mice. I climbed our as fast as I could and called an exterminator. I think these guests had actually been residents in the apple orchard long before the development started.

My job in San Jose was the most satisfying I had in my career. I had a staff of nine professionals, and direct involvement with operating management. Most of the work involved building nuclear power plants in Japan, Taiwan, Switzerland, Spain, Italy, and Mexico. My operation analyzed cost estimates and results, prepared budgets and forecasts, and assisted project manages in all financial matters. I enjoyed working with the project managers, and as their "bean counter" I became a trusted member of the management team.

$$\text{\Large ♪♪♪♪}$$

One day I found in the classified ads a 15-foot boat for sale; the package included a trailer and 35 H.P. outboard, all for an asking price of a few hundred dollars. I went to see this incredible bargain, had a sea trial in San Francisco bay where we almost capsized, came home with our first boat, and named her *Palu*—after Paco and Lucky. I should have remembered the rule that you get what you pay, which applies even more to buying a boat. Soon after my acquisition everything started to break down; I had to buy a new outboard and reinforce the trailer. Despite all the problems, I made a great investment: *Palu* opened the door to priceless adventures in California's beautiful lakes and mountains we would have never enjoyed without her.

Our first camping experience was going to a brand new campsite in northern California in the wild Whiskeytown Lake area. We were the first customers, and the owner gave us a remote site that was the most scenic in his property. When he casually mentioned that at night we would probably see a few bears roaming by, I asked for a site closer to his cottage. As we started pitching our tent, I had misgivings, and told the owner to keep my deposit: his place was just too wild for us. We put all of our camping gear back in *Palu* and headed for the next motel a few miles away near an airport; it had waterbeds and was pure luxury compared to our sleeping bags. We did not miss the bears.

Lake Tahoe was our favorite destination, and we visited this beautiful area year around. In the summer, we trailered *Palu*, pitched a tent in a campsite off the lake, and enjoyed cruising and swimming in the transparent waters of Emerald Bay. In winter, we went skiing to Heavenly Valley, where we skied east into the dessert, or west towards the lake at the bottom of the mountain. We also rented a beautiful condominium on the ski slope in the middle of a pine forest, a setting similar to our house in New Hampshire. At night, we would visit the casinos and staked around $100 playing dice or Black Jack. Yvonne, Alina, and Frank loved visiting the children's "casino," a training center for future gamblers, or "night school," as they called it; these night-care facilities closed sharp at 11:00 P.M.

❧❧❧

My father died soon after we returned from Geneva, in Thomasville, Georgia. He died of a heart attack with a book in his hands, sitting in his car at a parking lot and waiting for my mother to return from the pharmacy. He had retired from Towson State College, was in very poor health, and moved to Thomasville to be near Jorge and his family. Our three remaining parents came to California to visit with us. We took them sightseeing to nearby San Francisco, and the spectacular 17-mile drive which was in full bloom in the spring with its purple flowers. We also took my mother to Yosemite National Park, one of the first and most beautiful wilderness parks in the U.S. where you admire deep valleys, grand meadows, and ancient giant sequoias.

California has numerous breathtaking natural wonders. During our three years in San Jose, we visited some of them. In Lassen Volcanic National Park, we saw hissing fumaroles and boiling mud pots within peaceful mountain forests; it is the southernmost active volcano in the Cascade Range. At the Redwood National Park, we saw amazingly tall trees—icons that inspire visions of mist-laden primeval forests bordering crystal-clear streams. We visited many tourist attractions in Los Angeles, San Diego, and Tijuana. We, of course, went to beautiful San Francisco countless times.

❧❧❧

San Jose had many shopping centers, and one in Los Gatos was advertising a Cinderella contest with lots of prizes. Alina read this ad and wanted to enter the contest. They formed a line of girls to try a glass slipper on their right foot. Many girls tried, but their foot was just too big or too small. Yvonne's foot was almost right but did not make it. Alina was desperate to try her luck; she was one of the last and smaller girls on the line. Finally her turn came, she tried the slipper and it fit her like a glove. People were cheering and clapping, and she was pronounced Cinderella for the town of San Jose. They put a robe and a tiara and paraded her around the plaza and proceeded to award the prizes: $300 in clothes; $50 in toys; $500 in portrait photos from the area's best photographer; and the Title of Miss Cinderella for one year.

For the portrait, Lucky bought the girls very elegant white and green long dresses, and Frank got a toddler white knit outfit. The photographer took regal pictures of the three children with Bon Bon. Two months went by and Lucky heard on the radio that the photographer's shop had been vandalized. She got dressed and immediately went to the shop. It was full of people and a police line did not let anybody pass or enter. Lucky pleaded with the policemen and the owner to let her search for the negatives that had been doused with acid. Somehow she managed to recover them and gave them to the owner. She told him that our dog in the photo had died since the picture was taken, we were moving to New York, and it was important to have these pictures saved. The owner did not take the negatives with him, and, unbelievably, the vandals returned the next night and sprayed the photos again with acid. Lucky could not believe it had happened again; she returned to the store and became very upset with the owner. He finally promised to personally restore the pictures and mail them to us. After six months, when we were already living in Westport, the beautiful portrait arrived with minor defects; it now sits in our living room admired by all, especially Alina.

♪♪♪

As I was getting close to my third year in this position, I was invited to interview for a job opening in New York City as Tax Manager of the International Group; the position afforded a two level promotion. Howard Teaford knew me from my days in Bethesda, where I had a record of high performance and a high potential rating. He hired me after I was perfunctorily interviewed by his boss, the Group's C.F.O.

In our way to work in New York, I decided to take the family to Hawaii for a week. In Honolulu, the most interesting site to me was the Pearl Harbor memorial to "The Date of Infamy, December 7, 1941" when Japan sank the USS Arizona and killed 1,177 of her crew, among the first casualties of the Pacific War. In Maui, the second largest Hawaiian island, we admired Haleakala, off the coast of Lahaina, and the waterfalls along the roads as you maneuver the hairpin turns of the Hana highway. In preparation for our trip, I read James Michener's extraordinary novel about the islands.

WESTPORT, CONNECTICUT: 1977-1984

13 ENO LANE

WESTPORT, A BEAUTIFUL town in Connecticut's Gold Coast, was settled along the Saugatuck River in 1639, and incorporated in 1835. For many years Wesport was a prosperous agricultural community. During the American Revolutionary War, a British expeditionary force landed with approximately 2,000 soldiers. They were attacked by Minutemen and a statue was erected to commemorate the event. The town includes numerous locations and properties listed in the National Register of Historic Places.

Westport has excellent schools and recreational facilities. Compo Beach, restricted to Westport residents, is considered one of Fairfield County's best beaches. It has an extensive sand beach along the shore of Long Island Sound and the Saugatuck River, a boardwalk, pavilion, concession stands, volleyball courts, and children's activity playground. The Longshore complex includes swimming pools, a golf course, lighted tennis courts, ice skating rinks, snack bar, and a fine restaurant. In summer, our children went to beach school and had many activities; they also enjoyed the YMCA's Camp. Westport is home to two yacht clubs, Saugatuck Harbor and Cedar Point, and a beautiful equestrian center, the Fairfield Hunt Club.

One of the attractive features of Westport is the versatility and variety of its population; when we moved, it was particularly noted for its many actors and artists. The town was made famous by the *I Love Lucy* television show: it is where Ricky and Lucy Ricardo, played by Lucille Ball and Desi Arnaz, moved after purchasing their new home; the show's producer was a Westport resident. Desi was a fellow Cuban-American, and Zuni was a friend of the Arnaz family. It was also the fictional residence of Darrin and Samantha in the television series *Bewitched*. Some other shows, movies and plays with a Westport connection include *The Twilight Zone, The Girl Next Door, Rent, The West Wing, The Man in the Gray Flannel Suit* with Gregory

Peck, *The Swimmer,* and *Rally Round the Flag, Boys!* Yvonne recently had a photo shoot at her home, and the models were dressed as *Stepford Wives,* another Westport film.

Paul Newman and Joanne Woodward were Westport's most famous residents. We saw the Newmans' last performance, Thornton Wilder's *Our Town,* at the Westport Country Playhouse which was founded in 1930, and where they played a prominent role for decades. Michael Brockman, Paul's stuntman and fellow race driver, married Yvonne's friend Jennifer O'Reilly who lived with us for months in Italy. Newman was the best man and we met both of them at the wedding. Actress Gene Tierney grew up in Green Farms.

The town's attractiveness has kept real estate prices rising and increasingly restricted the town to wealthy Wall Street executives and entrepreneurs. Our new house was built in the Williams Phelps Eno estate. Mr. Eno lived from 1858 to 1945, and was a businessman responsible for many of the earliest innovations in road safety and traffic control; he is known as "The Father of Traffic Safety" despite never having learned to drive a car himself. Among the innovations attributed to Mr. Eno are the stop sign, the pedestrian crosswalk, the traffic circle, the one-way street, the taxi stand stand, and pedestrian safety islands. In 1921, he founded the Eno Foundation for Highway Traffic Control; its headquarters are located in a mansion at the entrance of Eno Lane where our house was built. Most of the land of Eno's estate was bought by Joseph Lotta who built the house for us; as it was under construction, we were able to customize it. It was a beautiful colonial in a one-acre lot, in an upscale neighborhood.

By coincidence, the number of our house was 13, we bought it on April 13, and years later we moved to a house located at 13 Via Piemonte in Gorgonzola, Italy. Some of our neighbors were older and had senior management jobs. Our house was the second one to be finished, and we effectively became the welcoming committee of the neighborhood. Our family settled quickly; in our seven years in Westport, our children were actively involved at the Assumption Church, and in many school activities.

Yvonne went to Bedford Middle School and Staples High School; took piano and bassoon lessons; worked part-time at Paron Chocolatiers; won a Richardson Vicks' scholarship; and, most importantly, found her lifetime partner in high school, Guy Claveloux. She was lucky to have five of her best friends and classmates as neighbors. Alina went to Saugatuck Elementary School, Bedford Middle School, and Staples High School; took piano lessons; played the violin at Staples' All City Orchestra; and was a member of the volley-ball team. Frank went to Kings Highway Elementary and Saugatuck Elementary; he was a member of the Westport soccer travel team.

Eno Lane's development required breaking ground to build the street, the sewage, and water systems. Alina has always been an amateur archeologist; she started digging for Indian relics with Lucky next to our house, and collected many artifacts: flints, spare heads, and smoking pipes and gave them to Norwalk Community College; they were considered important enough to be permanently placed in their museum. A N.C.C. teacher gave Alina a plaque and books in recognition for her discoveries and donations; she was nine years old and thrilled with the public recognition of her work.

I took the commuter train daily to New York which took one hour when everything went well. I walked four blocks from Grand Central Station to the G.E. building at 570 Lexington Avenue. This was an excellent commute by New York standards; I used the train ride to read the newspapers. Some commuters played poker in the smoking car which had an air quality so poor as to almost guarantee developing lung cancer. I was stupid enough to still smoke during these years.

At lunch, I went frequently to G.E.'s restaurant on the 17th floor. You could reserve a table, but I normally sat at the community round table. I still remember we frequently had intellectually interesting discussions on a wide range of subjects. To exercise, I went often for long walks to Fifth Avenue or swam laps at the next-door pool in the St. Bartholomew's building.

Once a week, I drove to corporate headquarters in Fairfield, Connecticut. I had meetings with corporate staff or other International

Group managers. These were tax-free days, as at that time you did not have to pay New York City or State taxes on days you worked outside New York. Needless to say, I tried to work in Fairfield as frequently as possible.

My job required international travel to affiliates around the world, and I reminisce about some of these trips later. The affiliates' financial managers were gracious hosts, and as a member of the Group finance operation I received special treatment. The biggest project I had in this job was the consolidation of Cogenel, G.E.'s unprofitable first tier Italian affiliate, and Sadelmi, its highly profitable second tier affiliate. This work proved valuable years later in facilitating my job transfer to Italy when I went to work for Sadelmi.

Lucky started to work at Richardson Vicks' Latin American Division in Wilton, which later moved its offices to a beautiful office in downtown Westport next to the Saugatuck River. She was an administrative assistant, enjoyed her work, and established a great relationship with her coworkers.

♩♩♩

When we left San Jose, *Palu* came in the van, which cost G.E. more than what I had paid for her. Soon after our arrival in Westport, I bought an 18-foot cuddy cabin for a few hundred dollars, named her *Palu II*, kept my new outboard motor and restored trailer, and prepared to enjoy Long Island sound with cruising ambitions in my modest small rig. One afternoon I met John Fogel, a neighbor two houses down, who was Commodore of the Saugatuck Harbor Yacht Club (S.H.Y.C.), a nearby yacht club with excellent facilities located in a beautiful cove within walking distance from our Westport home; the clubhouse was built in structures that originally housed a carriage house, barn, and stalls. John suggested that I apply for membership at the club, and we joined an exclusive institution where our boat was by far the smallest; the next boat in size was an ocean going yacht.

S.H.Y.C.'s history started in 1690, when William and Mary, reigning monarchs of England bestowed a royal grant for the tidal basin known as Great Salt March. It was established in 1958. Many exquisite wood carvings with the names of yachts owned by past Commodores adorn the clubhouse; they were carved by Stephen Otis, whose widow Joy was our friend. Our children participated in all the club activities, including the aquatic ballet and junior sailing programs. Yvonne was elected Junior Commodore. *Palu II* became the family's summer cottage; our children frequently brought friends to enjoy the club's swimming club, and Zuni spent many afternoons reading aboard.

We joined S.H.Y.C.'s first cruise of the season to beautiful Essex in the Connecticut River, some 100 miles northeast of Westport, a considerable distance for our little cuddy cabin. Other members could not believe the Sabins' *cojones* and welcomed us warmly. They probably thought I was a little crazy to take Lucky and three young children in these cruising adventures. We left my mother-in-law with our pet Black Jack at home.

A few weeks later, we bought a 28-foot Concord single engine cabin cruiser, which was the minimum for a family of five to undertake extensive cruises around New England; we named her *Palu III*. She was a bargain that required lots of tender loving care, and I learned that older boats are demanding mistresses. I spent countless hours and money working on my pride and joy, and added many expensive improvements to make life aboard easier; after many trips to West Marine, she was ready for her maiden voyage. New England has excellent cruising waters, but they can be treacherous and subject to sudden weather changes and heavy fog.

In our first sea trial, we headed for Shelter Island Yacht Club in Eastern Long Island with the fleet. As we were in the middle of the Plum Gut, where the current speed was close to six knots, we ran out of fuel in the first tank. I bought *Palu III* from an estate sale, and I did not know that the tank had to be closed before opening the second one, or it would get air in the fuel ducks. We were rapidly drifting towards the lighthouse when our anchor accidentally caught a cable on the ocean floor, and we thankfully stopped a few feet before crashing against the rocks. Eventually the Coast Guard came to our rescue and towed us to Shelter Island, a few miles away, in very choppy water conditions.

In another dramatic cruise, we took off from Newport to Martha's Vineyard; weather conditions in Narragansett Bay suddenly worsened from the remnants of a storm that sank several yachts in the Fasnet Race off England. We faced a ferocious following sea with 10-foot waves, allowing us to see the propeller of other big trawlers. We would go up and down in the mountainous waves and would disappear and come out of the depths after what felt like an eternity. We followed John Fogel, who claimed great marine expertise and knowledge of these waters. I learned that at sea you never follow anybody; the captain is always responsible for the safety of his crew and his ship.

In a cruise to Osterville, Martha's Vineyard, we went into a long dinghy ride with other S.H.Y.C. sailors, passing by the backyard of palatial homes. Two ferocious mastiff dogs thought the caravan of small boats was intruding in their properties and started swimming towards us with bad intentions. We had to press the small outboards to move full steam ahead to escape the attack.

We went to many parties at S.H.Y.C. including several custome parties. We dressed as Popeye and Olive Oil, a seagull and an inventive type of bird scarecrow, seaweeds, and a Geisha and Cuban Samurai; we won the first prize more than once. Other prizes included Fleet Safety Officer, given to me humorously in 1982 for cutting the wrong pipe; the Mermaid Award, given to Lucky in 1982 for her designs of the girls' attires for the aqua ballets; and the Maine Survival Award, given to us in 1983, a trophy which includes a sample bottle of Remy Martin cognac flanked by Cuban cigars.

In one of our many weekend cruises, we met a number of fellow club members at Port Jefferson, one of our favorite harbors; we frequently formed a circle with the boats, and went from boat to boat eating and drinking. While the adults were socializing, the children played in dinghies and similar water oriented games. In one of these occasions, Alina, with a face white as ashes, came rowing to alert us that Frank had been hurt in an accident. We immediately found out that he had slipped from the dinghy and the outboard propeller had cut his leg. He was bleeding profusely, and we feared that he had a serious wound. Somebody had radioed the Coast Guard; a Power Squadron volunteer appeared instantaneously in a fast boat, taking us to the emergency room of Port Jefferson's Hospital. Frank fortunately had a plastic bucket, and he shielded his body as well as he could. This saved his leg, which could have been seared, and even his life could have been jeopardized. Frank was used to our Dyer Dow but was at his friend's rubber dinghy that day. This accident demonstrated once more that boats and the sea can be sources of great joy, but dangers always threaten.

We noticed that food was disappearing from our boat's galley, and began suspecting that we had uninvited guests. I set up mousetraps and did not catch any mice. A friend suggested that I set bigger traps. I waited a couple of days and, sure enough, I found a big water rat in the big trap I had set on the cockpit. The animal was not moving, but I was uncertain as to whether it was dead or alive. My friend Tom came to help me, took the trap, and dropped the rat in the water. We did not want to scare Zuni and did not tell her about the rat. Other members would pass by, and ask how Mickey was doing. She politely would answer: "Just fine," without knowing the reason for their question. Years later, when we were given our farewell party before moving to Italy, we got a beautifully attired rat with the club's burgee as a memento.

We went to the Belmont Stakes every year, and saw Affirmed win the race by a nose in 1978, the last Triple Crown winner to date. This was the most exciting race I have seen as Affirmed was neck to neck with Alydar until the very last second. I bet two dollars on Affirmed and won $2.25. A Concorde, the French supersonic airplane, flew above the race track in a cloudless blue sky above the race track; the majestic turbojet flew from Paris to New York in less than half the time of other airlines and was considered an engineering marvel; it suffered continuous financial losses and stopped operating in November 2003 after a terrible accident in France.

♪♪♪♫

When I was growing up in Havana in the late 1940s, my family had three Boston Terriers, and I derived a lot of pleasure from these dogs. After Bon Bon's death when we lived in California, we missed not having a dog which I have always believe to be an important member of the family. We decided to buy a dog again and found one though an ad in a newspaper; we fell in love with the Boston Terrier puppy as soon as we saw him in a litter of several adorable puppies. We named him Black Jack because of his color and because I have always enjoyed playing the game. From the beginning, our new pet enhanced and complicated our existence. He was very smart and hyper.

Black Jack hated cats. One day there was a cat begging for food in our backyard. Lucky mentioned it to her boss whose family was looking for a cat. We managed to bring him into our garage; Lucky's boss arrived with his children, and it was love at first sight. Unfortunately, Black Jack also discovered the cat and his innate hatred of felines. We barely managed to restrain him, and the cat was adopted by this family. We saw the cat months later; he had gained weight and now had shinny beautiful hair. It shows a stray cat can become a fat cat if that is his destiny.

♪♪♪♫

After living in Philadelphia since coming from Cuba, Zuni and Carlos moved to our house in 1979. Carlos Alzheimer's continued to deteriorate; after living with us six months, we had to place him in the Roncalli Catholic Nursing Home in Bridgeport. Zuni went almost daily by train to see him. Sometimes Lucky was able to drive Zuni to the nursing home at lunchtime. These were hard times, and it was very sad not to be able to continue caring for a loved one at home. Carlos died on January 29, 1981, and is buried at Westport's Assumption Cemetery. Zuni helped us a lot with the children, and having her at home when they came from school was a big relief. She integrated well with our neighbors, joined the Y.M.C.A. where she took Yoga lessons, and accompanied us frequently in our boating and other outings.

My mother Esther visited us every year. She and Zuni had fun together, and went often to town in Westport's public bus system; luckily, the small bus stopped at the entrance of Eno Lane and Saugatuck Avenue. Their favorite restaurant was the Westport Pizzeria, a town institution where they loved to eat eggplant *Parmiggiana*. My mother also enjoyed going to our boat.

In June, 1983 my boss informed me that due to a department reorganization my job would be eliminated by year-end; I should immediately start looking for a job inside and outside G.E. For the past two years, I had repeatedly talked with Tim Daly, Manager Finance of the SADE Sadelmi Companies, about my strong interest to join his operation. I immediately informed Tim of my new job situation, and he had encouraging words, and a few months later he offered me the job of Manager, Auditing and Taxes.

We shared the good news with our family, and told Frank first; he said "Way to go, dad. Can I play soccer in Milan? When are we leaving?" Zuni responded: "How wonderful, Paco. Congratulations. I always dreamed to visit Europe before dying." Alina started to cry; she was going to be a junior at Staples High School next year, I understood her unhappiness, and told her: "Honey, you will see that this experience will be great. Italy is a wonderful country." Alina thrived in Italy. Yvonne was a freshman at the University of Connecticut, and we contacted our good friend Lee O'Reilly, Jennifer's mother, to help us look after Yvonne while we were gone. The hardest part of our move was to leave Yvonne behind, but the next year she came with Jennifer for her semester abroad.

Before we moved to Italy, we sold *Palu III* to a G.E. associate. There is a joke that the two happiest days in a man's life are first, when he buys a boat, and second, when he sells it. That was not our experience, and Lucky and I cried when we had to wave goodbye to a friend that gave us lots of headaches and many unforgettable moments. When we left for Italy, S.H.Y.C.'s Board appointed me Commodore of the Mediterranean Fleet on condition that I fly the club burgee in my office. It still flies in my office.

Tim Daly agreed that my family would join me in the summer, after finishing the school year in Westport. I spent six months traveling from Milan to the Company's offices in Madrid, São Paulo, Caracas, Santo Domingo, and New York. This was exciting, but hard on my family and me; we were delighted when we finally reunited in July.

SANTO DOMINGO, DOMINICAN REPUBLIC: 1984-1986

LA TALANQUERA

IN MY FIRST work visit to the Dominican Republic, I fell in love with the island and its inhabitants. It reminded me of the old Cuba, a quaint mixture of tropical exuberance with *merengues* and other Caribbean music always blasting in the background. I received a warm welcome from all the *Dominicanos* I met. In my second visit, I finished my work early, and was chauffeured to tourist attractions near the capital. We drove to a resort one hour from the airport called *La Talanquera* at the Juan Dolio beach, a few kilometers west of San Pedro Macorís, the hometown of many major league baseball stars.

The *Talanquera* was in its early phase of development by the wealthy Casasnovas family who owned extensive cattle farms and land holding in the area. The resort included a beautiful beach, swimming pools, tennis courts, and a country club with extensive facilities including horses and skeet shooting ranges. They planned to build a golf course. I thought the price was right. I bought a lovely fully furnished new three-bedroom house on the spot. I then called Lucky and told her: "Guess what? I have a St. Valentine's Day present for you. We are the owners of a villa in a tropical paradise." Lucky thought I was *loco*, and it was not until her first visit in the summer that she was reassured that my mind was reasonably sound.

The first family trip was dramatic. The movers had just finished packing our belongings for our move to Italy. Zuni went to visit her daughter Bibiana in Miami and then flew alone to Santo Domingo, where we had planned to meet. These plans were disrupted when torrential rains in New York forced the closing of the J.F.K. airport for several hours. We could not call Zuni to tell her about the delay because we did not have a cell phone during those years; she stayed alone at the Santo Domingo airport. At around 11:00 P.M., she was approached by a man who had noticed her frightened look in the empty airport. He suspected that she was awaiting her relatives' delayed flight from New York. He was a chauffeur, and offered to take her to her hotel; when she could not remember the name and address of my property, suggested taking her to a hotel owned by Cubans. She finally remembered that my house was located at *La Talanquera*, and that's where he took her. This drive takes about one hour in a narrow night bordering the ocean, is pitch black at night, and Zuni prepared to meet her maker as she understandably expected to be killed at any moment. In the meantime, we were extremely worried about her. When we finally arrived at the Santo Domingo airport at 3:00 A.M., a man approached us asking if I was Mr. Sabin; we were perplexed, and he was the same polite chauffeur that had taken Zuni to *La Talanquera,* who came back and was waiting for us. She had been temporarily given a house close to the office so she could feel less frightened.

ꓻꓻꓻ

Our children took daily tennis lessons from Pedro, a very funny tennis pro and Michael Jackson look alike who could do a mean moon walk; he represented Santo Domingo in tournaments in Japan, and did hilarious imitations of the Japanese. They rode for hours in the vast cattle ranch with Don Nino, the *mayoral;* we always brought clothing and school supplies to his children. His family was happy when we visited his humble dirt floor *bohío,* offering us *cafecitos.* Before we left, they wanted to give Frank and Alina a baby goat named *Tarrito;* Don Nino wanted us to adopt his niece, an adorable *negrita con trencitas,* whose mother was brutally killed with a machete by her jealous common-law husband.

Lucky and Alina again became amateur archeologists and discovered a *Taíno* burial ground near our house; they alerted the *Museo Antropológico Dominicano* and their experts came to mark it properly. We also bought many *Taíno* artifacts and relics of the Pre Columbian era from beach vendors, which at that time could be taken out of the country without restrictions; we plan to donate our collection to a museum. Whenever we wanted coconut milk, "Zancas", a boy with long legs, stood ready to climb one of the many trees around us and bring down a coconut for a few pesos.

We installed plastic screens in the windows of our villa which attracted rats. When we returned the following year, the screens had large holes. We started to notice early in the morning that food was disappearing from the top of the kitchen counters, asked the maid, and she said "Oh, my God, it looks as if you have rats. Let's move the sofa." Sure enough, we had rats and we found the food remains under the sofa. *Talanquera* workers put a poison called *tres pasitos* because the rat that ate it would take three little steps before dropping dead; this created a veritable ecological disaster as every animal that ate the poison would also die, and we found many dead lizards, frogs, and iguanas around the house.

When it rained the water inundated the holes where crabs lived, and they came out by the thousands. They literally covered the roads around *Talanquera*. We had to be careful every time we opened the door because they managed to enter our villa. There was nearby a restaurant of a *Dominicana* married to an American, who was an exceptional cook and frequently used sauces of mango, guava and other tropical fruits. The restaurant was a few kilometers away in a remote and isolated area with many bougainvillea and flamboyant trees; it had lots of character. To get to the restaurant, we had to sadly drive over the crabs making a very disgusting noise.

Our private beach was less than one kilometer from our villa, and you could walk or be transported by a horse drawn carriage. The beach extended for several kilometers and was lined by countless coconut trees. Frank and Alina took surfing lessons with limited success. Facilities for evening festivities were built the second year including a huge *bohío* with an area for disco dancing. We established friendly relations with several families that owned units in our development.

Santo Domingo, the Dominican Republic's capital, has many historical sites, including Columbus' disputed burial place. The city also had wonderful restaurants. We particularly enjoyed *El Restaurant Lina*, owned by Trujillo's former cook. We also drove around the island and visited the impressive Altos de Chavón in La Romana, a recreation of a medieval European village conceived from the imagination of Robert Copa, a former Paramount Studios set designer, and Charles Bludhom. Puerto Plata and Sosua were two unforgettable sites. Eventually, we cut back on these adventures as I was frequently stopped by a police car seeking a small bribe. These are unfortunate consequences of a tropical paradise with excessive poverty, where the only hope is to become a *pelotero* or join the thousands of fellow citizens that have succeeded in moving to the United States. When we visit New York and need a fix of *comida* Dominicana, we head for upper Broadway to satisfy our gastronomic desires.

When we returned to the U.S. in 1986, earlier than we had anticipated, keeping our beach house became impractical. The airfare for the entire family, previously reimbursed by G.E. as a stop in our trip from or to Italy, would have been very expensive. In addition, Alina had been accepted at the College of William and Mary, and we needed to devote all our resources to her education. We sold it back to the Casasnovas for the same price we had paid and has now appreciated considerably.

GORGONZOLA, MILAN, ITALY: 1984-1986

13 VIA PIEMONTE

I STARTED TO work for Sadelmi in Milan in January, immediately after being appointed Manager of Auditing and Taxes. In my first trip to Milan, I thought I had died and gone to heaven. Italy is a paradise, particularly if you are not Italian and not concerned about politics, and your income will allow you to enjoy all the enticing marvels that Italy offers. Milan is strategically located within a few hours' drive from the world's top ski resorts, the Riviera in the Mediterranean, and enchanting cities like Venice, Florence, and numerous towns easily accessible by driving. Another dividend for the family would be fluency in a foreign language.

During these six months, when I was in Milan, home was the Hotel Michelangelo, located across the street from the grandiose train station built by Benito Mussolini in the 1920s; the hotel had an amazing buffet breakfast, and I had to control myself with so many temptations. The hotel was conveniently located a few blocks from my office.

I bought a gray Mercedes station wagon for less than half what I would have paid in the U.S. It was equipped with an extra rear seat, as we needed the additional seats when Yvonne and Alina's friends visited us. Sometimes we were seven in the car and had to tie the luggage on the roof. We drove tens of thousands of miles in this beautiful station wagon touring all over Europe; tackling mountains in the Alps and the Pyrenees was a pleasure.

When we returned to the U.S., I sold it to a South African associate. He liked it so much that, when he was transferred to a new job in Fairfield, he decided to make the substantial investment required to meet E.P.A. and D.O.T. requirements. The station wagon was shipped to a garage in Stamford, Connecticut that specialized in this conversion. The garage went up in flames while the car was being refitted, and it was totaled in the fire.

I also began to look for a new house for my family. Although they would not move until the summer, my boss agreed to let me move to a house; renting a house or an apartment early would be cheaper than paying for a hotel room. Under G.E.'s compensation formula used for Foreign Service employees, I was responsible to pay rent for 15% of my salary, and had an incentive to get the best possible facilities I could find. I looked at great city apartments that would have been ideal if we did not want more of a country setting for Alina and for Frank. Such houses were scarce, and the company realtor and I took the commuters tram; she wanted to show me a property she thought might interest me in a nearby town: Gorgonzola, the place that gave the world one of the greatest cheeses.

Renato Montefusco, the owner of the property, was an engineer who worked in the Middle East for many years, had developed a Sahara mindset, and I pictured him leading a camel caravan. We later developed a warm relation with his Italian wife and son, whom he later abandoned for a young Romanian woman. He loved antique cars and took me to a garage that restored cars as only Italians can do: after the work is finished, the cars look better than when they were new. An Alfa Romeo owned by Benito Mussolini was in the shop when we visited.

His property was a new four-floor town house, with two-car garages in the back. It had four bedrooms in the first three floors, and two more rooms in a beautiful *manzarda* in the fourth floor; the first floor entrance had a *porta blindata*, or steel-door to protect against burglaries. At my request, Montefusco installed three air conditioners which did not endear me to the next door neighbors, who complained bitterly about the noise that our compressors generated.

I called Lucky about my find and carefully explained that the place had significant trade-offs. On the positive side, it was a large town house in an Italian town where we could taste the life of real Italians; we could also move to an apartment in *Milano Due,* where most foreigners moved, or a city center apartment, which was attractive to me but would deprive Frank from riding his bicycle and other similar activities appropriate for a 13-year-old boy, and Alina from meeting local teenagers. On the other hand, it involved a commute to the American School of Milan located in distant Mirasole, which did not provide bus service to Gorgonzola. Since a house-hunting trip to Milan would have been inconvenient, Lucky approved the rental sight unseen. In retrospect, it was an excellent decision, as the other alternatives would have deprived our family from the unique experience of living like Italians in *la bella Italia*.

Gorgonzola is part of Lombardy; once a rural community, and famous for the cheese which bears its name, it has become a commuter town with stops in the Milan Metro. According to local legend, in 879 few cows accidentally ate some cheese a farmer had discarded because it had developed green fermentation; the cows survived, and the farmer experimented by making more of the same cheese, gave samples to friends to try; everybody loved the new taste, and Gorgonzola cheese was gloriously born. It acquired its greenish-blue marbling in the 11th century. Whole cow milk is used, to which starter bacteria is added, along with spores of the mold *Penicillium glaucum*; the whey is removed during curdling, and the result is aged at low temperatures. During the aging process metal rods are quickly inserted and removed, creating air channels that allow the mold spores to grow and cause the cheese's characteristic veining. Gorgonzola is typically aged for three to four months. Gorgonzola may be melted into a *risotto* or served alongside *polenta*.

Its long and interesting history began in 453 when Gorgonzola and the nearby town of Argentia were attacked by the Huns; in 1176 it joined the Lombard League. The Naviglio Martesana is a canal and part of system of Milan's *navigli* crossing the town. The history of the canal begins on June, 1443 when the Duke of Milan approved an ambitious project put forward by a group of illustrious Milanese. In 1465, Francesco Sforza's edict marked the start of design work. The project was of great economic and military benefit; it was inaugurated in 1477. Today, it is a popular recreational area known for its tranquil cycling paths. The *Via Appia,* one of the earliest and most important Roman roads of the ancient republic, is Gorgonzola's main artery. According to local lore, in 1159 the famous pirate-turned-Ottoman Admiral Frederick Barbarossa stayed at a tower facing the town's main church; it is called the Barbarossa Tower.

Milan is located in the Po Valley, part of what Italians call *la pianura Padana.* It extends some 400 miles in an east-west direction, from the Western Alps to the Adriatic Sea, and effectively includes the flatlands of Veneto and Friuli. The geography of huge mountains and the River Po's flatlands creates perfect conditions for fog, which can be a challenge particularly in the winter. I drove from Gorgonzola to my Milan office and back every day and more than once missed my exit with pea-soup fog. I have encountered the same type of thick fog while cruising in Maine. Those familiar with the experience never forget it; it can be dangerous and hard to get your bearings even when you have radar.

ﮞﮞﮞ

One of my first priorities when we settled in Gorgonzola was to buy the Michelin Guide which still occupies a nostalgic place in my library. I immediately prepared to invest in culinary memories, which required considerable strategic planning. I had five full-time family members on my payroll: Alina, Frank, Zuni, Lucky, and I; in addition, I had two part-timers: Yvonne and many visiting guests in the Sabin Hotel. To pursue culinary delights with seven people requires a lot of lire—these were the years before the adoption of the Euro. We would splurge whenever possible in finer restaurants, and favor trattorias when going with the whole gang. I will reminisce about some of the gastronomic memories that enrich my senior years.

The French writers of the Michelin Guide were very stingy in awarding stars to restaurants outside France. Northern Italian cuisine is second to none and Milan is arguably a gastronomic paradise, but no restaurant in Milan received three stars and only one, Gualtiero

Marchesi, earned two. We ate at this center of nouvelle cuisine twice, and it was certainly superb; the décor was Milan ultra-modern, as you would expect. Giannino was our favorite restaurant with its open view of the kitchen and memorable *risotto e filetti di sogliola alla Giannino.*

Venice is approximately just a two-hour drive from Gorgonzola, and we visited this incredible city frequently. We often stayed at a nunnery, with clean rooms and reasonable rates for our large group. Venice offers a unique experience in each of the four seasons, and we were excited to get the *vaporetto* and cruise the canals. We drove to Mestre, a city just outside Venice, to eat at an excellent and reasonable restaurant named Valeriano; it had one Michelin star one of my favorite dishes was the *scamponi alla bussara.* Needless to say, the main purpose of our visits was to enjoy the city's unique atmosphere and countless art treasures.

Charlie Balfour was a Harvard graduate and Sadelmi's Treasurer who lived many years in Italy, married a Milanese *Dottoresa,* and had the brilliant idea to have the wedding in Venice. The bride was seven months pregnant; after the official ceremony, the group boarded a beautiful water taxi and headed to enjoy the festivities at a famous Torcello restaurant with great party facilities. We have never had so much fun at a wedding; Charlie was a unique individual. Under G.E.'s policy, expatriates were reimbursed for one trip back home a year. Charlie went to Colombia, rented horses for a few days to explore the mountains, and submitted the horse rentals in lieu of transportation expenses. I refused to initial the expense accounts which were rejected by my boss; I am glad that Charlie did not take it personally.

Charlie had lived in Italy for many years, and soon after our arrival he recommended that we visit Cinque Terre, the isolated region without good access roads in the Ligurian Gulf of La Spezia. The wild rugged coast has vineyards and fishing villages where the people remain strongly attached to old customs and traditions. Vernazza was the most attractive village with its tall colorful houses and its church clustered together at the head of a sheltered coast.

We frequently drove to the lakes of Northern Italy, including Lago di Como and its beautiful villages of Bellagio and Tremezzo; Lago di Garda and beautiful Simione; Lago Maggiore, Stressa, and the Borromean Islands, including Isola dei Pescaatori and Isola Bella, and Lago d'Orta. We have spent many days in this area since 1971, and we will always want to return.

Whenever we had visitors, we took them to nearby Certossa di Pavia to admire its rich buildings from the Romanesque and Renaissance periods. Many old feudal towers were built by the noble families of Pavia: the Visconti family built a castle and a famous Carthusian Monastery as a family mausoleum in 1396. We also took them to enjoy Bergamo's upper town, which was just a short drive from our home; we strolled around Piazza del Duomo and the Piazza Vecchia and showed them the remarkable Colleoni Chapel. This architectural gem was designed by the same architect that built Pavia's Cartusian Monastery. We always finished at one of the wonderful restaurants, including La Taverna del Colleoni, which offered a memorable *tagliatelle and piccata di vitello.*

Visiting Parma for a weekend was always a treat: sightseeing in the beautiful historic core and the Romanesque Episcopal Center, including the cathedral and baptistery, and surrounding palaces. Parma, of course, is famous for its food and rich gastronomical traditions: prosciutto di Parma and Parmigiano Reggiano cheese. Barilla and Parmalat, two food multinationals, are headquartered in Parma. Parma has two American twin cities: Milwaukee and Stockton. Famous music giants from Parma include Giuseppe Verdi and Arturo Toscanini; I am certain that their hometown prosciutto inspired to compose operas and handle the conductor's baton with unmatched artistry.

The names of towns and cities of Northern Italy and Tuscany have an inviting poetic quality: Florence, Lucca, San Gimignano, Sienna, Lucca, Verona, and others. We loved Milano, and Lucky became a tour guide for our many guests. She took them to see Da Vinci's *Last Supper,* the Duomo, la Scala, the *Pinacoteca di Brera*, the Sforza's castle, and other hightlights.

Yvonne was entering her sophomore year at the University of Connecticut, and could not wait to join us and participate in our adventures. She came to Milan for her semester abroad, and attended the *Instituto di Moda Marangoni,* a women's fashion design institute. Milan is one of the world's fashion centers; learning fashion design and Italian served her well in the future. Jennifer O'Reilly, Yvonne's Westport friend and classmate, spent six months with us.

Yvonne and Jennifer will always look back at this period as a great experience. They arrived two weeks before the start of *Marangoni's* classes, and we sent them to Rome. They stayed in a Catholic nunnery, where they were given room and board for a reasonable price, and had to be back at the house by 11:00 P.M. The food was so bad that they frequently pretended to eat, and later discarded the inedible concoctions. These two beautiful 19-year-old girls had a memorable time, and still talk about the fun they had in Rome.

Alina and Frank thrived at the American School of Milan. It is an excellent and expensive private school where one third of the students are children of American expatriates, and their companies pay for the tuition; one third are children of third country nationals working for multinational companies; and one third are the children of wealthy Italians. Lucky and I were actively involved in school activities.

Alina was an excellent student and class salutatorian; she earned several prestigious academic awards. Al Derry was A.S.M.'s Principal. In his college recommendation letter for Alina he states: "the goodness of this young lady is such that you must stand back in awe." We certainly agree with Mr. Derry's opinion. Alina also benefited from traveling throughout Italy to play volleyball against the teams of other schools.

We hired a piano instructor, *Signore* Liborio Lanza, who reported great success with Alina; with Frank, however, he told us that he was wasting his time and our money, thus ending Frank's musical career. Frank thought he could learn to play the piano without the need to study and practice.

❧❧❧❧

Most Northern Italian towns have great ski programs. Our town, Gorgonzola, had one of the best organized outings. Every Sunday, three buses full of children and some adults would leave at 5:00 A.M. and return at 6:00 P.M. from skiing. They would go to a different ski resort every week, in the nearby Alps. Alina and Frank really liked these trips; they improved their skiing as well as their fluency in Italian and were happy to integrate with their new friends.

For spring break we found a family resort, *Colere*, near Bergamo; it was reasonably priced and accessible only by ski lift. We left our children worrying they would miss us. When we came back one week later, they said that they would have liked to stay one more week. Both Alina and Frank had made friends with Italian students, had a great time, and kept the friendships they made for the rest of our stay in Italy. Frank was 13 and made his first romantic conquest with an older woman: Daniela. She was a pretty 15 year *signorina,* and later would call Frank and, when he was not available, say *"pacencia… pacencia!"* We thought that expression was hilarious, the voice of a young lady experiencing for the first time the need to have patience with hopeless men. Amazingly, they recently reconnected through Facebook.

A.S.M. had a week off in February for *settimana Bianca* and sponsored a ski week at the famous and charming resort of Courmayeur in the Valle D'Aosta. This area encompasses the Grand Alps of Italy, France, and Switzerland, which include Mont Blanc (4,807 meters), a majestic peak Germans call the Matterhorn and Italians call Monte Cervino (4,478 meters), and many other striking mountains. It is a paradise for mountaineers and winter sports lovers: excellent skiers can take interconnecting lifts, and ski from Italy, to France, to Switzerland, and back to Italy. We rented an apartment for the six of us for the week, but unfortunately, I had to return to Milan on Monday to work. On Sunday it started snowing, and it was still snowing early Monday when I had to leave. It turned out to be a historic snow storm, and I had a very difficult time getting back to my office; it took me approximately eight hours, three times the usual, but I thanked God for not having a serious accident.

When there is good snow, the Dolomites are my undisputed favorite mountains. It includes numerous massifs and extends mostly over northern Italy's German speaking Southern Tyrol. The 130 miles of mountain road from Bolzano to Cortina d'Ampezzo, certainly one of the most scenic in the world, passes through many resorts. It was at one of these that Alina, Frank, and I took off for a day of skiing and frolicking in the many chalets at the top of the mountains where you eat, drink hot wine, relax, and work on your sun tan. We somehow became separated in the miles of incredibly beautiful ski paths; I ended up alone many miles from our original take off and hitched a ride back. Lucky and Zuni were worried, and I could not account for Alina and Frank. We decided to go to mass at a nearby village and were in the middle of the service when they miraculously showed up in their ski gear after finding a ride back to town. Their ski boots made strange noises, and all the parishioners looked back to see what was going on.

♪♪♪

Our Boston Terrier Black Jack was the only family member to have a difficult transition. He stayed more than one month in a kennel while our belongings were en route, while most of the family was enjoying Santo Domingo. When I went to retrieve him at the Milan airport, found out that he had been sent down to Rome by mistake. A week later, he returned to Milan as an Italian citizen looking very thin and sad; he regained his health and appetite very soon.

One day a kitten somehow got inside our house; Black Jack followed him up and down our town house, and regretfully killed him. Lucky, Zuni, and our part time Italian maid were all horrified; many Italians, and some Cubans, are superstitious and will not touch a dead cat with a 10-foot pole. Lucky went to the butcher in the nearby market for his help figuring out he was used to killing rabbits, pigs, chickens, etc., but he declined saying it was bad luck. *Signore* Bindellini, who built our closets and cabinets, saved the day. He was walking by when he heard distress signals coming from our home; Lucky asked him to remove the poor dead kitten, and he solved the problem after asking for a plastic bag. Bindellini raised messenger pigeons on his rooftop and many times brought us some to eat; we were not used to cooking them, and gave them to our Sicilian maid. You can still admire some of Bindellini's closets in our Epping garage.

~ ~ ~ ~

I found a riding school for the children in the nearby town of Melzo and enrolled them to take lessons. The owner wanted to sell me a Russian thoroughbred that was ugly but a good jumper. I took the horse over a medium jump, and, after many years without practice, I almost fell when he stopped in front of the obstacle and then jumped. The owner told me his price was so low that I could sell the horse to a butcher and make a profit if I ever wanted. I, of course, rejected the offer. One day Alina had a fall, was scared, but I told her to get back on the horse and show she was the boss. She did and enjoyed more lessons later on. Frank and Alina preferred riding in the open fields in Santo Domingo, than the more restricted dressage lessons. Yvonne loved to ride and continued taking classes when she went back to college.

~ ~ ~ ~

Our fluency with Spanish and familiarity with Latin culture enabled everyone to integrate and learn Italian quickly. Fortunately, Alina's misgivings dissipated soon after moving to Milan. Between the American School of Milan and the town of Gorgonzola, she made many new friends and had a wide range of opportunities; she thrived in the new environment. Alina joined Gorgonzola's *palavolo* team and Frank the local *calcio* team. We immediately got to know all the parents of our children's friends and teammates and participate in their social activities.

On Sundays, we frequently joined a large group of parents for long lasting feasts. One of Frank's best friends from the soccer team was Miguele Chionfoli. His dad was a wine expert with great knowledge of the country; they were *terrones* as Italians from the south are derisively called, and came from Puglia—which we will visit this fall. The group was as varied as the wines and cheeses in Italy.

Frank became addicted to the *brioche con ciocolatte caldo* that he bought at the corner *gelateria,* where *Signora* Roberta made heavenly ice creams and sorbets. He would go straight to get these treats when he came from school. Alina frequently met her friends at this *gelateria.* I think we all took daily trips to this wonderful place that besides good ice creams they had excellent pastries and the best hot Swiss chocolate in town. It was situated next to the Mulino Vecchio, the only original windmill left in Gorgonzola.

Our neighbors, the Giordanos, Diottis, and Gallis were related and we became part of their extended family. In their backyard, they had a miraculous fig tree that seemed to always give plenty of the sweetest figs we have ever eaten, and we frequently got a basket of them. Mario used to run hotels in the mountains and in Rimini and was retired; Enrico had a big *embalaggi* business, where they packed industrial equipment for export. We attended the Diotti's daughter's wedding reception in the town of Monza, best known for its Grand Prix motor racing circuit, the *Autodromo Nacionale Monza.*

A few years ago, we visited our neighbors for a couple of days on our way to a three-week automobile tour of France. I had rented a small Fiat from Hertz, but Enrico insisted that I cancel the reservation and take his new and luxurious Peugeot turbo-diesel station wagon. We reluctantly accepted his kind offer, and he prepared the car for our long trip. A few miles later, we were driving in the turnpike and approaching a tollgate when the car was engulfed by smoke. Enrico came to our rescue, and towed the car to the dealer; it had some manufacturing flaws, and the major warranty covered repairs took weeks. Enrico wanted us to take another of his cars, but this time I thanked him but rejected the offer. I was lucky to finally get a small

Fiat from Hertz; it had a distinctly ugly pale green color but ran as a charm.

Gorgonzola had an annual country fair, where farmers brought their animals and artisanal products for sale: cheese, home-made pastas and pastries, rabbits, pigs, horse and mule meat, chicken, pigeons, frogs, and other delicacies. At our first fair, I bought a suckling pig and invited our neighbors for dinner to taste what I thought would be a delicious pork roast Cuban style. Unfortunately, the piglet almost disappeared in the oven as it shrank to the size of a big rat—certainly not enough to feed the crowd I had invited. We just had to call the local Pizzeria and order a few pizzas; as a result, the reputation of my culinary abilities suffered greatly.

ᴊᴊᴊ

My whole family was enjoying life in Italy, and I hoped to keep my job for years until retirement. We no longer feared that a long stay overseas would have a negative impact on our children, a concern that twenty-two years earlier made us seek a return to the U.S. Unfortunately, the SADE Sadelmi companies had gone into difficult times as the world economy turned downward severely affecting the construction business; G.E. sold the group to ASEA Brown Bovari months later. A new Finance Manager saw no need for my expensive services, and told me that my days in Milan were counted.

In seeking a new job, I immediately started networking within G.E. and identified a potential match in the Meter Department in Somersworth, New Hampshire. I knew the Manager of Finance since my Geneva days, and we had established good professional relations. He offered me the job of International Specialist reporting to his Financial Planning Manager, and I accepted.

ᴊᴊᴊ

I regret to finish this chapter of our days in Italy with a sad note. Tim Daly moved to Schenectady as General Manager of one of the Power Generation businesses. He had a heart attack while he was not even fifty, and died soon after waiting for a heart transplant as his last hope to stay alive. Denny Daigneault, my second American boss in Milan, also died recently; I think he was in his sixties. Howard Teaford hired me for my tax job in New York City; he had a heart attack shortly after joining Atlantic Richfield in California and died in his forties. These three men were chain smoker and compulsive workers. I quit smoking some twelve years ago, have not worked excessively for many years, and pray that these actions will keep me alive to enjoy my family and friends for a while longer.

During our years in Italy, we traveled extensively to other Western European countries. For our first Christmas, I rented a chalet in the mountains near Vienna. I will write about these trips later.

NEW HAMPSHIRE

I FLEW TO Somersworth to interview and was hired the following week. It has now been our main residence for 26 years—longer by far than the time I lived in any of my other homes. How can anybody help falling in love with a State whose motto is "Live Free or Die?" The longer we live in the Granite State, the more we appreciate its exceptionally fertile ground to pursue three of my interests: good cuisine, sailing, and skiing. We also appreciate the proximity to Boston.

I find their introduction to the Granite State's Southeastern region succinctly relates my passions to my adoptive home state: "New Hampshire's seacoast is the shortest of any state, but it's enough to give it an excellent harbor at Portsmouth, and access to good fishing and lobstering. The moderating effect of the ocean puts the coastal area in a warmer growing zone, which farmers have been taking full advantage of since the first settlements in the early 1600s. To the north lies the lakes region, better known as a summer playground than for its agriculture. But in this area you'll find an excellent working-farm museum. West of the coast, the Merrimack River flows down the center of the state. This waterway powered the largest mill complex in America and made New Hampshire an industrial state. This industry also gave New Hampshire its strong ethnic influences as immigrants came to work in the mills. Today these ethnic groups bring their flavors to the city's restaurants and food shops."

Its academic centers include Dartmouth College, the University of New Hampshire, and Phyllips Exeter Academy. Its history is long and rich: it became the first post-colonial sovereign nation in all the Americas when it broke off from Great Britain in January 1776, and was one of the original thirteen states that founded the United States of America six months later. The New Hampshire primary is the first in the U.S. presidential election cycle.

New Hampshire is comparatively small, and ranks 44th in land area and 42nd in population of the 50 states. For its small area, the geography is extremely varied. In addition to its coastline, the White

Mountain National Forest links the Vermont and Maine portion of the Appalachian Trail. The Old Man in the Mountain, a face-like profile in a rock at the top of Franconia Notch, was a state icon which sadly fell apart in 2003. In the north, it is bordered by Canada's Quebec and Montreal, which gives us the opportunity to occasionally enjoy *Crêpes Suzette* without traveling far.

In addition to beaches and ocean sports, major recreational attractions include skiing, snowmobiling and other winter sports, hiking and mountaineering, and observing the fall foliage. Motor sports are important: car races at the New Hampshire Motor Speedway; motorcycle rallies in at Lake Winnipesaukee's Weir Beach; and the Mount Washington auto road, where visitors drive or take the world's first mountain climbing cog-train to the top of Mount Washington's summit, 6,288 feet above sea level. The weather observatory at the top of the mountain claims that the area has "The World's Worst Weather," including hurricane-force winds every third day on average.

Lucky and I believe that New Hampshire's attractiveness influenced Frank and Minerva's decision to relocate to Exeter; having them and our two grandchildren ten minutes away is priceless. The same factor makes our home a favorite destination for the rest of our family, and for friends that visit us from all over the world, including former Italian and French neighbors, friends from our different homes in the U.S., and friends from Miami. We take them sightseeing to nearby places in the coast, the White Mountains, or the state's numerous crystal clear lakes.

4 COLD SPRING ROAD, DURHAM: 1986—1996

I started looking for a new house, and decided that Durham was the best location for us primarily because of its good schools. The town is the home of the University of New Hampshire, Oyster River High School, where Frank graduated, and a population with many academics and professionals; it is situated next to Great Bay at the mouth of the Oyster River and settled in 1635.

It was love at first sight when I found a beautiful two-acre waterfront lot with over 200 feet frontage on the Lamprey River and decided to build our home. It was part of a small thirteen-lot subdivision in an old farm; there were two-family cemeteries belonging to several generations of the initial landowners. Our house was custom built to our specifications as we had many large European furniture pieces. We built it contemporary colonial style; it had three floors, and each had large decks and lots of windows to enhance the view of the Lamprey River. We rented a unit at Oyster River Condominiums for nine months while our house was being built and had to put most of our furniture in storage.

The Lamprey, approximately 50 miles long, was officially designated a historical and scenic river at the time we lived in Cold Spring Road; it has slow meanders and rapids including nearby Packer Falls where we used to swim. It flows south from the Saddleback Mountains into Meadow Lake in Northwood, past the towns of Durham, Lee, Raymond, Epping, and finally New Market. There it meets Great Bay, a tidal inlet of the Atlantic Ocean, to which it is connected by the Piscataqua River; I kept *Dulcinea* at a mooring in Great Bay Marine for several years. The Lamprey is rich in history. Saw mills operated by water power were common along the river. The Wiswall Falls Mill site in Durham is on the National Register of Historic Places. It was originally used as a mill, and later to make knives, nuts and bolts, pitchforks, and carriages.

The river is perfect to practice the Olympic sport of two-oared sculling, a form of rowing—both competitive and recreational—in which a boat is propelled by oars held in the fingers of each hand. At dawn, we frequently could hear the sound of the shells cutting through the water and requiring to row with an efficient stroke; the cadence of the oars splashing at a consistent motion produces a beautiful sound, which frequently woke us up. A lady associate from G.E. and her husband were seriously into the sport, and imported shells from Italy; I occasionally helped her with translations. I tried sculling and quit after finding it hard to keep the shell from tipping over. Frank also tried the sport but gave up due to the need to practice at dawn and the ferocious mosquito attacks. Frank's friend and schoolmate, Graham Duncan, persisted and ended up competing at the 11th Pan-American Games that were hosted in Cuba when he was just 17 years old; I still smoked at the time, and he brought me several good Cuban cigars he smuggled as they are prohibited by American customs.

We planted many pine trees along the driveway, and did extensive landscaping in the grounds. We cleared trees and brushes, and removed wire fences; initially it was hard to see the river, where we owned 220 feet of water front frontage. I bought a chain saw and worked with Lucky and Frank to burn huge piles of debris. When we finally cleaned up the land, we could finally appreciate a spectacular and unobstructed view of the Lamprey River. On its west bank there were no houses so the whole place made you feel far away from civilization. We had a tennis court built directly in front of our house where we enjoyed playing frequently. Finally the house was finished and we were able to move before the snows came; the moving van had difficulty to maneuver to deliver the furniture, for it had been raining a lot and the driveway had not been paved yet and was very muddy.

Wiswall Dam is less than a mile from the property, and we used to go swimming and canoeing to the town of New Market some five miles downriver. Next to our lot were three acres of common ground with a dock for canoes. Everyone in our family enjoyed the river, and Frank's friends came frequently to swim and go for a canoe ride. In the winter the Lamprey froze, andwe went ice skating for miles with the kids and friends who came to visit.

The diversity of the Lamprey's habitat is remarkable: forests, open fields, quiet backwaters, rushing rapids, wetlands, and sandy riverbanks attract a wide variety of animals. Wild animals frequently visited, including countless squirrels, chipmunks, deers, raccoons, and even a moose now and then. Ospreys nested along the river pine trees; our small neighborhood association approved the construction of bat houses to control the mosquitos, and houses for blue birds to again attract them to the area. A bat once almost made us land in jail; one night, Lucky opened the attic door, a bat fell down in front of her face and started yelling for me to come to her rescue. As I am scared of bats and thought it could have rabies, I called our next-door neighbor to come to our help but he was not available. I then called 911; in the meantime, I got a tennis racket, a blanket, and leather mitts and proceeded to hit the bat. Thankfully, I was able to kill the bat. A few minutes later the police called asking to talk to my wife. They wanted to know if the call was legitimate, and she explained what had happened. Even after the call, the police was not satisfied that it was not a domestic abuse situation, and dispatched a patrol car. Lucky opened the door and reassured the officer she was not in danger from a mad husband.

Many beavers lived in the river, and were very active in constructing dams. We were amazed at the number of trees lost along the banks of the river. One day Zuni called Lucky at her office to tell her that while she was watering the garden she saw something moving, and thought it was a plastic bag of clippings that we had left the night before. She became scared as a head appeared from the bag, menacing her; she almost fell backwards, and realized she was being attacked by a snapping turtle. The turtle had just finished laying many eggs and was covering them while Zuni started to water the plants. These snapping turtles are very aggressive, and can inflict a tremendous bite. Zuni was scared, could not keep her eyes from it, and kept staring at the turtle from the window.

A pair of big beautiful swans lived in the Lamprey and often came to the banks of our house looking for food. They were named Priscilla and Ajax by the Durham Keeper of the Swans, our friend Dr. Marjorie Milne. She and her husband Lorus were long time former U.N.H. professors who came to Durham in 1948 to teach zoology, and purchased land adjacent to Mill Pond Park. They wrote more than 50 books on natural history and the land in Durham inspired them; it was their nature sanctuary, which they donated to the Town of Durham upon her death in 2009. We were friends of Marjorie from the International Group, and she helped me years ago when I first started to think about writing my autobiography. But going to back to Priscilla and Ajax; Priscilla was nesting nearby close to the town of New Market, when a couple in a canoe went by too close to the nest. Ajax became agitated, started pecking on the back of the man, and overturned the canoe; they were fortunately able to fend off Ajax with their paddles and called for help. Marjorie decided to relocate the swans.

Frank, Guy and I built a swing rope to jump into the river like Tarzan; we could swim a long distance in full communion with nature. Large flocks of wild turkeys visited the grounds around our house; some of them perched in the tall pine trees, and with their long black tails looked like monkeys from a distance. The first time Lucky saw them, she started yelling: "Paco, Paco. Hurry, I think we have some monkeys in the trees."

One reason we love New Hampshire is the interesting and compatible people we have met while living in this beautiful State. Many share our love of the ocean and the arts, and some have become cherished close friends including some of our neighbors. We have been members of the International Friendship Group since we came back from Italy. This cosmopolitan group meets once a month to enjoy a pot luck dinner, listen to lectures, and host graduate foreign students from the University of New Hampshire.

We have been active members of St. Thomas More Church in Durham and participate in many church activities. Lucky enjoys working in the fall and Christmas fundraisers. Four inspiring priests have been our friends and spiritual leaders; one of them, Rev. Daniel St. Laurent, officiated in Frank's and Minie's wedding. Rev. Andrew Cryans is the current pastor; his sermons are profound and eloquent. He is smart and a kindred spirit with whom I share many interests.

During many years I enjoyed winter sports with our children and friends. We occasionally rented apartments in ski resorts, drove to nearby slopes, and went cross-country skiing on the Lamprey River when it froze in the winter. Some ski loving retirees own property in Florida, rent their apartments in the winter while they are skiing, and go to their Florida homes in the summer: they are the opposite of us snow birds.

The last time I went skiing at Gunstock, a number of young children passed me in their snow boards; they were going recklessly fast and too close to me. I decided to quit early as was worried about a fracture or tearing a ligament, which I experienced while skiing in France and is a risk all skiers share. I still have my ski equipment and may still go skiing with my grandchildren, but Sophia and Andrew have already gone beyond my level of competence. I have also developed an allergy for cold weather. I should donate my ski equipment to St. Thomas' at their next rummage sale.

For my 50th birthday, we had a big Down East bash. We invited Modesto Maidique and the group of friends from his earlier 50th birthday party in Jamaica. We had a lobster bake, went for canoe rides in the Lamprey, and a fall cruise in Great Bay in the beautiful Isles of Shoals Steamship Thomas Leighton. Many of our Durham friends and family came; it was amemorable celebration.

❧❧❧

During the seven years we lived in Durham, we continued to cruise extensively with Dan Conron in Maine and Nova Scotia. In one of our cruises, I helped sail *Freyja* to Nova Scottia while Lucky took the overnight ferry from Portland and picked me up in Yarmouth. We explored the Cabot Trail by car; this scenic route is 185 miles long through the Cape Breton Highlands named after the explorer John Cabot who landed in Canada in 1497. We drove through beautiful Bras D'Or Lake where *Freyja* was headed with the Cruising Club of America, and returned to New Hampshire through interesting places, including Roosevelt's Campobello International Park and the Bay of

Fundy, which has the world's biggest tides. We visited Roosevelt's summer retreat where, in August 1921, the future President was stricken with poliomyelitis at the age of 39.

Frank joined me in another Down East cruise. We went to a jazz concert of Russian musicians in Bar Harbor. Conron was a friend of the manager of the Blue Hill Yacht Club, who retired from Pitney Bowes and built a beautiful house by himself in a spectacular property his wife's family had owned for generations.

We also did lots of day-sailing in our Laser Standard sailboat, a popular one-design class sailing dinghy which is one of the most popular single-handed dinghies in the world. It is a great classy little boat: robust, fast, and simple to rig and sail. It became a men's Olympic-class boat at the 1996 Summer Olympics in Atlanta; the first world championship was held in 1974 in Bermuda and entrants came from 24 countries. We often lifted the boat, put it on a ski lift on top of our car and took it sailing in the numerous beautiful New Hampshire lakes. Another favorite destination was Kittery Point across from Portsmouth at the entrance of the Piscataqua River, but we had to be very careful with the strong currents and tides. Frank and Alina frequently went sailing with me; they loved capsizing the Laser on purpose.

ﮋﮋﮋﮢ

The Meter Department experienced drastic changes as a result of new technologies, moving from labor intensive mechanical meters to electrical machines, outsourcing, and flattening of the organization. The Department had approximately 2,000 employees when I joined the business in 1986, and eventually dropped to around 100. The Department went through constant major cuts in personnel, with round after round of layoffs, an unforgettable experience that many workers and middle managers increasingly face in today's world. I was fortunate to qualify for G.E.'s Special Early Retirement Option (S.E.R.O.)—which required 25 years of service and 55 years of age and provided a pension enhanced to age 62 and health benefits.

I worked part-time for several years at Great Bay Marine, where I kept *Dulcinea* in the winter. We decided to permanently make New Hampshire our main residence, and to eventually spend winters in Miami. We started to look for a new house in the area.

153 OLD HEDDING ROAD, MELLING GLENN, EPPING: 1996-PRESENT

We found an ideal set up for our needs: a detached condominium in Epping, originally part of Exeter, one of the four original New Hampshire townships. In 1741 Epping was granted a charter and incorporated as a town, the last New Hampshire town chartered before the state separated from Massachusetts. The town claims three past Governors: David Morril from 1824 to 1827; William Plumer from 1812 to 1813, and 1816 to 1819; and Benjamin Franklin Prescott from 1877 to 1879. Because of this history, signs partly in jest read: "Epping, the center of the universe." Now, due to its strategic location at the crossroads of Routes 101 and 125, Epping is indeed becoming a retail center—and the center of the Sabins' universe. Fortunately, the town's antique architectural charm has been spared. Epping is also home to the Leddy Center for the Performing Arts, which since 1975 has been producing quality shows, concerts, and giving art classes.

Our home is well located, 15 minutes away from our Durham house, and large enough to accommodate the whole family for holiday festivities. Our children and grandchildren enjoy visiting with us. We have finished the basement, and made an entertainment room where they love to play. When we moved, we did extensive landscaping and planted many trees to ensure privacy. The complex reminds us of the condominium that we used to rent in Lake Tahoe, and coincidentally the Lamprey River meanders through the land where our property is located.

The move to our new home in 1996 coincided with Frank's graduation from the University of New Hampshire. Our house in Durham was considerably bigger, and we did not have time to rearrange our belongings and discard pieces that we no longer needed. We had to leave a number of large boxes outside our new house. When we returned, the condominium association warned us that we could not leave boxes outside our unit. We moved the boxes inside as soon as possible including a big one with items that belonged in the basement. When we opened it, we got a surprise: a large garter snake had taken residence inside the box, and somehow I had to keep the animal inside until I reached the garden.

When we moved to Epping, Lucky retired from her position as Administrative Assistant with Heidelberg Harris where she had many special associates and worked for seven years. I was able to keep a mooring at Great Bay Marina for our sloop *Dulcinea*. After a couple of years, Lucky went to work at the University of New Hampshire and enjoyed it tremendously. We stopped working completely and started spending winters in Miami beginning in the year 2000 to enjoy the warm weather and revive our Cuban roots.

In January 2009, Frank called us in Miami: "Dad, a pipe burst in your house, flooded the basement, and caused massive damage. You must fly back urgently." We decided I would fly alone to assess the situation and then determine what to do next. When I got to our home, it looked as if it had been hit by a tsunami. The pipes in the first floor bathroom had burst, and water came rushing for two days before the maintenance crew in charge of snow removal noticed that our water pump was running continuously; he alerted the President of our condominium association who then called Frank. The insurance situation was particularly complicated; responsibilities between the insurance of the condominium master insurance policy, and my own supplemental homeowners insurance had to be sorted out.

A crew came to clean up all the debris which required being loaded in two huge containers. The entire unit had to be gutted for fear of mold contamination. Carpeting, hardwood floors, and walls were removed; ceilings had to be torn down. The heating unit had been under water and had to be discarded. The damage exceeded $100,000, which fortunately was covered by the two insurance policies. Although the experience was extremely upsetting, we ended up by having an improved and updated house. A G.E. owned insurance company reimbursed us for contents, paid us the full coverage we carried, and did not even apply the deductible in appreciation that our loss exceeded our maximum limit amount.

Our antique upright piano made by H. Bord in Paris in the late 19th century, with two candleholders to provide light before the use of electricity and light bulbs, was severely damaged. We saw an identical piano in the National Palace of Portugal in Sintra, which dates back to 15th century reign of King John I and housed royalty for 500 years. I had surprised Lucky when I showed up with this piano when we lived in Geneva. We often went to buy antiques at an estate liquidator. My boss had bought a beautiful and very expensive liquor cabinet and bar made from an antique piano, and I wanted to do the same with my piano. Instead, Zuni was a good pianist and used the piano for its intended purpose; so did the children. I got a real bargain with this piano, that went with us around the world, moving from Switzerland, to California, to Westport, to Gorgonzola, to Durham, and finally to Epping. G.E. spent a lot of money moving this heavy piece from location to location, as I was continuously transferred to new jobs.

I filed a claim for the estimated value of this valuable musical piece, and contracted a handy man to remove the guts of the damaged piano. Our two bathrooms had to be torn, and replaced; we had lots of mirrors left over, and I took them to be cut to Portland Glass to line the lower and upper cabinets of the former piano. Ultimately, I refinished it, and the piano had a rebirth as a liquor cabinet/bar—which was my intention when I bought it 40 years ago.

⤳⤳⤳⤸

I bought a 1973 Sabre sloop without getting a survey; from previous experience, I should have known that old beautiful sailboats are demanding mistresses, and need lots of TLC. A friend helped me repair and enhance my sailboat and spent countless hours working on this project. We also discovered that the fiberglass hull had numerous blisters. After hundreds of hours of work and thousands of dollars, by the following June we got *Dulcinea* ready for the passage to Portland where I had bought a mooring and had it placed near the Portland Yacht Services. I discovered the "half" dinghy that a friend had given me and almost sank, was too small to handle the Portland Harbor's waves; soon after, I replaced it with a sea worthy Down-East Dolphin dinghy. We enjoyed sailing in Casco Bay and up and down the beautiful Maine coast for years.

We had initially planned to name the boat *Siboney,* after the first Indian inhabitants of Cuba. *Siboney* is also one of Ernesto Lecuona's most famous compositions; he was Cuba's foremost composer and one of Zuni's piano teachers. In 1989 Bill Butler, a retired G.E. employee, named his 38-foot sailboat Siboney, and set out to circumnavigate the world. After sailing a few days in the Pacific, dozens of maddened whales hammered through the hull of *Siboney*. Bill and his French wife Simonne ended up adrift in a six-foot plastic life raft, fought each other, and struggled for their lives for 66 days through storms, sharks, hunger and frustration. The odyssey is described in detail in his book "66 Days Adrift." Needless to say, the marriage did not survive. With this precedent, we decided *Siboney* was not the right name for our sloop.

We had recently seen the Broadway musical Man of La Mancha in Portsmouth's Repertory Theater; we immediately knew that we would name her *Dulcinea* after Don Quixote's lovely wench. We named the dinghy *Sancho Panza*, Don Quixote's loyal servant. Months later, while in Maine, we saw another sailboat named *Dulcinea*.

My S.H.Y.C. friends Dan Conron and Bill Brown helped me sail *Dulcinea* from Wesport to New Hampshire; although our passage did not quite match by any account Butler's adventure, it was nevertheless a memorable cruise. We left at night in a gentle breeze, which soon became a strong 30-knot-gale that required reefing. Sabers are excellent sailing boats, and the three of us enjoyed the feeling of *Dulcinea* cutting through the waves and foam splashing our faces. The wind died down by the time we crossed New London, and we had to start the auxiliary engine—a venerable Atomic 4 which had seen better days and started to overheat. We pulled into a marina in Stonington, where the Browns had moved, and found a mechanic to do a mechanical trick to increase the flow of water to cool the engine. From that day on, I knew I could never press this old engine that was supposed to have been totally overhauled; I also knew that my next sailboat would need to have a reliable diesel engine. We spent that night at the Brown's beautiful home in nearby Westerly, Rhode Island.

At dawn next day we took off again, anchored in Onset in Buzzards Bay south of the Cape Cod Canal to wait for a favorable tide, and took off again in the afternoon. I have crossed the Canal several times, and always find it an exciting passage with many points of interest, including Woods Hole. It is Cape Cod's main port and a center for oceanographic research; ferries to Martha's Vineyard operate year-round. You see a great variety of boats: motor yachts, sailboats, and commercial cargo ships. After crossing the Canal, we sighted a large family of whalebone whales which are frequently seen in these waters.

In the late afternoon, we were sailing under ideal conditions when *Dulcinea* came to an abrupt stop; we soon discovered the reason: we had picked up a lobster pot in the rudder. We immediately put down the sails, started the engine, and radioed a large commercial ship approaching at a distance to ensure the pilot could see us and knew that we could not move. As owner and captain, I was the logical member of the crew to dive, if necessary, to cut loose the lobster pot. We fortunately managed to disentangle the lobster pot by reversing the engine several times, and I never had to dive.

We finally reached the Portsmouth Yacht Club, and docked to refuel and prepare to proceed to our final destination, Great Bay Marina. While we were fueling, we saw a small single engine seaplane land near us; the pilot asked for permission to dock and fuel the plane, since the plane was out of gas. In the process of docking, the plane suffered a bump in one of its landing pontoons. This was a unique sailing experience, and even old salts like Dan and Bill had never seen anything like that.

I could not get a chart of the course from the entrance of Portsmouth to Great Bay, and left thinking that in a clear day we could navigate the small distance by carefully following the navigational aids. We were cruising at a good speed under power, when *Dulcinea*'s keel hit a rock sending us crashing to the floor. Fortunately, the keel absorbed the shock and the damage was minor. After this last incident, we finally limped to our marina and ended our odyssey.

We kept *Dulcinea* in Casco Bay for several years. Surprisingly, our mooring was near a monument commemorating the blowing of the Navy Ship Maine in Havana Harbor in 1898, which started the Spanish American War. Casco Bay is home to many small islands and seven beautiful lighthouses, including Pocahontas Light, which stands only 6 feet and is the smallest lighthouse registered with the U.S. Coast Guard. Among the many small islands, we frequently anchored at Great Chebeague Island, 10 miles from Portland. We visited two quaint Bed and Breakfast properties, the Orchard Inn and Great Chebeague, where we occasionally had lunch or dinner. We also bought lobsters from lobster fishermen, and cooked them in our boat; somehow, they always tasted better than the ones from restaurants. This island keeps a number of bicycles you can borrow for free, and cycle for miles exploring many great places. We also anchored at the Goslings, a few miles from Great Chebeague, where numerous seals came close to our boats, particularly at night.

〰〰〰

Eagle Island is particularly interesting, as it was purchased by the famous Admiral Robert Peary in 1881. On April 6, 1909, Admiral Peary, accompanied by Matthew Henson and four Inuit natives, planted the American flag at the North Pole. They were the first humans to reach the northern most point on the globe. We anchored

Dulcinea near Admiral Peary's cottage, which is a Maine Historic Site, and went ashore in our dinghy *Sancho Panza*.

We have an Antique Road Show connection to Admiral Peary. Every year in September, our church has a 650-family white elephant sale event, and rise over $30,000; parishioners donate everything from furniture to art works. A few years ago, Lucky paid $7 for an oil painting by John Richard Peary of a boat sailing between icebergs. She thought the artist might be related to Admiral Peary, and we immediately checked in Google. The painter turned out to be one of America's foremost Marine artists, and a seventh-generation artist with family ties to Admiral Peary. He depicts sailing ships with precise accuracy in all types of weather; his paintings appear in collections of the White House, Queen Elizabeth II, and President Ford. His studio is in York, and we immediately called him to ask for an appraisal, dreaming it would be worth thousands; he immediately recognized the painting and the original frame, and gave us a written appraisal of $700. We should have been delighted—but were somewhat disappointed as we expected an even higher value.

Admiral Peary graduated from Beaudoin College in Brunswick, Maine, which we visit frequently in our way to Sebasco Harbor. We subscribe to the excellent summer stock theater of the Maine State Music Theater, which uses the college's beautiful church-like building for its musicals. One of my favorite American Civil War heroes, Brigadier General Joshua Lawrence Chamberlain, was Beaudoin's President. He earned the Medal of Honor for his gallantry at Gettysburg, and was given the honor of commanding the Union troops at the surrender ceremony at Appomattox.

We sailed to Pemaquid to visit the Egberts, our good friends from our days in Geneva who own a summer cottage in Damariscotta. In one of our visits, we left *Dulcinea* at a nearby mooring, and upon our return found that the tide was too low for her keel; she was healing for a few hours, until the tide turned, and we had to sleep sideways. The coast from Portland to the Portland Yacht Club in Falmouth Foreside, Freeport, Yarmouth, Brunswick, and Bath offers great views and interesting coves.

To be closer to home, we moved *Dulcinea* to Great Bay Marina where I worked. While this harbor is lovely, the currents are strong; getting in and out of the ocean is time consuming and challenging, with three bridges. The University of New Hampshire has an oceanic research center in Great Bay. We occasionally docked overnight in Prescott Park in Portsmouth, and enjoyed the open air summer stock Broadway plays. Strawberry Bank Museum is next to Prescott Park, and offers an extraordinary opportunity to experience and imagine how people lived and worked in this typical American neighborhood throughout four centuries of history. It's restored houses, featured exhibits, and gardens tell the stories of the many generations who settled in Portsmouth from the 17th to the mid-20th centuries. A replica gundalow, a type of flat bottom cargo vessel once common in New England Rivers, is kept at Prescott Park. It is 70 feet long, and used tidal currents for propulsion, with a single sail to harness favorable winds. They were very important in the commercial and maritime history of the region.

We sailed frequently to the Isles of Shoals, a group of small islands situated six miles off Portsmouth, and straddling New Hampshire and Maine. The islands were used for seasonal fishing by Native Americans and were settled in the early 17th century. The first recorded landfall occurred in 1623, and the islands have a rich history. Thomas Leighton and Levi Thaxter opened a summer hotel on Appledore land around 1850; Thaxter married Leighton's fifteen-year old daughter Celia, who became the most popular American female poet of the 19th century. The Boston painter William Hunt drowned here in 1879, reportedly a suicide; Celia discovered the body. Appledore is maintained by volunteers, and each one spends one week in the summer caring for the terrain. We anchored in the harbor, and enjoyed walking in both islands.

Star Island is the only island served by a commercial boat from the mainland, and is owned by the Unitarian Universalist Association and the United Church of Christ. In the summer, they have numerous religious activities at the Oceanic Hotel and other facilities. We love walking in the beautiful island, and sit in rocking chairs they have in the wrap-around terraces; we buy ice cream, sip tea, and just look at *Dulcinea* and other boats at anchor in the harbor.

We eventually sold *Dulcinea*; the new owners had owned a boat with the same name—which helped seal the transaction. We have a busy life, and a boat became an expensive hobby for us. Frank fortunately inherited my love of boats and the sea. In 2010, he bought a beautiful 31 foot Pearson sloop, named her *Minerva,* and joined the American Yacht Club in Newburyport, Massachusetts. In the summer, he keeps her at Sebasco Harbor, one of our favorite harbors. It is located 50 miles north of Portland, at the tip of Popham Peninsula some 12 miles south of Bath. Sebasco was founded in 1930 by bakery magnate Nate Cushman and was frequented by Eleanor Roosevelt. The resort has two excellent restaurants which focus on homegrown and local food purchased from local organic farmers, lobstermen, fishermen, dairy farmers, and cattle ranchers. It includes a 9-hole golf course, saltwater pool, tennis courts, fitness center, and many other amenities including a day camp for children. In 2008, Sebasco was *Parents* magazine's Best Beach Resort for Families; in 2011, it was named Maine's Best Family Spa. Frank and Minerva are taking Power Squadron navigation classes, and we plan to embark on ambitious cruises in the future.

MIAMI, FLORIDA: CUBAN-AMERICAN SNOW BIRDS: LATE 1990s TO PRESENT

*"A mi me llaman
el negrito del batey
porque el trabajo
para mi es un enemigo,
el trabajar yo se
lo dejo todo al buey
porque el trabajo
lo hiso Dios como un castigo."*

Merengue Dominicano, M. Guzmán

SINCE THE LATE 1990s, we have adhered to *El negrito del batey's* philosophy and enjoyed leisure in Miami. We are snow birds from our main residence in New Hampshire, and our native nest is only approximately 100 miles away. Many of our friends are surprised that we have not become full time Miami residents, as we have some important reasons. We fear the reaction of our son Frank and his family who complain that already we spend too much time away. We also love our life in New England, where we have lived for almost three decades, longer than in any other location: we enjoy the seasons, friends, cruising, visiting interesting places in the northeast, culinary adventures, church and university functions. We are never bored.

Miami is a vital part of our Cuban third. The kaleidoscopic mix of our activities, and our many friends, make this city particularly attractive to us. Wikipedia defines a Cuban-American as a U.S. citizen who traces his or her national origin to Cuba. Cuban-Americans are also considered native born Americans with Cuban parents or Cuban born persons who were raised and educated in the U.S. Cuban-Americans form the third-largest Hispanic group in the U. S. and also the largest group of Hispanics of European ancestry. According to recently published data, at the beginning of 2007 there were

1,241,685 Cuban-Americans in the U.S., 833,120 of whom lived in Florida and 785 in New Hampshire—of which we have only met a few. Wikipedia lists hundreds of notable Cuban-Americans in many fields, including sports, business, education, entertainment, journalism, and politics. Under the entertainment category, the list shows numerous categories: actors, cartoonists, directors, screenwriters, producers, graphic designers, fashion, magicians, musicians, television personalities, and writers. Some of them are particularly relevant to our life in Miami.

I have visited Miami frequently since the 1940s when it was a popular destination for many Cubans. The city began a long process of decay despite its magnificent natural setting and countless Art Deco architectural treasures. The Cuban-American influx helped transform Miami into a vibrant world-class multi-cultural metropolis, and today it attracts business and tourists from around the world; despite problems, Miami is frequently called America's City of the Future.

We are fortunate our family shares our love of Miami and come to see us frequently; the Clavelouxs own an apartment at the Decoplage in South Beach and are spending increasingly more time during the winter. We expose our grandchildren to a few aspects of our *Cubanidad* and emphasize the importance of having a good knowledge of Spanish.

During many years, our visits to the Sanmartins' Summer Grove Apartment in Westchester off Coral Way enabled us to participate actively in Miami's Cuban life. According to the last census, Cuban-Americans constitute 66% of Westchester's population, the highest number in the Greater Miami area; Hialeah is second with 62%. It is an area where you can live without ever uttering a word of English, and there are posters half-humorously proclaiming "English Spoken Here" or "Parking for Cubans Only."

Cuban-American babies can be brought to life by a Cuba-American obstetrician in a hospital where you can buy *pastelitos de guayaba* and *croquetas de jamón* in the lobby, *go* to a Cuban-American nursery or kindergarten, and work their entire life among

Cuban-Americans. For a toothache, you go to a Cuban-American dentist; he or she will also handle implants, whiten your teeth, pull them if necessary, or install orthodontic gear if they are crooked.

Not feeling well? Your Cuban-American H.M.O. will dispatch a mini-bus to pick you up, be greeted by Cuban-American nurses, and eventually a Cuban-American doctor will see you. Your feet hurt? See a Cuban-American podiatrist. Your child is ill? Take him to a Cuban-Americn pediatrician. Not happy with you boobs? A Cuban-American cosmetic surgeon will enlarge or reduce them. Are you stricken with Cancer? See your Cuban-American oncologist. The Cuban-American doctor accelerated your demise? Your loved ones will call *Funeraria Caballero Rivero,* the two Cuban families who were prominent in the funeral business back in the 1950's; the *Funeraria Vior* handled funeral arrangements for Zuni and *Tía Bibiana,* which is owned and operated by descendants of the Caballero family. No money for the funeral? No problem. A Cuban-American banker will arrange the necessary financing. Want to marry? You can meet many eligible Cuban-American men and women; woo the ladies with flowers from a Cuban-American street vendor, or a florist if you want to spend more; buy the wedding cake at Jessy's Bakery; find a Cuban priest at St. Brendan's to confess your sins in Spanish; book a honeymoon cruise at a Cuban-American travel agency and be entertained by Willy Chirino. Your marriage didn't work? Find a Cuban-American counselor. Are the differences irreconcilable? See your Cuban-American lawyer specialized in divorce settlements.

Whenever my watch breaks, I take it to a Cuban-American expert well trained to do this job in Cuba. If your car breaks down, you take it to a Cuban-American mechanic; chances are he will have superb skills, like mechanics in Cuba who must improvise to maintain a fleet of antique cars and motorcycles running. In May, we go to Cuba *Nostalgia* at the Tamiami Park, where you find every conceivable memento from Cuba B.C.

Farmacia Navarro will sell you medicines, perfumes, and a wide variety of other goods and a Cuban-American will help you; you will even find *Agua de Violetas*, cologne favored by Cuban mothers to ensure their babies' fragrance. Next door you enter *Sedano's* grocery store, where you can buy your favorite Cuban supplies after enjoying a *cafecito*. Outside you will find vendors selling many items, from *tamales en hoja, granisados,* and shrimp packages at very attractive prices. If you want to visit your relatives in the island, send them necessities or *remesas* you will not have far to go. You will be greeted with the world's sweatest terms of endearment; anybody here is *mi vida* or, at least *mi corazón*.

Education is the key to advance, especially in today's ever more competitive world. Two Cuban-Americans have contributed greatly to make quality education available to countless young compatriots: my friend Modesto Maidique, who as President of Florida International University led this institution during decades of unparalleled growth, and Eduardo Padrón, who still does a similar job at Miami Dade College. They are both widely recognized as top educational leaders, and participate in education policy forums in the United States and abroad. These two Universities, and the University of Miami, are three anchors for Miami's progress in every intellectual and artistic pursuit.

F.I.U. is nearby at 107 Avenue, where you can study just about any subject at bargain prices, become a lawyer or a medical doctor, or learn how to play the trumpet. *Belén* is also nearby; this Jesuit school, Fidel's Alma Mater, was one of the best in Cuba and is now a preeminent prep-school with superb academic standards.

You want a break from so many Cuban-Americans? You can eat Argentine *empanadas,* a Brazilian *feijoada,* Mexican *tacos,* or specialties from every corner of the Americas and the world. We, however, generally favor Cuban restaurants; we never tire of our gastronomic heritage and will cover later this important part of our life in this city.

ᐳᐳᐳᐳ

During our months in Miami, we participate in many facets of the Cuban mosaic, probably more actively than most of our friends who are year round residents; this is similar to many New Yorkers who have never visited the Statue of Liberty, or Parisians who have never climbed the Eiffel Tower, or enjoyed a show at the Lido. Snowbird activities are also part of our life in Miami: we meet many of our Anglo friends at the beach where few Cubans venture in winter. We go to many musical shows and the theater, and particularly enjoy attending the many productions that focus on Cuban shows.

The Miami Dade Country Auditorium, which opened in 1951, has played an important role in fostering Cuban and Spanish performing arts including grand opera, *zarzuelas,* symphony, theater, concerts, ballets, and lectures. Sociedad Pro Arte Grateli is Miami's oldest Hispanic performing arts company, and Pili de la Rosa has dedicated many years to the preservation of these traditions. I occasionally receive phone calls in New Hampshire asking if I plan to attend their shows; the last call was to promote an Enrique Chía concert in September, and I jokingly told the caller that I would buy two tickets if they moved the show to January.

One of the many unforgettable performances we have enjoyed at Miami Dade was hearing the legendary Cuban diva Marta Pérez whose distinguished mezzo-soprano career included performances at Milan's *La Scala.* I like to joke that 60 is the minimum age to be admitted to the Miami Dade functions, as most of the audience makes me feel like a youngster; I regret younger Cuban-Americans do not sufficiently appreciate this institution's contributions to foster the important Cuban artistic heritage.

Talented Cuban-American artists regularly perform At the University of Miami, F.I.U., Miami Dade College, *Teatro Roca* at *Belén* Preparatory School, and many other theaters. Among them we have enjoyed performances by Celia Cruz, Olga Guillot, Cachao, Albita, Paquito Rivera, Gloria Estefán, Willy Chirino, Arturo Sandoval, Meme Solís, Marlena Burke, Enrique Chía, and many other jazz and pop musicians some of whom we have met personally. Many of these artists were famous in Cuba, like Maestro Marlene Urbay, who was music director of Cuba's National Ballet since age twenty and is currently Director and founder of the Florida Chamber Orchestra.

Miami has become an important Classical Music center. We subscribe to the Miami Symphony Orchestra, a world-class ensemble; Cuban Maestro Manuel Ochoa was the founder. After his death, Maestro Eduardo Marturet, a Venezuelan, took the baton and continues to improve the quality of the M.S.O. to ever higher levels. He is a generous virtuoso who inspires the orchestra and gives many encores. The New World Sympony and Maestro Michael Tilson Thomas prepare highly-gifted graduates of distinguished music programs for leadership roles in orchestras and ensembles around the world; the newly inaugurated Frank Gehry state of the art building is a landmark for American culture. The Cleveland Orchestra, one of the foremost American ensembles, features world renowned guest artists like the young Chinese pianist Lang Lang and the Japanese violinist Midori. The Chopin Foundation frequently offers free concerts on Sunday afternoons; some of these concerts are devoted to young pianists, and the talent of these young artists is simply amazing. In addition, the three major Miami universities offer many fine music programs.

Florida Grand Opera stages productions at the Sanford and Dolores Ziff Ballet Opera House located at the Adrienne Arsht Center for the Performing Arts. This world class art complex has given Miami a wonderful resource for a variety of artistic venues. We subscribe to the Florida Grand Opera, which typically produces four grand operas each year. Cuban-American singers like the young sopranos Eglise Gutiérrez and Elizabeth Caballero are quickly rising to prominence in the world's top opera houses.

We enjoy many wonderful ballet functions. Edward Villela, the former New York City Ballet star dancer, is the Founder of the Miami City Ballet where many Cuban-Americans serve as principals, soloists, and members of the Corps of Ballet. M.C.B. has become an important ballet company, and they tour around the world. The Cuban Classic Ballet Company, with the famous sisters Lorena and Lorna Feijo, frequently perform in Miami. Lorena is a San Francisco Ballet Principal

Dancer while Lorna is with the Boston Ballet. These two *prima bal-lerinas* are remarkable, and rarely have we seen their ethereal level of artistic beauty. We have been fortunate to enjoy many excellent ballet performances in New York, Boston, and Europe; we believe these sisters are a consolation for not having seen dancing legends like Nijisky, Pavlova, or Rudolf Nurejev.

Two newspapers cover Hispanics in general and Cuban-Americans in particular: *El Nuevo Herald* and el *Diario de las Americas* where Elio worked for many years. We also visit frequently the *Casa Bacardí* at the University of Miami's Institute for Cuban and Cuban-American Studies and the Cuban Heritage Collection.

I like to quote from the humorous song *Nosotros los Cubanos* by the popular singer Marisela Varena:

"Nosotros los Cubanos	We Cubans
no somos nada chovinistas,	are not chauvinists,
sólo somos realistas,	we are only realistic
el mundo se divide	the world is divided
exactamente a la mitad.	exactly in half.
Nosotros los Cubanos	We Cubans,
y el resto de la humanidad."	and the rest of humanity.

❧❧❧

Food is one of my passions and a significant element of any culture. Great civilizations produced the world's greatest *cuisines*, in-cluding the French, Italian, and Chinese—followed probably by the Spanish, Greek, and Japanese. I like to think that Cuban food is close to the top tier and ranks among the world's top ten.

Miami has the best restaurants in the world if you consider cost versus quality. Culinary offerings cover a wide variety of cuisines from around the world, but Cuban and Spanish restaurants predom-inate due to the large populations from Cuba and South America. We particularly favor Cuban establishments that generally offer good food, generous portions, and reasonable prices. We usually share entrees or take home some of the food to avoid developing an excessive girth. When we ask our Yankee friends where they want to go for dinner, they invariably choose a Cuban restaurant and ask for our suggestions.

Cuban food covers a broad range of recipes with primarily Spanish, Creole, and Asian influences. Before the Revolution, there were many Chinese in Cuba and they typically owned restaurants or laundries. Cuban-American-Chinese émigrés have opened Chinese restaurants in the U.S. that typically include typical Cuban fare in their menus; most Chinese left Cuba after the Revolution, draining the island of many of its smartest and hardest working people. One of these restaurants is in Broadway and the 70s and is named *La Caridad,* after Cuba's patron Saint. When Frank and Alina lived in the upper West Side of New York City we went to this restaurant frequently.

Some of the restaurants we visit frequently are the historical icon Versailles, where Presidential candidates go seeking Cuban-American votes, Havana Harry's, La Carreta, Las Culebrinas, Habano's, Latin American Cafeteria, Ayesterán, Habana Vieja, Casa Paco, Cacao, Garcías, Brisas de España, Sazón, Puerto de Sagua, Lario's, David's, El Exquisito, and many others including the Cuban-American fast food chain Pollo Tropical. Here are some of our favorite Cuban dishes:

APERITIVOS
Mariquitas   Tostones   Camarones al ajillo   Calamares frito
Croquetas de jamón o pollo   Empanadas de carne o pollo
Papas rellenas   Chicharrones

SOPAS Y POTAJES
Ajiaco criollo   Caldo Gallego   Fabada
Asturiana Crema de Malanga
Sopas: de pollo, de plátano, de frijoles, de lentejas, de chicharos

AVES
Arroz con pollo   Pollo con limón y ajo   Fricasé de pollo
Pollo en salsa de guayaba ó de mango

CARNES
Masas de Puerco Asado   Picadillo   Boliche relleno
Bistec de palomilla   Carne con papas   Ropa vieja   Vaca frita
Chilindrón de Chivo   Sesos   Lengua   Rabo encendido

PESCADOS Y MARISCOS
Paella   Enchilado de camarones ó langosta   Frituras de Bacalao
Pescados fritos o asados: Pargo o Cherna   Calamares en su tinta

ACOMPAÑANTES
Arroz y frijoles   Congrí   Platanitos maduros   Tostones
Yuca con mojo

BOCADITOS
Sandwich Cubano   Media noche   Frita Cubana   Elena Ruth
Pastelitos de carne, queso o guayaba
Churros con chocolate caliente

POSTRES, BEBIDAS Y CAFÉ
Buñuelos   Flán   Tocino del Cielo   Capuchinos
Panetelas Borrachas   Arroz con Leche
Daiquirí   Mojito   Sangría   Jupiña   Materva
Batido de mamey
Café Cubano   Cortadito   Café con leche

According to Jorge Mañach, my father's friend and one of Cuba's foremost thinkers, *AJIACO,* the national Cuban dish, is representative of the Cuban identity because of its adaptability and tolerance for new ingredients. There are many *ajiaco* recipes, but basically it is a thick stew with native tubers, vegetables and meat seasoned with herbs and spices. You can find a traditional *Ajiaco Cubano* in *tasteof-cuba.com*, which also provides information on other Cuban recipes and restaurants. I believe each person should develop his own *ajiaco* recipe, based on individual experiences. Below is my own *ajiaco* recipe:

- 2 pounds of *yuca* and *boniato*, for our Cuban roots
- 2 ounces of rum, for our Cuban spirit
- 3 lobsters, for the Down East infusion
- 8 ounces of grated Gruyere cheese, for our years in Switzerland
- 16 ounces of prosciutto, for our years in Italy
- 1 pound of stone crabs, for our winters in Miami
- 2 tablespoons of olive oil, for our Mediterranean heritage
- ½ gallon of fish stock, for mixing all the ingredients
- bring to a boil; stir frequently
- drink *mojitos* and lots of wine

ﻝﻝﻝ

For over fifty years, two million Cubans have fled the first Communist country in history to combine Bolshevik cruelty with Cuba's *choteo*. Many have been killed, tortured, or jailed. Yoani Sánchez, the Cuban blogger who bravely denounces the regime from her home in Havana, has won recognition for journalistic bravery; *Time* magazine listed her as one of the world's 100 most influential persons in 2008 stating "under the nose of a regime that has never tolerated dissent, Sánchez practices what paper-bound journalists cannot: freedom of speech." In November 2009, President Obama wrote: "her blog provides the world a unique window into the realities of daily life in Cuba."

Opposition to the Castro tyranny has been growing recently; a group of brave women dressed in white, *Las Damas de Blanco*, frequently demonstrate for the release of their family members who are arbitrarily held as political prisoners; these brave women are regularly attacked by pro-government mobs. Orlando Tamayo died after 83 days of a hunger strike in favor of human rights and his place was taken by Guillermo Fariñas. The Government abuses brought worldwide condemnation and demonstration in support of the hunger strikers and *Las Damas de Blanco* in cities around the world.

On March 26, 2010, Gloria and Emilio Estefán called for a march in Little Havana. We were all dressed in white to show solidarity with the opposition in Cuba, and tens of thousands joined the protest. We took the bus to *Calle Ocho* in Little Havana and talked to other Cuban-Americans also headed for the march. One of our new acquaintances was the nephew of a girl I dated in Havana, Ramona Rivera; I believe most of her family stayed in Cuba and supported the Revolution. Recently, I was surprised to see her picture and her name among the *Damas de Blanco* in the news. The young man lived near the zoo in Havana, and told us how the signs initially read "Don't Feed the Animals"; they were changed to "Don't Eat the Animals' Food"; and changed again to "Don't Eat the Animals." In fact, he said that the only remaining elephant died under suspicious circumstances, and the body was practically gone by the next morning. It is said that some may have added elephant meat to their *ajiaco*.

We bought little flags, and joined the march of Cuban-Americans and sympathizers from many other countries. In a sea of Cuban and American flags, the stirring Cuban national anthem was played through loudspeakers:

Al combate, corred Bayameses,	Run to the battle, people of Bayamo,
que la patria os contempla, orgullosa	make the motherland proud,
no temais una muerte gloriosa,	don't fear a glorious death,
que morir por la patria es vivir.	that to die for the motherland is to live.

It reminded me of the *actos cívicos* I attended at *Colegio Baldor* when I was a young boy. Over 60 years have gone by since then, but we felt strong emotions in the *Calle Ocho* and many of the marchers could not contain the tears hearing the anthem and cries of "Viva Cuba Libre. Zapata Vive." Many celebrities joined the march, and the Cuban Icon Olguita Guillot refused to be chauffeured and insisted in marching despite her poor health; she died a few months later. I suspect Celia Cruz also joined the marchers from her place of honor in heavens. Andy García organized a similar march in Los Angeles.

❧❧❧

On February 13, 2006, we attended a tribute to Solidarity and President Lech Walensa that was a moving experience for us. Walensa is a charismatic Polish leader who co-founded the Soviet Union's first trade-union, was Poland's elected President from 1990 to 1995, and won the 1983 Nobel Peace Prize for his key role in the demise of one of history's most despicable systems. At his keynote address, he spoke of the Polish transition, lessons for Cuba, and told us "Be patient, my Cuban friends. Cuba will soon be free." Six years have gone by, and Cuba is yet to be free; we need to keep hope that, sooner or later, Walensa's prediction will become a reality.

❧❧❧

La Ermita de la Caridad is located near Zuni's Brickell Avenue apartment, which we visit often. Our Lady of Charity is Cuba's Patron Saint. On September 8, 1961 an image of the Virgin arrived in Miami from a church in the town of Guanabo, a beach town near Havana. From 1968 to 1973 funds were collected to build a beautiful Sanctuary, and annually pilgrimages are made by Cuban-Americans representing 126 Cuban districts. In 1998, Pope John Paul II went to Cuba's Oriente Province and visited *La Basilica del Cobre* where a tiny statue is said to have been found by three fishermen, Rodrigo and Juan de Hoyos and the slave Juan Moreno, as their small boat was taking water on September 8, 1962 in the Bay of Nipe. Pope Benedict XVI will visit Cuba on March 26, 2012 to celebrate the 400th anniversary of the Virgin's apparition.

॰॰॰॰

Both Lucky and I have friends that we have known for decades and participate in many nostalgic activities. We have also made new friends among our fellow snow birds from the northeast, Canadians, Europeans, and South Americans who have also made Miami their winter Eden; many of these share our eclectic interests. In Frank Capra's classic movie, *It's a Wonderful Life,* George Bailey is a man close to commit suicide on Christmas Eve. Clarence, an angel in probation, is sent to earn his wings by showing George the lives he has touched, to appreciate family and friends, and value life. We all need a Clarence to remind us of what is truly important in life, and how blessed we are to have a close family and good friends.

TRAVEL MEMORIES

Travel Memories

(Clockwise from Top Left)
1. Lucky and Paco ready to fly a balloon, Cappadocia, Turkey
2. The Sabins vacationing in the Austrian Alps
3. Lucky and Paco in Key West
4. The Sabins and Zuni in the Italian Alps
5. The Sabins and Zuni in Portofino
6. Lucky and Paco in Jamaica

More Adventures

(Clockwise from Top Left)
1. Family portrait dressed in customes of the Old West, California
2. Paco and Lucky, Tower Eiffel, Paris
3. Lucky and Paco with Bayanas, Bahia, Brazil
4. Lucky and Paco at S.H.Y.C. as Olive Oil and Popeye
5. Parents coming to babysit daughters Yvonne and Alina
6. Tío, Zuni, Tía, Elio visiting Sabins in Durham, New Hampshire

Mohammed	*Don't tell me how educated you are, tell me how much you have traveled*
Solzhenitsyn	*Own what you can carry with you; let your memory be your travel bag*
Lin Yutan	*No one realizes how beautiful it is to travel until he comes home and rests his head on his old, familiar pillow*
St. Augustine	*The world is a book and those who do not travel read only one page*
R. L. Stevenson	*There is no foreign lands; only the traveller is foreign*
	For my part, I travel not to go anywhere, but to go. I travel for travel's sake. The great affair it to move
Mark Twain	*Travel is fatal to prejudice, bigotry, and narrow mindedness*
	Twenty years from now you will be more disappointed by the things you didn't do than by the ones you did do. So throw away the bowlines, sail away from the safe harbor.
	Catch the trade winds in your sails.
	EXPLORE. DREAM. DISCOVER
Rick Steves	*A tight budget forces you to travel close to the ground, meeting and communicating with the people. Experiencing the real Europe requires catching it by surprise, going casual....through the back door*
Paco	*The family that travels together stays together*

I am glad to confirm that many notable people agree that travel is an essential part of a well lived life. I was born with the travel bug and my addiction has not abated. Fate facilitated the pursuit of my passion and gave me a partner with identical interests. Travel has greatly enhanced our lives. My approach to "travel" is holistic: I view it as a medicine for the soul with interdependent parts. It encompasses key aspects of humanity and culture.

History: History has always been an abiding love, and I enjoy visiting locations where important events occurred, including archeological sites, battlefields, and other historical events of different civilizations.

Gastronomy: Many people around the world take food seriously and devote lots of time and effort to it. We have lived in countries with a rich culinary tradition, and the older I get the more important this passion becomes. Before and after a major and prolonged gastronomic adventure, I spend extra time at the gym and try to limit my caloric input.

Religion: I have considerable intellectual interest in religion, but your mother, as you know, is positively addicted to this important part of humanity. We have visited most of the world's cathedrals and places where the Virgin Mary has appeared, and I have a difficult time pulling my kindred soul away from these fascinating and emotionally powerful places and magnificent churches.

Arts: We love visiting the great museums of the world. I confess that my attention span and physical stamina now limits my visits to three to four hours. We also enjoy music, dance, and theater.

Nature: Sailing enabled us to enjoy many close encounters with nature. We have also relished visiting National Parks in the U.S. and Canada; some other places where nature's power and beauty astounded us include the Alps, Italy's Amalfi coast, and Turkey's Cappadocia landscape to name a few.

The money we have spent in traveling is a capital investment that belongs on my personal balance sheet's asset side and not an expense. It is not exposed to the risks of the stock market and yields a high return, as you enjoy the anticipation and planning, the actual trip, and finally you gain memories that you will take to your grave. Every time we return home, we feel our lives have been enriched. We are always happy to return home and are reminded of how lucky we are to live in America. We are not really surprised to learn in our trips that many people would like to visit or even relocate to the United States.

I was fortunate to travel before the world changed forever with the September 11, 2001 terrorist attacks which particularly encumbered air travel. In addition, airlines pampered passengers in the good old days: drinks, food, and amenities were infinitely better before cost-cutting efforts negatively affected the quality of life aboard an airplane—not to mention that youth and beauty were politically incorrect requirements for flight attendants.

A few years ago, my daughter Alina gave me a copy of Patricia Schultz' book *1000 Places to See Before You Die* as a birthday gift. According to its introduction "The urge to travel is as old as man himself. It's what drove the ancient Romans to visit Athens' Acropolis and Verona's amphitheater. It's what sent Marco Polo east in his momentous journey." I hope Marco Polo will continue to inspire me in planning new adventures.

UNITED STATES AND CANADA

DURING MY CHILDHOOD, I traveled extensively with my parents throughout the United States, including several months of driving around the entire continent in 1947, 1957, and 1958; we also visited Miami and New York countless times. Boston and New York are two of our favorite places, and we spend a few days in each of these cities every year. Since moving to the U.S. in 1959 after Castro's revolution, we have lived in six states, and enjoyed many travel adventures from each of our home bases.

We take several days on our way to and from Miami to visit friends and family and revisit many interesting places in the east coast. After enjoying the Christmas holidays in Westport and Ridgewood, we stop in Washington for a couple of days to enjoy Georgetown, the numerous museums, and excellent restaurants; one of our favorites is Acadiana, which specializes in flavorful Louisiana dishes. Our next stop is frequently Charleston, South Carolina, a city with rich history, classic elegance, and one of the world's best crabs; she-crab soup, one of their specialties, is simply heavenly. Another of our favorite stops is romantic Savannah, Georgia where handsome town houses, bedecked with fountains and statues which are beautified by live oaks and azaleas; the restoration of the warehouses and cotton brokerage offices along Bay Street, Factor's Walk and River Street have revived the city's historic waterfront. We then drive to my brother's home in Lake City, Florida and finally head for our final destination: Miami.

Every fall, we enjoy foliage trips in New England and Canada. The colors of the leaves are amazing, and the cool weather delightful. Lucky and I have driven thousands of miles in the northwest and southwest; we flew to Hawaii from California en route before moving to New York. During seven years, I worked in New York City, and still love to visit the Big Apple a few times every year. Before each of these trips, I always search for new culinary adventures. The only areas yet to explore are Alaska, Utah, and Colorado. Every American should get to know our fascinating country first, starting with our unique national parks.

In many occasions, I visited Canada for pleasure or business. I have seen many of Canada's attractions, including the principal cities and national parks. In my first trip shortly after the Second World War, I went with my parents and Jorge to the Canadian Rockies for the first time; we drove in an antique Ford that amazingly did not break down in the thousands of miles of our trip.

We have so many good memories of our trips in the U.S. and Canada that someday I may write a separate book about these trips.

LATIN AMERICA AND THE CARIBBEAN

ARGENTINA—1948; 1988

IN 1948 MY parents and I stayed a few days in Buenos Aires. I remember we had some excellent meals and desserts—reflecting the strong Italian influence. We flew to Bariloche, a mountain resort in Patagonia that resembles the Swiss Alps. Someday I would like to return to the *Parque Nacional Nahuel Huapi* and stay at the beautiful *Llao Llao* Hotel and Resort. I also remember the spectacular crossing of the Andes between Patagonian Argentina and Chile. The crossing is by land and boat, traverses two national parks, and four volcanoes can be seen at close range.

When I was the Financial Analyst in Geneva from 1971 to 1974, Vittorio Orsi was the C.E.O. of SADE Sadelmi, a group of companies involved in the installation of electrical power lines and similar infrastructure construction projects, primarily in Latin America and the Middle East. Vittorio was able to generate whatever profits were required to meet the Area Division's income commitments. A businessman of genius and relentless drive, he grew these second tier affiliates. When I was appointed Tax Manager of G.E.'s International Group in 1977, one of my most important projects was to merge these profitable companies with their parent company, G.E.'s money losing first tier Italian affiliate Cogenel.

When I went to work for Sadelmi in 1984 as Audit Manager, Vittorio had passed the torch to his brother Giorgio, moved to Buenos Aires, and married the widow of Pérez Companc—Argentina's wealthiest man. By this time, G.E. had sold the very profitable affiliate in Argentina after concluding that it was impossible to operate in Argentina in the construction business and comply with U.S. Foreign Corrupt Practices Act. Most of the financial managers at the South American affiliates of G.E.'s SADE Sadelmi Group were Argentines.

In 1988, I visited Buenos Aires at the request of G.E.'s partners in a small watt-hour meter company. They were gracious hosts, and took me to see the city's main tourist attractions, including the *barrios* of Recoleta, Plaza de Mayo, San Telmo, la Boca, and Plaza San Martín. I enjoyed walking in famous *Calle Florida,* celebrated by poets, tango singers, and shoppers. In the distinguished *Barrio Retiro,* the buildings remind you of the nineteenth century architecture in Italy and France.

BRAZIL—MANY VISITS STARTING 1948

IN 1948 MY parents and I boarded the *SS Brazil*, a McCormack Line luxury cruise ship, in New York and spent approximately two weeks at sea en route to Rio. The crossing of the Equator was celebrated by King Neptune with a special ceremony around the pool. The ship made a stop in Belem, a city founded in 1616 where the Amazon River reaches the sea. Most of the tourists went to the market, where the items for sale included monkeys from the rainforest of different colors and sizes. At my mother's insistence, we bought a tiny monkey which in Cuba was called a *mono tití,* and put it in a small cage for canaries. Upon returning to the ship in the afternoon, we discovered that many of the other tourists had also bought monkeys—but these were large simians that were rejected for lack of proper documentation. Our monkey was so small that we were able to smuggle him. On arrival to our cabin, we opened the door of the small cage and the monkey quickly went out and started jumping all over the room, before finally landing on my mother's shoulder. She started screaming, my father grabbed the monkey, and the monkey bit my father. At this point, it was obvious that the purchase of the monkey was a grave mistake. We kept the monkey hidden in a drawer, brought him food and water, smuggled him out of the ship in Rio, and gave him up for adoption to the veterinary clinic where he was tested for rabies.

I traveled frequently from 1977 to 1983 to São Paulo as Tax Manager of G.E.'s International Group. From 1984 to 1986, I returned to São Paulo repeatedly as Audit Manager of the SADE Sadelmi companies. During these trips, I always visited *Tía* Bibiana and *Tío* Darcio, who were living in Sâo Paulo at the time. I was taken by the local

AROUND THE WORLD IN 70 YEARS

management to excellent restaurants, gained a few pounds eating scrumptious *feijoadas,* and enjoyed many amazing nightlife shows including the famous *Oba Oba.* After joining the Meter Department in 1986, I went to Rio on two occasions.

In April 2011, we returned to São Paulo. We visited the *Instituto Butantan,* a scientific center to study the venom of Brazilian snakes which was still operating at a lesser scale than in my first visit; in 1947, I witnessed how they extracted the venom but this is no longer shown to visitors. We visited Heloísa Rivadavia, one of Alina's best friends from the American School of Milan. Their home in Morumbi had numerous security features; nevertheless, burglars had vandalized the house four times in the past. In the last incident, the family had been gagged and held at gunpoint. The Rivadavia's hospitality was memorable, but we were happy to leave as soon as we could to safer sites.

We visited with Augusta Tanaka and stayed at her apartment in *Jardins.* She is the second wife of our dear friend Ramonín Flórez who introduced me to Lucky. Augusta, a plastic surgeon, is a distinguished member of São Paulo's important Japanese colony, and owns a cosmetic products firm. Her father was transferred by a Japanese financial firm to open a bank In São Paulo; her mother was a master of the Japanese tea ceremony and taught this art form in Brazil and throughout South America.

Our chauffer drove us to Paraty, a beautiful historic town that had its heyday in the 18th and 19th centuries as a prime shipment point for gold, coffee, and slaves; we stayed at the restored *Pousada do Oro,* which date back to that era. We chartered the schooner *Terra Morena* to sail the bay, and enjoyed eating in the Kontiki Restaurant at the *Ilha Dos Irmas* while our schooner waited at the dock; we were the only customers at this very romantic setting. At night, we explored the cobblestone streets of this World Heritage Site of great architectural beauty and excellent dining. The Masons were important in the history of this city and engineered the streets with an inclination to allow ocean water to flow and wash them.

We went to Rio by bus, in treacherous mountain roads that straddle the numerous bays. We visited Sugar Loaf, Corcovado, the Cathedrals of *São Sebastião* and São Pedro de Alcántara, Petropolís' Imperial Museum, and Buzios, a sleepy fishing town discovered by Brigitte Bardot in 1964 that has become Rio's premier beach resort.

We toured the infamous favelas *Rosinha* and *Vila Canoas* where we were touched by meeting young artists that painted excellent land-scapes; they asked that we tell the world that not everybody at the favelas was a bad person or a criminal. Very recently, in November 2011, the army moved to these favelas to control the narcotics lords who rule like kings. The Government has now provided services to them including electricity, water, and sewage. They are governed by their own police, appointed by drug lords, run their schools, and function autonomously. We walked through the narrow pathways and were instructed of what to do including when to take pictures. In the evening we went to Plataforma, which is now Rio's most famous folklore show; Lucky and I were photographed with two tall beautiful *mulata* showgirls.

A visit to Salvador was a chance to step back in time and to stroll through a well preserved city from the 16th and 17th centuries with close connections to Africa. We stayed in *Perourinho* at the *Convento do Carmo,* a former convent where rooms have been converted from former monk cells. We attended a *Caporeira* show that mixes dance and martial arts. After visiting the Church of Bon Fim in the park across, a *Bayana* performed a *despojo* ceremony on Lucky, an ancient African rite that is popular in Cuba; it is supposed to cleanse you from *malos ojos* and improve your odds of finding happiness.

On the ground floor of the Convent of Saint Francis' cloister, we saw thirty-seven remarkable tiles; these artistic expressions reflect on the human condition. The *Dannemann* cigar factory has a reforesta-tion program named "Adopt a Tree," and later received a certificate showing that we had adopted a *Pau Pombo (Tapirira gulamensis Aubl.)* on the farm Capivari; our tree is numbered 45815, and was planted in lot 55.

We flew to Recife and stayed in *Olinda*, founded by the Portuguese in 1530 on a steep hill overlooking the harbor which grew rich on sugar exports. Restoration work began in the 1970's, and in 1982 the historic center was declared a World Heritage Site. We stayed at the *Pousada do Amparo,* a restored 200-year old building in the heart of the city. We had three memorable meals: seafood *moqueca mixta; jerimum recheado com langosta au coco*—pumpkin filled with lobster in coconut milk; and a seafood concoction cooked in a coconut. Across our *pousada* was *Nova's* atelier; he is a well-known *naïve* painter. We purchased a number of his very colorful artwork and enjoyed meeting his wife and daughter. Our visit took place during Holy Week, and the procession passed by the window of his atelier. It reminded us of similar processions we had participated in Cuba as children.

CHILE—1948

CHILE IS A narrow strip of land on the western edge of South America with a stunning variety of terrain. Santiago, the capital, was founded in 1541 by Spanish Conquistador Pedro de Valdivia. It gained independence from Spain in 1817. It has gained economic prosperity and has emerged as probably the safest country in the region, despite suffering natural calamities like the major earthquake in 2010. Chile has a long viticultural history dating back to the 16th century, and we frequently buy Chilean wines. The country is now the world's fifth largest exporter of wines.

During our few days in Santiago my parents went out to dinner with Dr. Ricardo Nuñez Portuondo, my father's friend and famous surgeon who had run for President in Cuba's 1949 elections; he was defeated, and Carlos Prío Socarrás won the election. We have enjoyed the friendship of several *Chilenos,* and plan to visit their country in the future to enjoy its stunning natural beauty and warm hospitality.

COLOMBIA—*Many visits starting 1977*

I VISITED BOGOTÁ frequently, first from 1977 to 1883 as the International Group's Tax Manager, and starting in 1984 as Sadelmi's Auditing Manager. It is Colombia's capital, largest city, and has become known as "The Athens of South America" for its many universities and libraries. Its history dates back to the Chibcha Indians, which had an advanced culture. The Spanish conquistador Gonzalo Jiménez de Quesada founded the city in 1537, became a Viceroy-ship in 1739, and became independent in 1819 under Liberator Simón Bolivar.

At the Gold Museum, which was particularly interesting to me because of my passion for Indian cultures, I bought reproductions of this attractive jewelry for Lucky. The Salt Cathedral, a large church built inside salt mines, was impressive. I commissioned rugs with the colors of the Sagautuck Yacht Club burgee from Indians in nearby villages which we still have.

Sadelmi's Finance Manager, my main contact, had a small farm in the vicinity of Bogotá. He enjoyed visiting the farm with his family, but he had to pay the guerillas for access to his property. Colombia's political climate has improved, but during the years of my visits I had to be extremely careful to avoid problems and retreated to my hotel room early in the evening.

JAMAICA—*1995*

MODESTO MAIDIQUE, MY friend from Cuba and Boston roommate, rented a beautiful villa in Ocho Ríos for a week to celebrate his 50th birthday; he invited a very diverse group of approximately twenty of his best friends and their wives. It was located in one of the most scenic spots on the island with a bird sanctuary and a private beach in front of Dunn's River Falls. Ian Fleming used this mansion as a setting for James Bonds' novels and movies. We visited the Blue Lagoon and had reggae musicians entertain us. We will always remember the wonderful time we had, the setting, and interesting group of friends.

MEXICO—*Many visits starting 1947*

IN 1947, MY parents and I visited Mexico for two months. We drove to Acapulco in the treacherous old two-lane mountain road with numerous crosses at both sides to mark the site of many people killed in traffic accidents. To make matters even worse, we went in the middle of a major storm. My parents brought two Indian servants to Cuba, but they became homesick, disliked Havana's heat, and returned to Mexico after a few months.

In 1958, after buying a Mercury Monterrey in Miami, I drove to Mexico with my parents. In San Miguel Allende we stayed with Felipe Cosío del Pomar, my father's friend from the Habana Yacht Club. Don Felipe was a scion of a wealthy and distinguished Peruvian family who had gone to Paris in the early years of the 20th century to study law at the Sorbonne. After graduating, he stayed in Paris and made a living as a painter. His friends included Pablo Picasso and Salvador Dalí. He frequently organized artistic *soirées* to entertain wealthy art collectors, and invited Spain's *infanta* and other royalty members to impress the customers. He was a friend of Haya de la Torre, an important Peruvian political figure and founder of the APRA. He married a Cuban lady, and spent several months in Cuba and in San Miguel de Allende where he founded the art school which has become world famous.

Another favorite memory of this visit occurred in Chapultepec Park. I drove our Mercury with an American girl to a romantic site near the lake, it was late and the park had been closed. A policeman came to give me a ticket, and I asked if there was some way to take care of the problem. He instructed me to follow him in his bicycle to talk to his boss near the monument to the *Niños Heroes*. After the two policemen finished their conference, they informed me that I had to pay a *mordida* of 20 *pesos*; in the future, I should pay the *mordida* first so I would not be bothered later.

From 1977 to 1983, I went back to Mexico frequently for business, and again in the late 1980's when I worked for the Meter Department in Somersworth. We had a joint venture to build watt-hour meters. G.E.'s American representative, Mike Mehan, was a unique person and I stayed with him during these visits. The Mexican partner had been Provincial Governor and was one of Mexico's wealthiest men; he had a lion as a pet and his statue inside a water fountain was placed strategically at the entrance of the plant. Mike eventually relocated to Las Vegas to try his luck as a professional gambler.

In 2010, Lucky and I toured Mexico for three weeks. In Mexico City, we visited the major sites, including the Basílica de Guadalupe, the Pyramids of *Teotihuacán*, the recently discovered amazing Maya ruins near El Zócalo, the Colonial Museum and remarkable church in *Tepotzotlán*; bought silver jewelry in Taxco; stayed at La Casa de la Marquesa in Querétaro, a restored 18th century palace situated in the heart of the city. In San Miguel de Allende, I called the art school to inquire about Cosío del Pomar; they knew he was one of the founders, had died a long time ago, and had no information to help me locate the mansion where I had stayed in 1958.

In Guanajuato, a World Heritage Site, we visited a unique museum of mummified human corpses, and we were surprised at the number of well-preserved mummies. In Pázquaro, we stayed at the Mansión de Iturbide, a 17th century mansion located on the city's main plaza. In Morelia, also a World Heritage Site, we enjoyed the colonial flavor permeating the streets; we wanted to visit the nearby mountains to witness the annual migration of the Monarch butterflies, but unfortunately could not go because floods had made the area difficult to reach.

The following year, we returned to Mexico with our friend Margarita Halikias, flying to Cancún. We snorkeled in beautiful Isla Mujeres and in Cozumel, where I saw a huge and brilliantly colored parrot fish. I had a taxi take us around the island; he had two married daughters and said their husbands were "fine fellows, and did not beat them too frequently." The *Costa Maya* coast streaches down to the Belize border with Chetumal as its capital. The Maya ruins of Tulúm are one of Mexico's most important archeological sites. We stayed in a lovely beachside *cabaña* with a *palapa* roof and without electricity, just a few feet from the sea. Two handsome gay male models shared a hut next to ours, and had many interesting tales, including stories about their numerous visits to India. We went to a nearby hotel to watch a hilarious movie that had been filmed there, with the employees acting as the main characters; it was projected on the hotel's wall, and the young man sitting next to me kept telling me that he was one of the actors, but initially I doubted it because he had grown up and had a mustache by now.

In Uxmal, another vast and well preserved Mayan archeological zone, we were carried in a kind of Mexican rickshaw, and toured la ruta Puuc where you find numerous important ceremonial ruins. We took a detour to visit the Hacienda Temozón, a beautiful restored old *henequén hacienda*. It was a super-deluxe facility where several Mexican Presidents, Bill Clinton, and George Bush had been guests.

In Mérida, the city's main promenade, the *Paseo de Montejo,* bears the name of your distinguished ancestor, Don Francisco Montejo. In 1519, he joined Hernán Cortés' expedition from Cuba and was Yucatán's Conquistador. Lucky's great grandmother, Catalina "Catunga" Montejo, was a direct descendant of this aristocratic Mexican family. The *Casa de Montejo*, originally Don Francisco's house, faces the southern edge of the central plaza, and was constructed between 1543 and 1549. It is the city's oldest building, now a cultural center and museum. Thirteen generations of Montejos lived in this house. Many schools, avenues, and other public buildings bear the Montejo name.

We drove to Progreso, where we enjoyed meeting interesting local people in the attractive waterfront, and were taken by a guide to an unforgettable tour of the Reserva Ecológica de los Petenes, home of the flamingos' largest colony. Thousands of other birds and waterfowl nest in the wetlands and mangrove forests, including numerous blue herons. The habitat is extraordinarily diverse, and I went swimming in a crystal clear water hole not far from where we had sighted crocodiles. A few Italians were my swimming companions; there were no other Americans. The main pyramid in the Maya ruins of Cobá is the second tallest of the Yucatán Peninsula, and one of the few you are still allowed to climb.

Chichén Itzá and its majestic ruins are one of the most attractive ancient cities in the world, and the regional capital of the Mayas from A.D. 750 to 1200. We stayed at the *Hacienda Chichén,* which abuts the ruins, and was initially used to house the archeologists that documented this important site. Some of the important guests at this facility included the Mexican tenor Plácido Domingo. We enjoyed swimming at the *Cenote Xkekén,* a deep water hole under enormous stalactites that was turquoise on the bright day of our visit, with a shaft of sunlight filtering through the opening. The area has many of these *cenotes,* each one at different depths.

PERU—1948

WHEN I WAS a child, I visited Peru's capital, Lima, with my parents for a few days. As I mentioned earlier, my father was a friend of Felipe Cosío del Pomar, a Peruvian with a fascinating life story whom I knew well in Cuba at the H.Y.C. and Mexico. He was a friend of Victor Raúl Haya de la Torre, who founded the *Alianza Popular Revolucionaria Americana, APRA,* in 1924 with aspirations to become a continent-wide part. It subsequently importantly influenced other Latin American political movements.

Lima is a fascinating city, the fifth largest city in Latin America. It was founded by Francisco Pizarreo in 1535, and became the capital and most important city in the Spanish Viceroyalty of Peru. It is home of one of the oldest learning institutions in the New World, the National University of San Marcos.

Frank was awarded a scholarship to study his semester abroad at the *Universidad Católica de Quito,* in Ecuador. After finishing his studies, had a month to take an additional courses for extra credit, or go in an adventure to Peru; he asked, "Dad, what do you think?" At the time, the Marxist revolutionary guerillas *Túpac Amaru* were very active in Peru, and I was concerned about Frank's safety. I reluctantly told him, "Frank, that's a difficult question. I can only tell you what I would do." He went to Peru, thankfully nothing happened to him, and he gained priceless memories: visiting Machu Picchu, the pre-Columbian 15th century Inca site located over 2,400 meters above sea level near Cusco. Frank tells us we must visit Machu Picchu, and we plan to follow his exhortation. Frank also went to the Amazon River without our knowledge, and brought back a photo of him with a group of students, and a giant Anaconda wrapped around their shoulders.

PUERTO RICO: 1972; 1996

IN 1893, A Puerto Rican poet wrote Puerto Rico and Cuba are two wings of the same bird. The culture and history of the two islands have much in common, including music; Puerto Rican artists like Tito Puente and Cuba's immortal Celia Cruz collaborated to enrich the islands common heritage. Many Cubans settled in Puerto Rico after 1959 after the Castro Revolution.

We visited *la isla del encanto* for the first time in 1972 when we were returning to Switzerland from a trip to the U.S. to visit our parents. Our main purpose was to visit Carmen Pidal Torruella, Lucky's neighbor in *la Víbora* and one of our dearest friends. During this trip we acquired a number of limited edition signed cerographies from the painter Manuel Hernández Acevedo, a Puerto Rican self-taught Naïve painter that lived from 1952 to 1985. He focused primarily on the streets and houses of Old San Juan, with their characteristic details of daily life, laundry, overhead power wires, and kites. His work has been exhibited in museums in New York and Puerto Rico. One of his most important paintings, Plaza San José, was selected for Puerto Rico's Census 2000 poster.

In 1993, we returned to San Juan with our family to attend the wedding of her daughter, Carmen Beatriz. It was held at the *Catedral de San Juan Bautista,* in Old San Juan, which dates back to 1520.

One of the cerographies mentioned above depicts children playing in front of this Cathedral. The wedding reception was held at the Hotel *El Convento,* where Carmelite nuns lived for approximately 350 years and was featured in the 2002 Architectural Digest.

WESTERN EUROPE

AUSTRIA—Several visits starting 1971

IN DECEMBER 1985, we rented a chalet for a week in a mountain approximately 60 miles from Vienna. I planned to ski a few days and drive to Vienna the other days. It was a long drive from Milan, and we arrived at dinner time at a country restaurant where the owner of the chalet, Mr. Meisner, was waiting for us. We were starved and all the other restaurants were closed, and the cook offered us the only thing they had left: cheese omelets, sausages, and fresh baked bread. It was the best omelet we have had, probably because we were famished. After dinner, we followed Mr. Meisner to the chalet that was a mile up hill in a country road; we have never seen so many deers flanking the road, and their eyes were like light bulbs in the dark. It was a beautiful huge chalet, suitable for three families, and had a central chimney, an antique Austrian stove, and wood carvings all around. We went to bed exhausted but with full bellies.

When we woke up the next morning, we could only see pine trees around for miles. The property was located at the top of the mountain and it was totally isolated. We realized that we had nothing for breakfast. Zuni came to our rescue, as she had brought a supply of Toblerones®. She melted them, and made enough to make a cup of delicious hot chocolate for each of us. We still think about that special morning every time we see Toblerones® in a store.

There had not been any snow for few days so we had to change our plans. As we could not ski, we drove daily to Vienna during the whole week. On the way, we passed by fields full of rabbits and hunters; we learned that we were in the middle of the hunting season. They recorded record-breaking cold weather and extreme winds the week we were there, but no snow. We had to buy heavier coats, and Lucky found a beautiful fur coat to keep her warm.

It was Christmas week, and the decorations in the street and stores were dazzling. We drank lots of hot chocolate and apple cider, ate lots of venison and rabbit, had to run from store to store for cover and faced blizzard conditions. Despite the frigid weather, we visited tourist highlights, including Schonbrunn Palace, the Danube Valley, the Opera House, the Tiergarten, the Belvedere Palace, and the Hofburg. We also visited Salzburg, and followed Wolfgang Amadeus Mozart footsteps, imagining his being five years old when he first showed his prodigious musical ability performing in front of Europe's royalty. We enjoyed listening to a concert of Mozart's Piano Concerto Number 24 in C minor, which is considered one of his finest masterpieces; its clarity, balance, and transparency are hallmarks of his work.

Looking for snow, we headed to the Pitztaler Gletscher, Austria's highest Alps in Tirol with approximately 70 kilometers of slopes from intermediate to expert levels. The resort is known for their fantastic powder and spectacular alpine scenery. It has one of the fastest ski lifts in Europe carrying approximately 40 people traveling in a tunnel inside the mountain. The ski season goes from September through early June; Yvonne, Alina, and Frank had by now become excellent skiers and had to slow down for me. We skied on a glacier at the top where pines did not grow because of the high altitude.

For New Year's Eve, better known as the Feast of Saint Sylvester, we were in Innsbruck. Our hotel had a big celebration, and all the guests were invited to participate. They had a large group who were drinking a lot and became very friendly. At midnight, the sound of St. Stephen's Cathedral Mass in Vienna was broadcast, followed by Johaan Strauss' Blue Danube. Fireworks started in the plaza, everyone kissed, exchanged good luck greetings, and toasted to absent relatives and friends.

We spent a few days in Vienna in 2010 and enjoyed a training session of the Spanish Riding School at the Hofburg. In our prior visits the School had been on tour, and we actually had seen the show in Dover, New Hampshire. We met a fine young Colombian studying in Barcelona, who is an accomplished Gran Prix rider in Bogota; his grandfather founded an important equestrian center, and his whole family is actively involved in the sport and in breeding open jumpers.

They brought two horses from Argentina, which reminding me of a similar experience when several Argentine horses were imported to Havana when I was a teenager. Our visit was made even more enjoyable by being able to discuss the exercises with a fellow horseman, who invited us to visit him in Bogota.

BELGIUM—Several visits starting 1972

WE VISITED BRUSSELS for the first time in 1972 with Yvonne and Alina. We walked around the *Grand Place,* which has been a UNESCO World Heritage Site since 1988; the girls giggled when they saw the *Manneken Pis,* a bronze fountain with a small peeing boy, which is a famous tourist attraction and symbol of the city. We loved the Belgian gastronomic delights, characterized by the combination of French cuisine and the more hearty Flemish fare; we consumed lots of waffles (*gauffres*), chocolates, and French Fries and mussels (*moules frites*). Lucky and I drank lots of Belgian lambic style beer, which is brewed only around Brussels, and the yeasts have their origin in the *Senne* valley. Another version is called cherry beer or *kriek.*

In 1973, G.E. started planning to move its European headquarters from Geneva to Brussels, because of two important reasons: its strategic location at the center of Europe, and the home city of the new Vice President. I had to visit the new office frequently, and in one of these occasions stayed with our friends the Egberts that had already moved from Geneva. We had dinner at the famous franco-belgian restaurant *Comme Chez Soi,* which is rated as one of the best in Europe. A Google search shows the current menu and prices; the *menu degustation,* which includes seven courses, is almost 200 Euros, or approximately U.S. $280. With a reasonable wine or two, a *digestif,* coffee and service you are looking at well over $400 per person. It's a good thing I went in 1973 when a dollar was worth a lot more than now, and I do not plan to return as I believe there is no meal worth $800 for two.

We drove to Brussels in the early 1990s, and stayed in a beautiful country house near the fields where the famous battle of Waterloo took place, approximately eight miles south southeast of Brussels. It was fought on June 18, 1818 between Emperor Napoleon's forces and an Anglo-Allied army under the command of the Duke of Wellington. Waterloo was a decisive battle, ending the series of wars that had convulsed Europe since the French Revolution and Napoleon Bonaparte's political and military career.

Bruges is one of our favorite cities in Belgium. It is the capital and largest city of the province of West Flanders in the Flemish region. The historic city centre is a UNESCO World Heritage Site, and is frequently called the Venice of the North for its many canals. It has a rich history, and at one time was considered the world's main commercial city. For us, the site is particularly important: Frank became engaged to Minerva in this romantic town. They rented bikes, had a romantic picnic next to a canal, and he gave her a diamond ring. She lived as a teenager in Belgium with her family, and her dad worked as Chef for the U.S. Navy Admiral and Attaché to NATO.

DENMARK—1972

ON ONE OF my visits to work in Stockholm, I managed to escape for a weekend to Copenhagen. I visited the famous Tivoli Gardens amusement park that date back to 1843, and took a cruise of the harbor. I saw the famous Little Mermaid statue, which was a gift to the City of Copenhagen by brewer Carl Jacobsen. He had seen Ellen Price dance the ballet "*The Little Mermaid*," at the Royal Theater, and asked her to pose for a statue that he planned to donate to the city of Copenhagen. She agreed in principle, but had prudish reservations about posing nude when she found out where the statue was going to be placed. Instead sculptor Edvard Erichsen's wife stepped in and modeled for the body. On August 23, 1923 was unveiled, and its birthday is celebrated annually to symbolize the fairy tale by Danish author and poet Hans Christian Andersen; it describes how a young mermaid fell in love with a prince who lived on land, and often came to the edge of the water to look for her love. The statue has become iconic of Copenhagen, 75% of tourists go to see the statue, and I suspect few have learned her lovely story.

During this visit, I fell in love with Danish modern art and bought an impressionistic Scandinavian rendition of a lioness and a cub. The two lions moved with us around the world but unfortunately the cub perished in our move from Milan to New Hampshire. It was so small that it got stuck in one packing box that was unintentionally burned, believing it was already empty, when we were clearing the forest where our house was being built.

FRANCE—MANY VISITS STARTING 1971

WE LOVE FRANCE, appreciate many aspects of the French culture, and have visited the country countless times. After we finish our remaining adventures around the world, France is one of the few countries that we will return frequently for the rest of our lives. I believe our command of the language and Cuban origins help us to frequently enjoy a friendly reception.

The Michelin Guides, my gastronomic bibles when I was an expatriate with G.E. in Switzerland and Italy, helped me plan many of our itineraries. My 2003 Guide lists 10 three-star restaurants in Paris, and 25 in France; they are in a class by themselves. To eat at these restaurants you need to apply J.P. Morgan's answer when asked how much his yacht cost him: "if you have to ask, you cannot afford it." To put it in perspective, there were 72 two-star restaurants with an excellent table, warranting a detour; 407 one-star restaurants with a good table in its category, and 452 *"bib gourmand"* establishments, offering simple tables at a moderate price. During a visit to *Chez Jean-Francois* in Lyon, a patron was receiving special attention; I was curious, and asked our waiter if the gentleman was a frequent guest. He said: "Monsieur, that gentleman is a former Prime Minister of France."

Our first visit to Paris was in 1971, en route to our house hunting visit to Geneva, soon after I was appointed Financial Analyst of the European Division. We decided to splurge to celebrate our reentrance in an affluent and deliciously decadent world, and had dinner at the famous restaurant *Tour d'Argeant*. According to the Michelin "on regale ici les tétes couronneés, et les autres, depuis le 16e siècle! Salle á manger en plein ciel, vue unique sur *Notre-Dame et la Seine*. Un lieu mythique!." I could not resist leaving this description in French, which uses musical language to describe the experience of a meal at this legendary place, which the crowns of Europe have visited since the 16ᵗʰ century. We, of course, had the house specialty: *Canard "Tour d'Argeant."*

We went to the *Troisgros,* in the town of Roanne near Lyon. Many critics consider Lyon to be France's gastronomic capital; the *Troisgros* in nearby Roanne is one of the reasons for this reputation. The *auberge* is relatively modest, located near the train station, and has thirteen rooms. We stayed overnight, and left Yvonne to baby sit Alina while we marched into the downstairs salon to indulge in what Italians would call a *pecato de gula;* in between courses, Lucky and I took turn checking on the girls, who mercifully fell sound asleep.

According to the Michelin, "Troisgros: three generations; three stars." The *Tour d'Argeant* lost its third star years ago; in contrast, a visit to *Troisgros* is always a perfect and unmatched dining experience. Just to read their specialties makes me salivate like Pavlov's famous dog: *Anguille chemise de noisettes et romarin, emin*é *de cornichons. Pigonneau et foie gras croustillants, "Café Pouchkrine", Contraste á la Péche blanche et verveine. Vins Saint Joseph rouge, Santenay.* As the guide indicates, this is culinary art carried to a high dimension.

During our first visit to Cannes, I rented a sailboat the size of a tub. The boat did not move an inch, and the owner asked Lucky if I had ever sailed before. There was little wind, and it was right on my bow so the world's sailor would not have fared better. In the evening, we went to have *bouillabaisse* at a restaurant that had one Michelin star for their art in making this glorious seafood creation from Marseille;

I believe this dish is particularly patriotic, since when it is properly made you want to sing the *Marselleise*.

A few years ago we spent a week in Nice, visiting the many important collections of works by Picasso and Matissse, and the countless breathtaking sights that abound in the Cóte d'Azur. We were walking in Vieux Nice when we noticed a restaurant named *La Caridad*, specializing in Cuban food. It was not open for lunch, but the door was open and a man was arranging the tables. It turned out that he and his friend were Italians, retired and in their 60s, had sailed in their yacht to Cuba, and brought two young *Cubanas* to open the restaurant in Nice. He was very friendly and invited us to return for dinner so we could meet his Cuban girlfriend; the other Cuban woman was visiting relatives back in Havana. We were sorry that young Cuban women had to use old Italians to escape their hell. We did not return that night to meet her.

We visited the beautiful town of *Talloires* to have dinner at the famous *Auberge du Pére Bis* with Yvonne and Alina, when we lived in nearby Geneva. Lucky has kept two mementos from this visit; here is the handout menu of our dinner:

> *Feuillete de ris de veau; homard grille beurre cancalais; foi gras sayte ayx navets;*
> *sauce perigueuex; tous les fromages; le grand dessert; petit fours*

Yvonne's hand written note, shown as written when she was only six years old, with misspellings:

> *Une carte d'un restaurant qu'sappelle Auiberge du Pere Bis dans Talloires sur le lac d'Annecy.*
> *Son menu es compose du: un hors-d'oevre, une entré; un roti ou grillade avec legumes; depuis les fromages, un plateau des fruits, accompagne avex les petit fours et des patisseries.*

(Il dis dans la carte que ils fasons toute pour satisfaire les persones.)

I believe her note vividly shows the value of an expatriate assignment for the children to learn a foreign language and to gain an appreciation of the local culture, not to mention an introduction to one of the better things in life: the art of good eating. In those years, Yvonne and Alina started snacking on *escargots* when they came home from school, which Lucky used to buy in frozen bags of 100 snails in garlic and butter. Lucky and I bear some responsibility for the taste for delicacies our six grandchildren have inherited.

We visited the Châteaux de la Loire when we lived in Geneva, and again in the mid 1980s, when we lived in Milan. The Loire Valley occupies close to 300 kilometers in central France, and is called the cradle of the French language and the garden of France due to the abundance of vineyards, fruit orchards, artichoke, asparagus and cherry fields which line the banks of the river. Notable for its historic towns, architecture and wines, the valley has been inhabited since Paleolithic times. We enjoyed many light and sound shows at the spectacular castles of Chambord, Blois, and Chenonceaux.
We stayed at several delightful chateaux-hotels, making each stay an unforgettable experience. France is uniquely endowed in many of these residences that offer special character and atmosphere.

Provençe is one of our favorite regions, and we have been fortunate to spend weeks at different times enjoying the many magnificent sites, including Aix, Avignon, Arles, and Marseilles. Provençal cooking is characterized by garlic, which poets have called the truffle of Provence, and olive oil. Culinary specialties include *bouillabaisse*, the most famous Provençal dish, aioli, and a variety of local fish and crustacean dishes. Avignon's history includes seven French Popes that succeeded each other from 1309 to 1378, and we enjoyed galleries, chambers, chapels and passages that comprise the *Palais des Papes* and imagined how they would have looked at the time of the pontifical court. Arles was a Roman capital and major religious center in the Middle Ages, and preserves important amphitheater, and the doorway and Cloitre of St. Trophine. It is particularly exciting to trace the lives of Vincent van Gogh and Gaugin in this city; van Gogh was hospitalized, his fortune went from bad to worse, and he was finally interned in the asylum at St. Remy de Provence. We visited this asylum, all white, clean, and a very peaceful atmosphere. Too bad he had such a sad ending.

In 2005, we drove to Normandy and made an overnight stay in Caen. We stopped at a gas station at the city's entrance and asked an attractive French lady for directions to our hotel. I also asked her for restaurant recommendations, and she told me that there was an excellent two-star restaurant nearby but it was pricy. I answered that it did not matter as we were celebrating Lucky's birthday, and then chatted for a few more minutes. We had dinner at the excellent restaurant, but I do not remember the restaurant's name or what we had. What we will always remember is that on our return to our hotel, we found a birthday present left by our newfound friend. We will always look back in awe at this kind and pleasant surprise which made us feel very welcome.

During this trip we visited each of the *Plages du Débarquement,* where the Allied troops came ashore during Operation Overlord on June 6, 1944: Juno, Gold, Omaha, Utah, and Sword. Many movies and books have been inspired on this historical invasion, but visiting the actual sites leaves you with a deeper appreciation for the bravery of these soldiers. There are several vast cemeteries in the area, and the American cemetery in Colleville-sur-Mer contains row upon row of identical white crosses and Stars of David, immaculately kept, commemorating the American dead. A massive memorial monument in Caen faces the Dwight Eisenhower Esplanade, and is marked by a fissure which evokes the destruction of the city and the break-through of the Allies in the liberation of France and Europe from the Nazi yoke. I believe this would be a fine place to take our grandchildren when they are older, to gain an appreciation for the price that at certain junctions must be paid for democracy.

Lucky is keenly interested in fine laces and tapestries, and greatly appreciated the famous *Bayeux* tapestry displayed in the William the Conqueror Centre. This jewel of the Romanesque art consists of five sections, covering the exploits of the Vikings, the Battle of Hastings, and the Conquest of England. *Bayeux* was the first French town to be liberated, and was fortunate not to have been damaged during the war.

From Normandy we drove west to Brittany. We visited Mont St. Michel, which has been called the Marvel of the Western World due to its island setting, its rich history and the beauty of its architecture. At any season of the year it leaves an indelible impression. The movement of the tides in the bay is very great and the difference in sea level between high and low water is tremendous. Construction of the Gothic Abbey started in the eleventh century, and the exceptional *Marveille* buildings were used by monks and pilgrims, and for the reception of important guests. We drove on to the port of St. Malo, one of Brittany's main tourist centers, but fortunately could not find a place to stay as we ended up enjoying a unique religious ceremony in the nearby small resort of Dinard. We also found a cozy hotel nestled at the end of the town. It was Easter Week; the mass was celebrated in French, of course, with a beautiful choir offering Gregorian chants; after Mass, we joined in a procession around the church and all the parishioners carried lighted candles.

Lucky had always talked about her devotion to Our Lady of Lourdes, and always mentioned her desire to go on a pilgrimage to that holy site in the Pyrenees. As a child, she attended *el Colegio de Nuestra Señora de Lourdes,* located near her home in *La Vibora,* and has fond memories of her relations with the nuns; Yvonne's middle name is Lourdes. In 1985, we drove to the Santuary from our home in Milan with our family, Zuni, and Yvonne's friend Jennifer O'Relly. It was an emotional visit. Thousands of bricks, crutches, and silver objects commemorated miracles ascribed to the Virgin. Each brick in the two basilicas has the name inscribed of someone who has received one. Many believers pray, kneel, light candles, and drink the miraculous waters that flow from the spring in the grotto where the Virgin appeared to Bernadette. Many sick and infirmed are brought by the thousands. Unfortunately, the town is overcrowded with vendors and commercialism, but still remains one of the most important and revered shrines for Catholics in Europe.

In the early 1990s we drove to southwestern France and visited Dordogne, an area with a wide range of delights: a rich history, caves, underground rivers, cathedrals, abbeys, castles, and unparalleled gastronomy.

The region of Périgord and Quercy is a kingdom of gastronomic delights. Its very name conjures images of truffles, *fois gras,* and *confits*—specialties that rank high among France's culinary marvels. The region's specialties have resulted in a massive increase in the number of geese, which are raised primarily for the production of these products. The fat livers are obtained by force-feeding geese or ducks. After three months in the fields on a diet of grass, the ducks and geese are put on a diet of flour, meat and corn, before undergoing a three-week force-feeding regime. During this period, they are made to ingurgitate vast amount of maize mash three times a day through a funnel. Their livers grow to enormous weights, and can be served as goose liver in a variety of ways. *Confits* are still prepared using traditional methods, cooking the pieces of goose in their own fat for hours, and then preserving it in large earthenware pots. Stuffing and sauces, flavored with liver and truffles, are also use to garnish poultry, game, suckling pigs, and stuffed gooseneck. The underground mushroom or Truffle is considered to be the "fumed soul of Périgord." There are around thirty different types of truffles; the best is known as the *Périgord truffle,* the black diamond of gastronomy. The vineyards of *Bergerac* and *Cahors* were already famous in the Gallo-Roman times.

This area is home to the famous Paleolithic art in the Caves of *Lascaux.* The original caves are located near the village of Montignac in the Dordogne. They were discovered in 1940 by four teenagers, and the caves opened to the public in 1948. They contain paintings of animals made approximately 17,000 years ago with an amazing modern technique of color and movement. In 1979 they became an UNESCO World Heritage Site. The caves were affected by fungus and closed to the general public. *Lascaux II*, an exact replica of the caves, was opened in 1983, 200 meters from the original one.

The Village of *Eyzies-de-Tayac* is located in a grandiose setting of steep cliffs crowned with evergreen oaks and junipers. Shelters cut out of limestone piles served as dwellings for cavemen in the Ice Age. You can observe the many interesting sites where the troglodytes once lived.

We have visited Alsace Lorraine in several occasions; it is France with a German accent. The Verdun battlefield gives a vivid impressions of the horrors of World War I, when over 300,000 soldiers died and over half a million were wounded in indecisive battles in 1916. We visited the trenches of the battlefield, which became a symbol of French determination to hold the ground and then roll back the enemy at any human cost.

We headed east to Strasbourg, the capital and principal city of Alsace, which was classified a UNESCO World Heritage Site in 1988. From 1943 the city was bombarded extensively by Allied aircraft, but the city has been restored to its former glory. It is known for its Gothic Cathedral with its astronomical clock, and its medieval streets. Our next stop was Colmar, situated along the Alsatian Wine Route 60 kilometers southwest of Strasbourg. The medium size city has impressive German architecture, fountains, monuments, and museums. This is a great area to taste the local wines, which are typically white; because of the German influence, it is the only region in France to produce mostly varietal wines, from similar grapes as used in Germany. It produces some of the most noted dry Rieslings in the world, and is particularly famous for its highly aromatic wines. We stayed at an 1839 hotel in the small town of Thann, with commanding views of the famous Rangen vineyards.

Burgundy is a delightful place to taste wines, and in our last visit we stayed at the Domaine Borgnat le Colombier, a fortified 17th century farmhouse that presides over a superb wine growing estate. Bistro tables, a piano, and a terrace around the swimming pool, set the scene for breakfasts. Meals are invariably served with a choice of homegrown wines, and the establishment has 12th and 17th century cellars for tasting sessions. Visiting Burgundy takes you back through time to an era when its mighty Dukes rivaled even the kings of France. Born of an uncompromising desire for perfection, their stately castles and rich abbeys bear witness to a golden age of ostentation and prestige. Burgundy claims to have the best wines in Christendom, and their cool and canny wine growers guard the secrets of their fine vintages.

For Christmas 2002, we visited the French Alps with the Swansons. We stayed in Arêches, a typical Savoyard village in the route of Grand Mont; our hotel was a small charming chalet, *Le Christiana*. After arriving at Arêches, ski plans changed as they had not had any snow that month. We dropped off Kurt to ski in Val-D'Isére, one of the most prestigious Alpine ski resorts, where in 1968 the famous champion Jean-Claude Killy won medals in downhill, special slalom and giant slalom. We drove to nearby Chamonix , and went to the top of Mont Blanc.

Mass at the town church made us feel transported to another world and felt the warmth of the community. We celebrated New Year's Eve at our hotel with the friendly owners and many of the other guests. Music and dancing went on well after midnight. The traditional cuisine of the hotel's restaurant was well known in that area as "the best and remarkable site for a great meal." The shopping in the town was amazing; we walked up and down the main road and watched the nearby farms with their typical log buildings and chimneys fuming with smoke. All these stores offered unusual souvenirs and beautiful craftsmanship. The local cheese factory offered incredible assortments of their Savoyard samples, all of which are typical in the Beaufort tradition. We drove to Albertville, the location of Winter Olympics; it was adorned with lights and ornaments for the Christmas season.

Our last trip to France was in 2008. In Paris, where we have gone on many occasions, we spent the whole week walking and taking public transportation—a rewarding approach to this enchanting city. We always enjoy visiting this fascinating city again. We walked in sections, which one of our guides classifies as ancient and medieval

Paris, royal Paris, and artistic and literary Paris. Our first destination was the nearby *Place du Teatre*, near the *Sacré-Coeur* Basilica, which has become almost a holy site for us to visit every time we are in Paris. This longstanding meeting place has an almost village atmosphere, with numerous café restaurants and tourists glancing at paintings of unknown artists. It is in this location where twenty-two years ago Guy Pierre Claveloux declared his love to Yvonne Lourdes Sabin and asked her to be his wife.

One of our walking priorities was to visit the Montmartre and Pére-Lachaise cemeteries, which are probably the world's most romantic cemeteries. Trees teeming with black crows droop over elaborately carved mausoleums, while stray cats roam through the foliage and around the tombs. Scarcely a sound disturbs the calm of the graveyards. It is no wonder that they have become the final resting place for France's most prestigious names. In Pére-Lachaise we saw the tombs of many of history's great giants in every field of endeavor including Moliére, Bálzac, Chopin, Corot, Proust, and Zola. At the Montmartre cemetery, some of the highlights included Stendhal, Degas, and Berliotz. We could not find the tomb of the novelist Alexandre Dumas, known around the world for his high adventure novels, including *The Count of Monte Cristo* and *The Three Musketeers*. We asked an old gardener for directions, he insisted in accompanying us to Dumas' grave and us a lesson about the writer. We have experienced frequently the kindness and hospitality of the French people, despite the fame—occasionally deserved—that they have among *les Americains*.

After Paris, we rented a car and drove to the beautiful town of Chantilly, approximately 40 kilometers northeast of Paris to visit the Saabs, a Lebanese and French couple who worked with Lucky at Heidelberg; Saib now works designing printing presses in France for Goss. Veronique works for the famous Aga Khan; every year his subjects give him his weight in gold and jewels. His father was married to the famous Hollywood star Rita Hayworth, and the family has always owned a stable of superb racehorses.

Chantilly is known for its horse racing track and the Living Museum of the Horse with amazing stables built by the Princes of Condé. Chantilly gave its name to the Chantilly cream, popularized by the maître d'hôtel of the Princes. The city grew out of its chateau, and in 1673 Louis II de Bourbon, Prince de Condé, built a new road; the land ceded on both sides formed the embryo of the new town. We enjoyed the opportunity to visit this famous equestrian center, the fine horses, and the hospitality of our friends.

Next we drove to the country house of Philippe and Laurence Thevenet, our French friends from Heidelberg in Durham. He is a mountain climber and just retired, and she is an accomplished oil painter. They live in a charming working farm in Vers-sur-Launette, north of Paris.

We stayed at Le Château, a sumptuous 19th century castle in the outskirts of Paris, laden with furniture and objects the owner brought back from all over the world. Each of the rooms is styled on a different theme: Moroccan, Indonesian, Louis XIII, and even Coca-Cola, which has a collection of items going back to its origins. The garden is full of ducks, ganders, dogs, horses, and ostriches, giving the place a distinct Noah's Ark flavor. One of the ostriches liked Lucky and followed her; she gave him a piece of stale bread, and Lucky almost lost her hand when the huge bird stretched its long neck looking for more bread and bit her. She ended up the day with a bandaged hand. Beautiful models were filming a commercial in this amazing setting when we arrived. For the fabulous breakfast, we will never forget the collection of jams served in fine porcelain cocottes on a table some thirty feet long.

GERMANY—SEVERAL VISITS STARTING 1971

I VISITED FRANKFURT and Munich a few times on business from 1971 to 1974. We also drove to the Black Forest, where we bought two carved tree trunk used as flower basins; they traveled with us until they rotted in New Hampshire. In Heidelberg, a bus of Japanese tourists took pictures of Yvonne and Alina, thinking they were German girls as they were both blonde and attired in the traditional Bavarian Dirndl dresses. We went to Ulm, home of Lucky's maternal ancestors: Zuni's last name was Ulmo. The city, situated on the Danube River, is primarily known for having the church with the tallest steeple in the world, the Gothic minster, and the birthplace of Albert Einstein.

In 1985, Lucky went to Berlin with Alina and a group of students from the American School of Milan; they flew on the Aereoflot Airlines at the time when the Communists were still in power. Upon arriving, the agents took a long time studying Lucky's American passport, which shows Cuba as her birthplace. They isolated her from the group at gunpoint and released her after an hour, very scary. They went back and forth through Checkpoint Charlie several times. The group of students was able to see the wall that separated East and West Berlin since 1961 to 1989, and witness how sad and somber the East was at that time. A week after, an American tourist was killed teasing the guards that he was trespassing.

On the way to Berlin we stopped one day in Gorlitz. The joy of Gorlitz is simply wandering the Old Town and appreciating the 15th century late Gothic architecture. Our hotel was directly across the small square right outside the former city walls. In the Church of the Trinity we found an exhausted Jesus, reminiscent of Auguste Rodin's *The Thinker*, who ponders the fate of man.

One more stop. As we had one more day before Berlin, we got off at the Neustadt train station in Dresden. Its Golden Age in the mid-18th century under Augustus the Strong is palpable when you stroll next to the Elbe River. First, we stopped at the Zwinger; this palace complex is a Baroque masterpiece—once the pride and joy of the Wettin dynasty, and today filled with about five fascinating museums. We walked to see the Parade of Nobles, a mural painted on 24,000 tiles of Meissen porcelain. Longer than a football field, it illustrates 700 years of Saxon royalty.

After lunch, we went to see the Historic Green Vault. The famed glittering Baroque treasury collection was begun by Augustus the

Strong in the early 1700s. It evolved as the royal family's extravagant treasure trove of ivory, silver, and gold knick-knacks. The last stop was a visit to the Church of Our Lady; destroyed by the Allied firebombing in World War II and reconstructed like a giant jigsaw puzzle, 90 % of which came from donors around the world. On our way out, we noticed the copy of the twisted old cross, which fell 300 feet and burned in the rubble. Our visit to Dresden was worth the detour.

When we visited Berlin in 2010, we were surprised to find a rebuilt city full of life and vitality. Several magnificent museums had just reopened in Berlin's Museum Island, a UNESCO World Heritage site: the Bode, Pergamon, Neues, Altes, and the National Gallery. Together they present outstanding archeological collections, early Christian art, Islamic art, Egyptian antiquities, Asian treasures, Byzantine art, 19th century German works, and one of the globe's largest coin collections. With the 1990 German reunification, the government began major restoration for the structures. The work continues, having already cost $2 billion. We also visited The Jewish Museum, which documented the atrocities of the Nazis and their forced labor.

We paid to have a photo in front of the Brandenburg Gate with the American and Russian flags; they provided uniforms to make believe we were American soldiers. We were touched by the Wall Museum at Checkpoint Charlie, documenting the horrors of the Communist era and the different methods Germans used to escape to the West; two of the ones we remember are a seven-mile balloon escape, and a woman who hid like a contortionist in a tiny Volkswagen.

We took a day trip to Postdam, a World Heritage Site, which is the site of the Postdam Conference between the victorious Allies. The Sans Souci Gardens are magnificent with their elaborate stairs and statues and well-manicured terraces.

As we were leaving our hotel, a maid surprisingly asked us: "Are you Cubans?" When we answered affirmatively, she became emotional and told us her life story. She married a German to escape Cuba, had lived thirteen years in Berlin, divorced three years ago, visits her daughters in Cuba whenever she has the money, dreams of Miami, and wanted us to take her with us in our luggage. Her sad story is, unfortunately, not uncommon to Cuban women desperate to leave the island.

GREECE—1980 AND 2007

IN 1980, I attended a business meeting in Athens while I was working in New York, and saw a magnificent show of lights and sounds at the Parthenon. In 2007, I returned with Lucky and the Clavelouxs for two weeks to celebrate Alexandra's 16th birthday, one of our happiest weeks ever. After a week in London, we flew to Athens in August, and a heat wave prevented us from sightseeing with more time the Parthenon and its surrounding areas. The temples and the museums were opened only in the morning.

The Hilton Athens, where we stayed, has magnificent views of this ancient and historical city, known as the inspiration of the Gods. We visited the Acropolis, the National Archaeological Museum, and Plaka, with its Byzantine domes and cobbled streets. We thought of Melina Mercouri's effort to motivate Athenians to return to the historic heart of their unique city. Kolonaki, with its luxury boutiques and chic outdoor cafés, is the most fashionable part of central Athens. We had lunch at a friendly Lykavittos Hill tavern, Athens' fashionable section, with vines dangling from the trees. At night, we ate at a restaurant offering entertainment; after a few glasses of *retsina*, we all danced until late.

We took a highspeed ferry from the Port of Pireaus to our first island, Paros, in the town of Naoussa. It is small island but very colorful. Our hotel, the Astir of Paros, had beautiful gardens with bouganville flowers of intense fuschias, red, and white blossoms; the gigantic pool had a wonderful view of the Aegean Sea. Izzy enjoyed the numerous cats roaming the property. We had most fun renting A.T.V.'s to drive around the island, stopping for lunch and visiting the typical white dome churches and monasteries.

Mykonos was next; it is next to Delos, one of the Greek world's revered religious centers. Our hotel, Petasos, was situated on a cliff, with superb views from the swimming pool; we could see the beaches of Platis Yialos and Psarou, and amazing Greek private yachts. We could go by water taxi to the famous Paradise, Agrari, and Ella beaches. Guy, Alex, and Izzy tried speed inner tubing; I was the photographer from the speedboat pulling them; none of us will ever forget this priceless adventure. We had a gourmet Greek dinner at the Alefkandra restaurant, overlooking five big white windmills in the front of the Catholic Church. The town was very near our hotel, and we took the bus that conveniently stopped at every corner. There were many people strolling through the narrow streets, and eating *al fresco*. It was a beautiful night to enjoy the walk and atmosphere.

Our final destination was the island of Santorini, where we arrived by ferry. Santorini is one of the southernmost islands of the Cyclades in the Aegean Sea, and one of the most beautiful. It offers a glorious view of the sea with its deep blue waters filling the volcanic crater. Its gradual formation was due to the activity of local volcanoes around 1,500 years B.C. An earthquake preceeded the eruption, based on archeological evidence. The name Santorini, or Thera as locals call it, is derived from the island's church of St. Irene; foreign seamen used to call her Santa Irini, and over time became Santorini.

The Hotel "La Perla", white clusters of cave houses, is in the heart of the caldera. To our amazement, the owner was Aristotle Onassis' former assistant; she was finishing a book entitled *Onassis' Women*, which included, of course, Jacqueline Kennedy Onassis. They were also filming a movie of her book at the hotel.

To go to our cave villa, we had to climb up and down steep stairs with narrow steps. We debated whether to ride the donkeys up the caldera to the town, but decided just to wait for them when they reached the top; they looked tired from climbing many steps up and down the whole day. We had fun seeing them pass while having dinner in our comfortable chairs. I pray I do not reincarnate as a donkey; if I do, hopefully it will not be in Santorini.

ITALY—Many visits starting 1971; I cover separately our adventures when we lived in Italy—1984-86

AFTER MOVING TO Geneva in 1971, we took several long week-end trips to Italy. We drove to the scenic Borromean Islands, three small islands in the Italian part of Lake Maggiore, between Verbania to the north and Stressa to the south. A boat took the four of us to *Isola dei Pescatori*, the only inhabited island with a population in 1971 of about 200 people; actually, we saw more cats than people. In another, we headed for San Gimignano, a small walled charming medieval hill town in Tuscany. In our first visit to Florence, we had a memorable lunch at a trattoria that offered a big bottle of Chianti for the patrons; after lunch, we started faking that we were drunk. Yvonne and Alina did not think we were funny, and sat down in the corner of the street in front of the Baptistry.

In the fall of 1971, we were returning to Geneva from Italy and approaching the Mont Blanc Tunnel. There was black ice on the road that I had not noticed. Suddenly, our Mercedes started spinning out of control; thankfully, the car stopped on the snow covered embankment to the right and not to the left, where there was a huge precipice. This is a very busy north south artery, and we were very lucky that there were no trucks coming at that moment. I turned back to a gas station five kilometers south for help in putting snow chains in the tires; we then returned north to the tunnel, where chains were not allowed. I had to take the chains off by myself before proceeding.

In the summer of 1972, we invited my parents to come to Geneva and join us for a long trip of Italy. After all they had gone thru after leaving Cuba, this trip was like a dream. We were four adults and two children in the car, with the space in the rear seat a little bit tight.

We stopped at a gas station near Pompeii to ask for directions and were approached by two locals selling "Swiss" Omega watches for a pittance. Lucky and my mother fell in the trap, and after examining the watches pronounced that we could not pass on this unique opportunity.

Each bought one for a total of around $100, and the two Mafiosi told us to get away quickly as the *carabinieri* were coming. We drove away in a hurry; afterwards, we examined the watches more carefully, and it was apparent that they were made in China. Lucky and my mother were so upset that they started to cry; this lesson taught us to be aware of anything that is too good to be true. Amazingly, the watches still run to this date.

The beautiful Amalfi coast to Positano was unforgettable; women were selling lemons, we noticed many had missing teeth due to the acidity of the lemons, and we decided not to buy any. We left the car in a parking lot and took a ferryboat to visit the island of Capri. We spent time at Axel Munthe's breathtaking villa at the top of Anacapri; he was a world famous Swedish physician who wrote *The Story of San Michelle,* a best seller in 1929, about his experiences in Paris and Rome and his relations with colorful friends like Guy de Maupassant and Louis Pasteur. On our return we found that our car's door had been forcibly opened by burglars. Fortunately only petty cash was stolen. There is a striking difference between the north and south of Italy; in Naples stealing from foreigners was considered a respectful activity since the times of the Roman Empire.

MONACO— SEVERAL VISITS STARTING 1972

THE PRINCIPALITY OF Monaco, a sovereign state on the French Riviera, has been ruled by the House of Grimaldi since 1297. Prince Rainier III married Hollywood star Grace Kelly in 1956; the event was widely televised and covered in the press. In 1982, she died in a car crash in Monaco after suffering a stroke. Prince Rainier died in 2005 after 56 years of reign, and his son Albert II, succeeded him as Prince of Monaco.

After our visit to the palace and a fantastic lunch, we did not notice that the back door of our car was not properly closed. As we were negotiating one of the many fearful curves of the French Riviera's dangerous roads, precisely where Grace Kelly's car crashed, the door opened, and Lucky was able to grab Alina; she would have gone out of the car since in those days cars were not equipped with safety belts. Our digestion was affected by this experience, but we thanked God for the good fortune in avoiding a possibly tragic accident.

We have visited the famous Monte Carlo Casino a few times. It is owned by a company in which the ruling family has a majority interest, and has a long history. When I was a child I saw David Niven's movie *It Happened in Monte Carlo*, where a playboy gambler's luck suddenly changes and he starts to win; the casino workers to whom he owes a lot of money hit him on the head when he starts losing; at the end, he is able to get a new engine for his beautiful motor yacht. Other movies include James Bond's *Say Never, Golden Eye*, and *Casino Royale*.

I had never before staked $100 at a Black Jack table, a pittance compared to others gamblers at the table. I was slightly ahead after an hour, and decided to leave as Lucky and the girls were waiting at a nearby restaurant. For sure had I stayed longer, I would have lost more than the initial bet.

One of our visits to Monte Carlo accidentally coincided with the running of the Monaco Grand Prix, one of the most prestigious automobile races in the world. It is a dangerous place to race, and dates back to 1911. Juan Manuel Fangio, five-time world champion, won his first World Championship race in Monaco. It was exciting to hear the thunder of the sleek cars, but we left after an hour concerned that the cars were racing too close to us and did not feel safe.

PORTUGAL—Several visits starting 1971

DURING MY YEARS as Financial Analyst in Geneva, I visited Portugal frequently and was entertained by local management. They took me sightseeing around Lisbon, to Sintra and Estoril, a resort where royalty and others sought refuge during World War II.

In 2009, we went to Portugal and Spain with the Clavelouxs to celebrate Isabella's 15th birthday. After our stay in Spain, we stopped in the busy town of Gibraltar to see the famous "Rock", and headed for Portugal. First we visited the Algarve, a very colorful beach resort with great food; the Moors named this land Al-Gharb al-Andalus, to the West of Andalusia; you still see white dome buildings with traditional *azulejos*. We drove to Evora, which became a World Heritage Site in 1986; this little town has a long history from Romans, to Moors, to Portuguese Kings. Our friend from Durham, Dr. José Evora, is a direct descendant of the families of this town.

In Lisbon, we went to the remarkable Gulbenkian Museum. We had dinner at the *Restaurante Trovador*, where we enjoyed a fine fado performance. We danced and had a lot of fun; fado is Portugal's unique, mournful traditional music, generally performed by women.

Guy unfortunately had to return to work, and the Clavelouxs returned to the U.S. after two weeks. We stayed one more week touring the rest of Portugal, and Salamanca, in western Spain. We visited the beautiful shrine of our Lady of Fátima, where we were able to hear mass; on May 13, 1917, the Virgin Mary appeared on an oak tree to ten year old Lucia dos Santos and her cousins Jacinta and Francisco with a message: peace was coming in the midst of World War II. The three of them are buried in this basilica, one of the three Virgin Mary sights in Europe. On October 13, 70,000 people assembled near the oak tree where Mary first appeared, and a miracle happened. It was raining hard and everyone was wet; all of a sudden, the sun came out blinding all, danced in the sky, plunged to the earth, and suddenly disappeared, leaving everyone perplexed and completely dry. In 1930, the Vatican recognized the Virgin of Fátima as legitimate, and today countless pilgrims come here to rejoice.

We spent a few days in Porto, Portugal's charismatic second city, with a magnificent position down the steep slopes on the north bank of the River Douro. We enjoyed tasting wines and wine lodges, and sightseeing in Ribeira, the fishermen's district with narrow streets and gaily painted houses rising above riverside arcades. At *Solar de Mateus,* we admired the building that graces the *Mateus Rose,* a splendid Portuguese Manor house with fine furniture, paintings, for-mal gardens, and a family chapel; it offers a glimpse into the lives of Portuguese aristocracy. In Coimbra, Portugal's oldest University City, we admired the grandeur of the *Biblioteca Joanina* and the *Sala dos Capelos*. The city's high hills and narrow corridors full of steps made us exercise vigorously, and kept us in shape.

At *Nazaré*, an Atlantic-coast fishing town turned resort, I discussed the price of lobsters with the owner of a seafood restaurant I discovered that the price of a pound of native Portuguese lobster was approximately U.S. $140, while an imported one was cheaper—just around U.S. $90 a pound. I told my new friend that back home in New Hampshire and Maine, we pay as little as U.S.$4.99 a pound of excellent down east lobster at our local grocery store; they will even cook it for you at no additional charge. This experience reminds me of how lucky we are in New Hampshire. The women in this town wear seven long petticoats, and the widows still dress in black. Nowdays, they have become the tourist bureau of the town, directing people to hotels and restaurants.

SPAIN—*Many visits starting 1971*

IN DECEMBER 1971, we drove to Spain for our first Christmas in Europe. Barcelona was our first stop; we had become friends with an elderly couple of *Catalanes* that visited Geneva to help relatives in a wine festival. We bought two cases of Rioja wines. They came back the next month to visit us and extended an invitation to babysit for us when we visited their city in a few weeks. The girls stayed with them for two days and had lots of fun playing with their nieces.

We went to *La Barceloneta*, the port area of Barcelona, with many seafood restaurants. Yvonne and Alina were fascinated watching the lobsters and a wide variety of mollusks and other ocean creatures that Spaniards appreciate. The waiters liked playing with the girls, took two lobsters from the water tank, and chased them. We explored Gaudi's *Sagrada Familia,* climbed Mount *Montjuit,* and enjoyed walking in *Las Ramblas*—which were particularly exciting at Christmas. We visited the Benedictine monks' Monserrat monastery and the famous Black Madonna; I love their motto: "Hora et Lavora," pray and work. In the altar, they had flags from all nations; as we were having our pictures taken, we stood next to the Cuban one just by coincidence.

We then headed to Alicante, for a family reunion with Lucky's grand aunt Rosa América Ulmo and her family, who were all Spaniards and had not visited Cuba. Lucky had corresponded with her for years, as she was her grandfather's closest sister. It was very emotional to finally meet relatives who Lucky had only known through pictures and letters.

In Madrid we went to the main tourist sites. At the Prado Museum, we bought a large canvas of Eraclitus, one of Rubens' masterpieces, from a painter at the museum; he was doing a study of Eraclitus' powerful arms. We had it framed in Geneva, and ever since has graced our living rooms in the many houses we have lived. From Madrid to Geneva is a long drive, but in our younger years we were tireless.

In 1972, I went to Bilbao frequently to work with the financial staff of General Electric's big plant. In one of these business trips, I drove to Guernica, which Picasso made famous for his canvass depicting the bombardment of the city during Spain's Civil War; then headed for *San Sebastian*, a beautiful resort town in the Basque region, and stayed at a hotel at the top of *Monte Igueldo*. At night I ate tapas at the city's numerous restaurants and cafes. I still remember the best *calamares en su tinta* I have ever eaten.

When we were transferred back to the U.S. from Italy in 1986, we decided to take a trip to northern Spain with Alina, Frank, and Zuni; at that moment, Yvonne was still in Storrs in her last year at the University of Connecticut. In Asturias, we visited Nicanor and Blanca Gutiérrez, the parents of one of Lucky's best friends, Blanca; they were neighbors and close family friends for generations back from *La Víbora*. We visited the important northwestern seaport of El Ferrol in Galicia, home of my paternal grandparents and of Generalísimo

Francisco Franco. *Las Rías Bajas* reminded us of the low tides and good seafood in Maine.

The last town we visited was Santiago de Compostela, one of the most important Christian pilgrimage destinations over a thousand years; according to tradition, remains of the Apostle Saint James were carried from Jerusalem and are buried there. We stayed at the *Parador de los Reyes Católicos,* a veritable museum and one of our favorite hotels in Europe. Someday, we plan to do the St. James Way, *el Camino de Santiago,* from the French Pyrenees to Santiago; it takes at least a month, and we will have to carry walking canes and lots of Celebrex, and perhaps we may have to rent a car.

In our 2009 trip with the Clavelouxs to Southern Spain and Portugal, Guy rented a van big enough for the six of us. He drove to Iznagar, some 60 kilometers from Córdoba, where they rented two extraordinary hilltop hideaways called *Casa la Loma* and *Casita la Almendra,* which a British couple restored. The houses were set among olive groves with panoramic views over the village, the lake, and surrounding mountains that are the setting for *cotos de caza* to hunt rabbits during the season. As we drove at night, many rabbits crossed the narrow mountain road; when we got to our hideaways, we enjoyed the swimming pool and lots of *vino tinto.*

From this site, we drove to Córdoba, Granada, Antequera, and Ronda. In Seville, Guy had an accident backing up in a very narrow street, and hit a one-foot metal bar protecting pedestrians which damaged the radiator. Thank God he had excellent insurance, the van was replaced, and we were able to have a great time after all. The hotel sent porters to help us carry our suitcases. We visited the *Hotel Alfonso XIII,* where we had stayed in 1974 when we were relocating from Geneva to California; that night, we left Yvonne and Alina with a babysitter and went to enjoy a great dinner at the Hotel. Upon our return, the sitter informed us that Yvonne had called room service to order a filet mignon, assuring her that we would not mind. Our children were exposed to good things and developed a good taste early in life.

SWEDEN—SEVERAL VISITS IN THE EARLY 1970'S

IN THE EARLY 1970's, I visited Stockholm several times regarding financial issues of G.E.'s small operation in Sweden. The financial manager was a young Swede named Per Anderson, and he was a most gracious host. He is an avid sailor, and took me to the Vasa Museum, which houses the famous 17th century warship that sank on her maiden voyage in 1628. It was found and raised in 1961 after 333 years lying at the bottom of the sea. The ship requires dim light, correct temperatures, and no sunlight for long lasting preservation. It is the most visited museum in Scandinavia.

Stockholm is the most populated urban area in Scandinavia, but at the time of my visits it was a relatively small city with a population of approximately 750,000. It is a very attractive city strategically located on 14 islands, where Lake Malaren meets the Baltic Sea. I always stayed at the Grand Hotel, a luxury establishment that has been home to many celebrities: movie stars, Nobel laureates, politicians, rock stars and royalty. It is situated in an ideal waterfront location overlooking the Royal Palace and Gamla Stan, Stockholm's old town. Due to the city's high northerly latitude, daylight varies widely from more than 18 hours in the warm and pleasant summers to only around 6 hours in the cold and snowy winters. This temperature differences greatly impacted my visits.

I had memorable gastronomic experiences at Stockholm's famous smorgasbord restaurant Operakällaren, located in the Royal Opera House. This traditional Swedish buffet was popular from the 16th century, when it was called aquavit spread, and became famous in the mid-19th century. Tore Wretman is one of the great icons of Swedish artistic cuisine. He presented a replica of Operakällaren's buffet at New York's 1964 World Fair, which was a great success. He divided the buffet in five tables: the first was devoted to herring specialties; the second to other fish "smoked, cured, salted, and poached"; the third to cold meats: sausages, preserves, aspics, patés, and salads; the fourth to hot dishes, including reindeer, pheasant and other Swedish delicacies; and the fifth and final to desserts, cheeses and breads. I washed these gigantic meals with Swedish beer followed by shots of aquavit.

THE NETHERLANDS—1972 AND 2005

LUCKY AND I drove to the Netherlands in 2005, and stayed a few days in Monnickendam, a small town a few miles from Amsterdam that was an artist's colony; locals still wear Dutch attire and wooden clogs. Lucky bought typical red clogs and Dutch fabrics to make dresses for the girls. The Netherlands is a low-lying country and approximately 20% of the population lives below sea level, and 50% of its land lyes less than one meter above sea level. Significant land area has been gained through land reclamation and preserved through an elaborate system of dikes.

The Nazis invaded the country in 1940, and during the occupation over 100,000 Dutch Jews were rounded up and taken to concentration camps in Germany, Poland, and Czechoslovakia; only 876 survived. We were touched by our visit to Anne Frank's house, where she hid during the war before being arrested in 1944; she was sent to Auschwitz ending up in the same barracks as her mother and sister. She wrote her world-famous diary while in hiding, and died at Bergen-Belsen in 1945 at age 15.

The Red Light District or Rosse Buurt is an interesting place, where numerous prostitutes try to entice customers behind big glassed windows. Most of the action takes place around 11:00 P.M.; the district swarms with crowds and red neon lights illuminate the inky canals. It has existed since the 14th century.

At the Rijksmuseum, we admired highlights of the Dutch Golden Age, including masterpieces by Fran Hals, Vermeer, and Rembrandt. The Van Gogh Museum houses the world's largest Van Gogh collection, and an extensive collection of his contemporaries and friends, including Paul Gauguin and Toulouse-Lautrec. We enjoyed this museum's different setting in the woods. In Paris, he got acquainted with the Impressionists painting style, the handling of light and color, and treating themes from the town and country.

UNITED KINGDOM—Several visits starting 1971

WE WERE IN our way to look for a house in Geneva in 1971, and stopped in London for a couple of days of intensive sightseeing; we were young and could not wait to see for the first time London's countless wonders. Over the years, I visited London on business a few times.

In 2007, we accompanied the Clavelouxs to celebrate Alex's sixteenth birthday in Greece with a stopover in London where we stay for a few days and had a very special time. We saw the British production of the smash musical hit *Wicked,* and revisited the principal sites, including the changing of the guards at Buckingham Palace, Westminster Abbey, The Tower, Big Ben, Harrods's, etc. As usual, it was a rainy gloomy day, but to us all it was a great experience to do this as a family. Guy's office is one block from the London Bridge. Churchill's Museum and Cabinet War Rooms were of particular interest to me as a history buff; he was a prolific writer, and said "I have always earned my living by my pen and my tongue."

EASTERN EUROPE—2010

POLAND

OUR TRIP TO Poland was memorable. The country suffered greatly under Communism, like our native Cuba, and under the Nazis. Poland has been fertile soil for giants in religion, mysticism, and spirituality.

The Old Town Market Square in Warsaw has been rebuilt exactly as it was before it was destroyed following the revolt near the end of World War II. We met Anton, a student from Ukraine, who spoke English and joined us; our guide, Kasimir, had lost both legs when conscripted into the army at age thirteen. We were amazed to see him driving the car with such ease and walking without a limp. He drove us to the major sights and explained them in detail: Castle Square, the Royal Castle which is Warsaw's best palace, Jewish Ghetto, Marie Curie Museum, Barbican, and Chopin House. After Kasimir dropped us, we walked down the Royal Way and its numerous historic sites.

Train transportation is great; we stopped at the Jasna Góra Monastery on the way to Kraków. We left our luggage at the lockers in the train station, and took a taxi to the Basilica where the Black Madonna is venerated. It was packed mostly with young devout students; we noticed countless votive offerings on the walls. The Treasury included rosaries made with bread crumbs by concentration camp prisoners in Siberia in 19th and 20th centuries, and a cross of Polish American firemen made with steel from the World Trade Center. When we went to get our luggage back, I put key in wrong slot, and could not get it out. I prayed to the Black Madonna, and she sent help in the form of two nice young Poles: a minor miracle, as they managed to get my key out as the train arrived five minutes later.

We arrived in Krakow two hours later; it is Poland's most important tourist destination: a beautiful, old-fashioned city buzzing with history, and enjoyable sights. Even though its capital moved to Warsaw 400 years ago, Krakow remains Poland's cultural and intellectual center. In the Old Town, we visited the splendid Wawel Cathedral and

Castle grounds; Main Market Square, the heart of Krakow; St. Mary's Church with extraordinary Gothic altar piece; St. Francis' Basilica, a beautiful Gothic church, which was Pope John Paul II's home church while he was archbishop of Krakow, featuring some of Poland's best Art Nouveau. The Cloth Hall is still a functioning market dating back to the Middle Ages.

In the afternoon, we visited the Lagiewniski Monastery: the shrine of St. Mother Faustina, the cell where she lived, and the Basilica of the Divine Mercy. Pope John Paul II visited this place often, and canonized her. Zuni, Lucky's mother, always prayed *La coronilla* of the Divine Mercy to St. Faustina until her death in 2010. We went to hear the Royal Cracov Quartet's concert in the Church of St. Adalbert, one of Kraków's oldest Gothic churches.

Our most unforgettable experience in Poland was the visit to Auschwitz and Birkenau. Auschwitz I was a base for the Polish army. When Hitler occupied Poland, he took over these barracks and turned them into a concentration camp. By 1945 when the camp was liberated, at least 1.1 million people had been murdered there—approximately 960,000 of them Jewish, out of a total 4.5 million murdered in all of Poland. An exhibit shows huge piles of belongings of the murdered: eyeglasses; fine Jewish prayer shawls; crutches and prosthetic limbs; shoes and suitcases with the names of the victims. It takes an emotional toll to see these exhibits. One thing is what you think you know from pictures you have seen or books you have read; this visit raises your awareness of what humans are capable of doing to other humans. We will never forget and hope our entire family will go one day there too. By 2010, 29 million visitors, 1.3 million annually, had passed through the iron gates crowned with the infamous ironic motto, *Arbeit macht frei* —Work Makes Free.

HUNGARY

ON THE NIGHT train trip to Budapest, our compartment had bunk beds and a small sink. At 4:00 A.M. four uniformed police men woke us up to ask for our passports; they were not polite, did not apologize for waking us up, and behaved as if they still were under communist rule.

My first experience in Budapest was not a good one. Upon arrival at the Nyugati Train Station, I went looking for a taxi and fell down on the cobbled stone street, hurt my wrist and right hand badly, and bruised my left cheek; I looked as if I had been in a fight. Thank God I did not break any bones, but the pain persisted for weeks. Budapest has 118 natural thermal springs, and I decided that a good remedy might be to head promptly to the Gellért Baths and Hotel Spa hoping that the curative waters would help me; it did not, but we still enjoyed the bath at the famous hotel.

This city is split down the center by the Danube River. On the west side of the Danube is hilly Buda. On the east is flat Pest (pronounced "pesht"). We walked to Matthias Church, a landmark Neo-Gothic church, and the Royal Palace, a reconstructed fortress on Castle Hill. We had a wonderful brunch at the ritzy Gundel Restaurant, which is across the Széchenyi Baths. At night we went to the Hungarian State Opera house to see *"The Marriage of Figaro"* by Wolfgang Amadeus Mozart. It was an incredible artistic production with superb acoustics and refined voices. Across the Opera house was the Callas Café, which has one of the finest Art Nouveau interiors in town. We had a delicious hot chocolate with pastries, and very romantic live piano music.

We took a Hop on Off Bus, which was a good way to see the city, allowing us to meander through Vaci Street and the Charles Bridge. It was a clear night with the moon reflecting on the Danube. We took a cruise in the Danube Legend, an evening sightseeing boat; it offered a great view of Buda and Pest.

SLOVAKIA, BRATISLAVA

WE ARRIVED AT Bratislava's Main Train Station, Slovakia's capital. We looked for the lockers to leave our luggage and overheard a couple speaking in Spanish; we recognized their Cuban accents, and sure enough, they were from Miami. They had left their daughter studying in Barcelona. We had a hearty lunch in a typical tavern in town, and continued together to visit the small, colorful Old Town and the Castle above it; they are the only parts of Bratislava worth visiting. It was raining, and we shared our umbrella with our new friends.

THE CZECH REPUBLIC

PRAGUE IS THE only Central European capital to escape the bombs of last century's wars and one of Europe's best preserved cities. The Vlatava River divides the west side from the east side. *St. Vitus Cathedral* is the Czech Republic's most important church, and one of the most impressive and beautiful Catholic churches, with a history going back to 973 when it was founded. Here the kings of Bohemia were crowned and lie buried. Prague Castle is the traditional seat of Czech rulers. The Loreto is a religious pilgrimage site that was built to commemorate the legend of a cottage said to have been the home of the Virgin Mary, which was transported with divine help to Loreto, Italy, centuries before Prague's 18th century Baroque Loreto Church was built.

We had an early dinner at U. Fleků, a brewery and restaurant established in 1499; the food and beer were great, as well as the music. At night we saw a delightful performance of Verdi's *La Traviata* at the Národní Divadlo Theater.

The Old Town Square with dozens of colorful facades, the dramatic Jan Hus Memorial, Týn Church, and fanciful Astronomical Clock were as enchanting as we had pictured it. A walk across the Charles River, with its statue-lined crossing, and connecting the Little Quarter and Prague Castle was very inviting; we crossed it several times. We walked down Wenceslas Square to St. Nicholas Church, famous for having the miraculous statue of the Baby Jesus of Prague, well known all over the world. The priest in charge of the church, who is also a missionary in Africa, gave us as a present a beautiful Baby Jesus of Prague of butterfly wings made by one of his parishioners.

At the Museum of Communism you see many stories of atrocities commited during the communist years, and reminded us of the same tactics pursued in Cuba. That night we went to the National Theater to see Mozart's Opera *Cosi FanTute*; I bought cheap seats in the fourth tier and left with stiff necks but still loved the production.

At the Hotel Intercontinental, we rented a car with a G.P.S. to help us drive around the Czech Republic where few people speak English. The Town of Karlovy Vary is the biggest and most famous spa in the Czech Republic; about 70,000 patients from 77 countries come every year for the curative powers of the town's mineral waters. We tasted them at the Svoboda Spring, directly across from our hotel, and the taste was terrible. They have special pitchers to collect and drink the waters. The town is beautiful with its steep streets and thousands of luxury hotels. We drove next to another spa town, Mariánske Lázne, but we did not drink the foul tasting water again.

The history of Kutná Hora is inseparably connected with the mining of silver ores at the end of the 13th century. The Cathedral of St. Barbara was intended to equal the Prague Cathedral of St. Vitus in its magnificence. We were tremendously impressed with this cathedral, which lasted more than 500 years before its completion in 1905. The Ossuary at Kutná Hora has its origin in the Cistercian monastery founded in Sedlec. The bones come from 30,000 bodies buried there at the time of the great plague of 1318 as well as from many other wars. The wood carver Frantisek Rint was the author of the unique decorations made from human bones. We have never seeing anything like these in any of our trips, beautiful but macabre.

Our last stop was Český Krumlov. It is a fairy-tale town with its natural moat in the Vltava River, settled first by the Celtic tribes a century before Christ. The Pension Olšakovský were we stayed was strategically situated on the bank of the river; our room faced the impressive Krumlov Castle, and the Horni Bridge. The Church of St. Vitus, in the Market Square, was built as a bastion of Catholicism in the 15th century. After a wonderful week driving around the Czech Republic, we returned the car without a single scratch.

ASIA AND FAR EAST

AUSTRALIA—1980

WHILE I WORKED in New York as G.E.'s International Group Tax Manager, I had to visit Sydney to counsel on tax aspects of a corporate reorganization. My flight was delayed due to a snow storm, and when I arrived in Honolulu I missed the connecting flight to Sydney, and the next flight was overbooked. Passengers were offered to stay at a luxury resort in Waikiki for free if they voluntarily surrendered their ticket and accepted to leave two days later. Unfortunately, I had to be in Sydney to work on Monday and could not accept the airline's tempting offer.

After exhausting flights, I arrived in Sydney without my luggage. It was Saturday morning and planned to recover during the weekend from such a long flight. I could not sleep, and finally decided to go shopping for a swimming suit, took a taxi, and told the driver "please take me to Bondi beach." The beach is beautiful; a swim helped cure my jet lag; unfortunately I did not buy sun tan lotion, and got my life's worst sun burn.

Sydney is one of the world's most beautiful cities, particularly for sailors. It is Australia's biggest city, and the site of the first British colony in Australia established in 1788 as a penal colony. The city is built on hills surrounding Port Jackson, which is commonly known as Sydney Harbor, where the iconic Sydney Opera House and the Harbour Bridge feature prominently. I enjoyed a cruise of the area, and visited Hyde Park and the Royal Botanic Gardens.

HONG KONG AND NEW TERRITORIES—1977

I ARRIVED IN Hong Kong in the middle of the Chinese New Year celebrations for the year of the tiger. In the evening I boarded a ferry to colorful Aberdeen, where fishermen and their families live in sampans. In the ferry I met a Swiss on his way to Thailand, where he spent his vacations probably to participate in that country's prostitution trade. We decided to stick together for the rest of that evening, and went first to have dinner at the famous Jumbo floating restaurant. As part of the celebration, every sampan was lit with lanterns and firecrackers illuminated the evening.

After dinner, we took the tram for Victoria Peak, the city's highest point, for a breathtaking view of Hong Kong's New Year's Eve. The French submarine Joanne d'Arc was visiting, and my French enabled me to chat with the sailors and their Chinese "girlfriends." Finally, we headed for Victoria Park, large grounds named after Queen Victoria, which is home to the Lunar New Year's Fair. I was squeezed in the middle of a huge crowd of Chinese, many carrying flowers, and prayed that my Cuban-American journey would not end prematurely in a Chinese stampede.

On a day tour from Hong Kong, I visited the New Territories, which is located in Mainland China; it is one of Hong Kong's main regions along with Hong Kong Island and the Kowloon Peninsula, and makes up 86% of Hong Kong's territory. The United Kingdom leased them from China in 1898 for 99 years, and sovereignty was transferred to the People's Republic in 1997, together with the Qing ceded territories and the Kowloon Peninsula. I had my picture taken with an old Chinese couple that looked like the quintessential peasants of *The Good Earth*, Pearl Buck's famous novel and movie; I have seen it several times, and it is a epic story of humility and bravery of a farmer and the amazing freed save Wang Lung receives from his father as wife. Years later I saw the same couple in a magazine advertisement of Scotch Wiskey. They were smart entrepreneurs, and asked for a substantial donation to pose for the picture. I believe this was a precursor of China's free enterprise system.

JAPAN—*1976, 1978, AND 1980*

I WORKED FOR G.E.'s International Nuclear Operations when we had to provide clean up services to a power plants under construction in remote locations in Fukushima; this site became notorious when Japan's 2010 tsunami created a major disaster as a result of leaks in one of the early nuclear plants. The project required bringing some forty specialized hourly workers from the U.S. because of stringent regulatory and safety requirements that limited the number of hours of authorized exposure to radiation. I was responsible to set up administrative support programs to handle this project, including guesthouse arrangements.

At night, I visited a small bar where some fifty Japanese and a few of my associates gathered to eat Japanese snacks and drink beer and sake. After an hour everybody was drunk. Several Japanese adopted me as their Cuban-American brother; we all sang and laughed, the Japanese formality disappeared and we all became very friendly. I always tried to leave before they became ornery—which was the last thing I needed. One night I felt a hand in my pocket, but was too high to worry about being burglarized—and, in any event, these Japanese were extremely honest. When I got back to the guesthouse, I found a small sake cup given to me as a gift and token of my Japanese brothers' good will.

In another visit to Japan, I took the bullet train to Kyoto, and in three hours arrived in Japan's most interesting and historic city. After a few hours in an organized tour visiting Shinto shrines and tourist sites, I left the group to roam the winding narrow alleys of this charming place. Shintoism is a set of practices to connect present day Japan with its ancient past. It mixes folklore, history and mythology, and was first codified in the 8th century.

PHILIPPINES—1980

I BELIEVE *FILIPINOS* are among the friendliest people in the world, a feeling reinforced by the temperament of my grandchildren Lucas and Emma; their maternal grandfather is from the Philippines. A second personal connection with the Philippines is that, as a Spanish colony, the country gained its freedom with Cuba in the 1898 Spanish

American War. I enjoyed working with my financial counterparts at G.E.'s affiliate, and I still remember their hospitality during my visit.

Manila has probably the world's most colorful vehicles and one of the world's worst traffic conditions. Metro Manila has become the 11th most populated area in the world; the whole atmosphere is utterly chaotic, most of the population is poor, and the country has a history of corruption and incompetence—just like Cuba. Dictator Ferdinand Marcos ruled from 1965 to 1986; his wife Imelda, a former beauty queen, owned the world's biggest shoe collection. I also visited Pag San Jan falls, where Francis Ford Coppola filmed the Vietnam War movie *Apocalypse Now* in 1979; the movie was nominated for the Academy Award for Best Picture, and was selected for preservation by the National Film Registry in 2001.

SINGAPORE—1977

WHEN I WORKED at G.E.'s International Information Services Department, we sold one of our first computer time-sharing businesses to the Singapore Government.

At a harbor cruise I took in 1977, I became acquainted with an elderly Chinese-American who owned a chain of dry cleaners in Los Angeles. All his children had graduated from Ivy League schools, and were Doctors, Professors, and Scientists. He spent a month in Singapore every year to "de intoxicate" his digestive system from American food. I asked him for dinning suggestions, and he suggested I should try "steam boat," an Asian version of *bouillabaisse*, at his favorite restaurant. He declined my dinner invitation, but accepted a taxi ride in the direction to his recommended restaurant. My friend and I entered the taxi; the taxi driver did not crank up the meter; my friend objected vociferously in Mandarin; the driver ejected my friend and me from his taxi. I eventually made it to the restaurant and had a delicious sea food concoction surrounded by some fifty Asians.

TAIWAN—1977

G.E. WAS BUILDING a nuclear power plant in Taiwan, which I visited. I stayed at the properly named Grand Hotel, and asked the concierge for written directions for Wahid Street, famous for its restaurants and snake recipes. The taxi dropped me off, and I asked for suggestions from a fine looking young man that happened to speak excellent English, as he was the representative of an American company in Taipei. He told me I was lucky, as a nearby restaurant was having a special of cobra soup. I went there first for the novelty, and then went to another restaurant where I had a Chinese feast.

I flew to the mountains where Generalissimo Chiang Kai-shek drilled his armies by building mountain roads after fleeing Mao's advancing Communist Army in mainland China in 1949. He was a political and military leader, and key member of the Nationalist Party. Chiang agreed to a temporary truce with the Communists after Japan invaded China in 1937, and the Civil War resumed after the Japanese surrendered in 1945. Chiang retreated to the island of Taiwan, where he ruled until his death in 1975.

THAILAND—1977

I VISITED THAILAND to take advantage of a business trip to Japan and Taiwan. I visited a variety of Buddha statues of all sizes and shapes, including the huge reclining Buddha. This religion and philosophy emcompasses traditions, beliefs, and practices largely based on teachings attributed to Siddhartha Gautama, commonly known as the Buddha, "the awakened one." He lived in the eastern part of the Indian subcontinent between the 6th and 4th centuries B.C. His insights help sentient beings end ignorance of dependent origination, thus escaping a cycle of suffering and rebirth. It is estimated that 300 to 500 million people are Buddhists, primarily in Asia.

I took a bus to visit a floating market near Bangkok. On the way, we were taken to see a mongoose fight a cobra. For this show they probably only needed one mongoose, but a large supply of cobras—as the mongoose always killed the cobra. I wondered whether the Cuban *jutía*, a cousin of the mongoose which I shot in my childhood's hunting expeditions, would be as adept at fighting snakes.

TURKEY—2011

WE TRAVELED AGAIN with the Clavelouxs and accompanied them to Turkey to celebrate Izzy's sixteenth birthday. Turkey is a unique country of unending fascination; its Asian and European conquerors have crossed its soil, but it has remained proudly independent. Its history is as ancient as Byzantium. We will always remember this trip, and the unforgettable adventures we had with Yvonne, Guy, Alex, and Izzy.

We flew from Istanbul to magical Cappadocia in Central Anatolia, where wind and rain have shaped soft volcanic rock into a fairy-tale landscape. Early Christians turned caves that abound in the area into homes and churches. We stayed at an elaborately newly renovated cave hotel in Urgup, where found two small scorpions that terrified Isabella and Alexandra, and had to move to another cave-room. They were advertising a show, that although was not the real thing, we went anyway. We wanted to see the dervishes, always dressed in long white skirts, who whirl in graceful spinning dances; it is a way to fill them with love, which they believe is the essence of the divine. The show was, of course, for the tourists, but very diverse and entertaining.

Cappadocia has the weirdest natural landscape we have ever seen, with giant elaborate cones, needles, pillars, and pyramids. We rented three ATV's, hired a guide, went for a ride of many miles, and raced in our vehicles; I had to slow down because Lucky was getting dizzy. We had a marvelous time, and returned covered with dust and ready to enjoy a Turkish bath. The girls went their way, and Guy and I headed for the boys' baths. We swam in a hot pool and then in the cold one; they gave us clean robes and made us relax for ten minutes while enjoying a cup of tea and get ready for the experience. They applied a dark mask of Turkish mud in our faces. Next, we laid down on a marble surface, while one attendant rubbed aromatic oils on our body. They proceeded to cover us with undulating towel movements spreading foam over us, and then poured buckets of cold water to rinse the oils and foam. We showered again, and were taken to a room with music and aromatic herbs. They gavbe us a forceful half an hour massage, which left us hurting for two days. The girls had the same treatment.

One of the highlights of the visit to Cappadocia, was flying on a hot air balloon; we will always remember dangling high above the rock-littered valleys, sailing past rock cones and fairy chimneys. Approximately fifty balloons, each carrying some 24 people in each basket from all nationalities; we took off at the crack of dawn for the ride. I prayed that we would not end up like Matías Pérez, a Portuguese pilot, canopy maker, and Cuban resident who was carried away with the increasing popularity of an aerostatic aircraft. He disappeared while attempting a flight from Havana's Central Park on June 28, 1856. A few days earlier, he had made a successful attempt flying several miles. His second try, however, became part of Cuba's folklore: when somebody disappears, they say: "*Voló como el globo de Matías Pérez.*"

Guy rented a van, and we headed for Pamukkale Travertines, an enormous chalky white cliff rising 330 feet from the plains. Mineral-rich volcanic spring water cascades over basins and natural terraces, crystallizing into white curtains of solidified water seemingly suspended in air. These hot springs are believed to cure rheumatism and other ailments, and we relaxed with a long bath in these medicinal waters. Immediately after, we experienced an exotic and effective "pedicure." We dipped our legs into water tanks full of Garra Fufa fish, better known as "doctor fish", which gently remove dry and hard skin from your feet and legs, leaving them feeling silky soft and rejuvenated. This natural therapy started over 400 years ago in Turkey.

Especially in the Roman Empire period, Hierapolis and the surroundings were a health center. The ruins were amazingly standing, despite the terrible forces of nature. They date from the time of the Roman Empire as far back as the 5th century B.C. Todays Antique Pool was shaped by the earthquake, which happened in the VII century A.D. It as very impressive to walk in the slimy sibmerged ruins, full of Roman columns and estatues; the water was envigorating. We then drove to the ruins of Aphrodisias, the city of Aphrodite, goddess of love, which is a large and well-preserved archaeological site. High up on a plateau and ringed by mountains, Aphrodisias has a spectacular setting.

Our next stop was the Central and Southern Aegean coast where we stayed in Kusadasi at a hotel appropriately named *La Vista* for its breathtaking view of the ocean. We chartered a gulet, a converted antique wooden fishing boat; went snorkeling and exploring the warm azure waters and secluded coves. The Clavelouxs went cliff diving, and I was appointed the official photographer. The yacht's capitan prepared an escrumpious lunch, and we returned while taking a nap rocked by a gentle following sea. Next to our hotel, we found a small restaurant situated right on the beach, and had a romatic dinner, sitting so close to the water that the waves were splashing us. There was a full moon shining on the horizon.

Next on our trip, we visited the Roman ruins of Ephesus, the City of the Gods, where we marveled at how well they were preserved. They were previously visited by great historical figures from Alexander the Great to the Apostle St. Paul. Ephesus was one of the world's wealthiest cities in the Greco-Roman era. A visit to the Virgin Mary's last home was particularly emotional, and Lucky collected some earth from the location. Our wishes were left on little papers on the fences.

We flew to Istanbul and checked at the Conrad Hilton Hotel, after going through a thorough extreme security check as in the airports. The next day, we noticed that security had doubled with many armed soldiers in the lobby. We inquired as to what was happening and found that an important meeting of Middle-East ministers was taking place at the hotel. We were concerned for our safety, but finally decided to stay at the hotel since the meeting was ending the next day.

From the Conrad's penthouse, we delighted at the magnificent view. Istanbul is the only city in the world which stands upon two continents: the main part of the city is in the southeastern tip of Europe, and is separated from it suburbs in Asia by the Bosphorus

Sea. I have never seen a busier port, with so many diverse ships waiting for entrance. It is a beautiful city, with many important sights and monuments of the Byzantine and Ottoman empires, including the historic Sultanahmet Historic Center where you admire the Blue Mosque, Hagia Sophia, the Topkapi Palace, the Mosque of Süleiman the Magnificent, the covered Bazaar and countless other sites.

The Turks are extremely friendly, and we were able to establish warm interchanges with many locals despite the language barrier. At a cruise we took from the Golden Horn, connecting the Old Town to the New District, we met a Turkish family from Ankara: a father and two attractive daughters 16 and 20 years old—just like our own granddaughters. Their mother had died in an automobile accident; their father had recently married an older American woman with the idea of obtaining an American visa, which had been already been rejected five times. They insisted that we see them in our next visit.

During our stay in Turkey, they were celebrating Ramadan, the 9th month of the Islamic calendar in which Muslims fast, and refrain from eating, drinking, smoking, and sex during daylight hours. It is intended to teach patience, spirituality, humility, and submissiveness to God. They fast the whole day and only eat at sundown. Muslims are adherents of Islam, a monotheistic, Abrahamic religion based on the Quram, which Muslims consider the verbatim word of God, as revealed to Prophet Muhammad. The founder of Islam was born in Mecca in the year 570 and died in Medina in 632 after returning from his farewell pilgrimage. "Muslim" is an Arabic term for "one who submits to God."

After shopping at the nearby Spice Bazaar, we had dinner at the Hamdi Restaurant, where we had a memorable grilled eggplant; we were not allowed to order meat or alcoholic beverages. We crossed the Galata Bridge with countless restaurants under it. It connects Beyoğlu—the city's modern, European heart—and the old peninsula. There were also three beautifully decorated barges serving delicious food.

We were surprised by the striking contrast between devout

Muslims who pray five times a day, as they respond to calls to prayer from the numerous minarets that you find in every city. Many nights we were awakened around 4:00 A.M. by the Imam's call to prayer. Many of old Turkish women and some young ones, wear burkas, or at least have their heads covered with a scarf, and others dress in black with only their eyes visible. On the other hand, we found that a majority of the young people wear modern Western clothing and sexy bathing suits at the beaches. This conflict between religion and modernity has defined recent Turkish history, and remains a major issue of contention long after the death of the Father of Modern Turkey, Kemal Attatürk.

TUNISIA, NORTH AFRICA—1972

I SPENT YEARS working very hard and needed a week of rest in a remote beach with no notable sights or compelling histories. The Swiss newspapers had an infinite number of vacation ads to destinations ranging from nearby locations to exotic and remote islands like the Seychelles. One resort attracted my attention: Hammamet in Tunisia. The ads showed amazing beaches and prices that wetted my appetite. One of our friends suggested swapping baby-sitting. We immediately agreed this was a great idea, and bought tickets to spend a week in a Hammamet resort.

Tunisia is the smallest of the nations situated along the Atlas mountain range. The south of the country is composed of the Sahara desert, with much of the remainder consisting of fertile soil and 1,300 kilometers of coastline. The country played a prominent role in ancient times, first with the famous Punic city of Carthage. It was proclaimed a republic in 1957; Habib Bourguiba became the first president, who was still in charge during our visit. The country was ruled by dictator Zine El Abidine Ali from 1987, and fled during the 2011 Tunisian revolution that launched the Arab Spring.

Although I cannot claim to be Lawrence of Arabia, our first time in North Africa was a new experience for us. We rode bicycles to the town, a few kilometers away, and were surrounded by small children eating from the garbage and begging for money. They addressed the tourists in whichever language they heard them speaking; we marveled at their language ability. We gave them a few coins; they were insulted with our paltry offering, and starting cursing us in Arab. A rug vendor came to our rescue, and he may have paid the kids to ensure the tourists went to his store first. The rugs were very attractive, and we bought a runner approximately 3 feet by 12 feet; the store owner had a young man carry the rug on his back to our resort, as we walked back; he also arranged to return our two bicycles to our resort. We never again went bicycling in Tunisia. The runner perished in 2009 when our home flooded because the pipes burst in the harsh New Hampshire weather which I describe separately.

One day we decided to give camel riding a try. We rented two camels for an hour, with two separate camel handlers to control the nasty animals. Charm is not a necessary attribute for any creature that can survive in the Sahara for days without water or attention, and camels exemplify this condition. After we managed to mount, my camel developed an irresistible urge to bite Lucky's butt, and the instructor was hard pressed to contain him. Lucky started yelling for help, and our ride was cut short after a few minutes. Perhaps it was all a show and the camels and handlers conspired to minimize the time and efforts on both the beast and the humans. We have never again been enticed to ride a camel, although I considered giving it a new try when we visited Turkey in 2011; we wisely decided against it.

PEARLS OF WISDOM

"Tantas idas	"So many goings
y venidas,	and comings,
tantas vueltas	so many turns
y revueltas,	and returns,
quiero amiga,	my friend,
que me digas,	please tell me,
son de alguna utilidad?"	are they of any value?"

Fable "The Horse and the Squirrel"
Tomás de Iriarte, Spanish Writer, XVIII Century

Now that I have finished telling my life experiences, I will address the question the horse asked the squirrel: "What, if anything, did you learn in seventy years?"

Over the course of my journey, I have dived deep to fish for pearls of wisdom in the oceans of the world. I must tell you that finding the most precious pearls require lots of work, and you have to overcome obstacles to find them. Throughout history, philosophers have written about happiness and a well-lived life, and entire libraries have been written on advice books on how to reach these elusive goals.

Many books on the subject of happiness are disappointing. Eric Weiner's New York Times Bestseller *The Geography of Bliss* is a rare exception on this important topic. Mr. Weiner spent years searching for the happiest place in the world and analyzed ten countries, including Switzerland and America. I was particularly interested in his conclusions about Miami and Cuban-Americans:

"I've tried to like Miami. I really have. I've done my best to fit in. I've gone to the beach. I studied Spanish. I've drunk large

quantities of Cuban coffee. I briefly considered getting breast implants. And yet all of the sunshine has left me feeling cold. Maybe I would like Miami if I were Latino. Latin American nations are unexpectedly happy, given their relative poverty. Some studies suggest that Latinos retain this happiness bonus when they immigrate to the United States. I asked a Cuban-American friend about this. He thinks there's something to it. Partly it's the Latino focus on family. And there's this emphasis on living in the moment. A Cuban expression says: que me quiten lo bailao, or, nobody can take away what you have danced."

Family is the essential element of human happiness, but it takes work. Look at your family as you would a garden: to grow beautiful flowers requires constant work and attention. We are blessed to have frequent and meaningful interactions with our family. We value our tradition of having each of our six grandchildren spend one week with us every summer. This one-on-one time affords us the opportunity to spoil and bond with them, and give each undivided attention. It helps develop close and loving relationships which is an important part of our happiness and theirs. It is a win-win tradition with high returns for everyone. We also attend many of their games and important events in their lives.

"Que me quiten lo bailao" is the Cuban equivalent of Horace's *Carpe Diem*, or seize the day. It was popularized by Albita Rodríguez, the Cuban-American Grammy winning singer, who named one of her hits after this idea. For Horace, mindfulness of your mortality is essential to realize the importance of the present and the uncertainties of the future. I am increasingly conscious that the clock is ticking ever faster; I am trying harder than ever to live every day as fully as possible.

At critical junctions in my journey, I have had to temporarily suspend lighthearted life attitudes, which Italians call *la dolce far niente* and the French call *la joie de vivre*. In facing life's storms, I had to batten down the hatches and follow Yankee values of austerity and hard work. America is a competitive meritocracy that demands hard work to succeed; in business, you must always be ready to answer a ubiquitous question: What have you done for me lately? Over the years I adopted a Protestant work ethic, and did some heavy lifting to earn the opportunities that enabled us to have a privileged life, and I was fortunate that my work efforts were richly rewarded. In life there is a time for everything.

Cubans, I believe, are among the most outwardly emotional people in the world. We share this trait with Italians, particularly the ones that inhabit in the south: they tend to be louder, darker, funnier, warmer, and closer to the Italian image portrayed by Sophia Loren or Vittorio De Sica; they are derisively called *terrones* by the *Lombardos*. In the northern latitudes, where I have lived most of my life, some question our relative loudness and gesticulations; weather influences character. This zest for life is a main reason for our loving Italy, and the Mediterranean and Cuban mindsets; it adds spice to life. I believe the ability to express what you feel inwardly, yell if necessary, and then let go probably helps longevity and certainly happiness.

❧❧❧❧

Zuni wrote a small booklet of *consejos* to her two daughters in 1981. She was one the wisest, smartest, and funniest persons I have ever met; I have translated some of her pearls of wisdom:

Abuela's Consejos

- Eat balanced meals, exercise daily, and keep an active mind.
- Develop discipline in your daily activities. Your efforts will be rewarded when you look at the mirror, your sincere friend for as long as you live.
- Develop a good posture through daily exercise. Stand straight. Watch your weight. Take care of your hair. Ensure the clothing and colors you wear befit you, and are simple and elegant. It is important to always look attractive.

- Keep good manners in the family, sit down for dinner every day, keep a good and pleasant conversation, and thank God for your food and ask for his blessings. Children should always ask to be excused if they leave the table. These actions will help to develop a happy home and self-respect for all members of the family.
- Have self-confidence, face life's adversities with strength and character, control your emotions, keep a pleasant expression, admire and respect nature, and love everyone you meet.

In my student days I struggled with physics, and Einstein's famous equations still cause me heartburn. Under these circumstances, I surprisingly developed an algorithm that has helped me in life: "The height at which you set your bar should be indirectly proportional to your age." My algorithm will not revolutionize the world, but I believe it should be better understood: the younger you are the higher you should aim; if you fall short, you will still have accomplished a lot; as you age, you must accept your limitations and appreciate what you have.

I recently came across these wise words about the importance of living well each day:

Sankscrit teaching:

Old Jamaican saying:

"Today well lived makes every yesterday a dream of happiness and every tomorrow a vision of hope."

"Yesterday is a cancelled check; tomorrow is a promisory note; today is cash in the bank."

We found the most precious pearls when our parents arrived in

America as refugees at an old age. We had forebodings on how they would be able to survive, and benefited from countless lessons on how they faced gigantic challenges with courage and optimism. They showed us you should never lose hope, were kindred spirits of little orphan Annie, and believed there will always be a **tomorrow**.

Our children and grandchildren have become an increasingly important source of wisdom. We do practically nothing without asking advice from our three children and their spouses. To remain young at heart we embrace youth and are open to the fresh ideas of all the members of our family.

(Left to Right)

Front first row:
Lucas Sabin, Sophia Swanson, and Andrew Swanson

Second row:
Isabella Claveloux, Francisco "Paco" Sabin, Lucila "Lucky" Sabin, Emma Sabin, and Alexandra Claveloux

Third row:
Minerva Sabin, Frank Sabin, Alina Swanson, Kurt Swanson, Yvonne Claveloux, and Guy Claveloux

YESTERDAY, TODAY, TOMORROW

Dear Children:

Our family is our greatest pride and joy and has logged an enviable record of almost a century of married bliss: Lucky and Paco 50; Yvonne and Guy 22; Alina and Kurt 14; and Frank and Minerva 12. Our grandchildren are representative of the American melting pot, with a diverse heritage: Cuban, Spanish, English, Scottish, Basque, French, German, Swedish, Irish, Filipino, and Puerto Rican. We have stressed the importance of Spanish fluency; our family loves Cuban food, and for Christmas, *pierna de puerco, frijoles negros,* and *yuca* are part of our tradition. We are fortunate you settled in the Northeast: Westport, Connecticut; Ridgewood, New Jersey; and Exeter, New Hampshire. We visit you frequently, and include side trips to visit friends and enjoy the area's many attractions. In winter, you visit us in Miami, and we Skype frequently.

You have surpassed our expectations, reflecting good luck and parenting skills, and have been fortunate to find great partners. Like many Cuban-Americans, we talk almost daily and frequently more than once a day which surprise many of our American friends. By now you have become our best friends, and we hope the next stage, when we become your children, is years away. Old age has its compensations, and one is bragging with impunity about our family. As grandparents, we exercise this fundamental and inalienable right to brag about our clan; it is music to our ears when our children tell us "the fruit does not fall far from the tree." According to a wise saying, a parent is as happy as his unhappiest child; we are proud of your accomplishments.

As I indicated at the beginning of my memoir, you asked us to write about our lives; I hope you are not disappointed. Little did we how much work it would it entail, but it turned out to be a wonderful family project. We were also pleasantly surprised to learn that to remember is to live again, as the old Spanish proverb says—*recordar es volver a vivir*. It also reminded us how fortunate we have been. As we come to these final pages, I will ponder upon my yesterday, today, and tomorrow.

YESTERDAY

YOGI BERRA, THE legendary Yankee catcher and American thinker, offered advice on the art of living; according to one of my favorites "When you get to a fork, take it." During my whole life, I have adhered to Yogi's dictum; I am happy to tell you I chose the right fork in three critical decisions I made early in my journey—by careful analysis or fate.

The first decision was leaving Cuba to study at B.U. The second was choosing my profession. A Brandais University Professor teaching Far East History at a B.U. summer session saw I had aptitude for this subject, and offered help to get the scholarships necessary to pursue a Ph.D. and an academic career in this subject. I inherited some of my father's interest in the humanities, but not the money to pay for studies that require lengthy preparation and modest financial return. I decided to study finance, launched my professional career in less than three years, and obtained an extraordinary rate of return on our modest financial investment. In addition, I am very active and needed to live history. I never had a passion for finance, which was a means to an end—and passion is not an attribute applicable to how most of humanity earns a living. You pay for life's pleasures, are paid for work, and work is hard. At this stage of my life, writing my life's history for my family has been rewarding; my interest in history helped me create this family legacy, and I will indulge my passion one last time with a look at world events and technological breakthroughs that directly impacted me.

Choosing a mate was the third. It was my destiny to win life's most importat lottery; my decision was unplanned and risky, and we and our families were navigating gale force winds. It was my life's best decision. I value my *media naranja* more as we age; our backgrounds and personalities are amazingly compatible, and we discuss and plan for every eventuality—even what to do if death separates us temporarily. We own a lot at the Assumption Cemetery where the Sabins will be near the Gardiners and the Sanmartins. Our gravestone will have a cross and a two-word inscription: *Together Forever*.

My interest in history has enriched my life, and I always try to learn as much as possible about the past before I visit a country which enhances the value of each trip. I particularly like to read about the amazing personalities that created culture and civilization, as well as others who tried to enslave and destroy the human spirit. My memoir gives historical overviews of some of my trips, and hopefully my future generations will appreciate the importane of this fascinating and important subject. They should remember that those that do not learn from history will repeat the mistakes of the past.

꙳꙳꙳

The Cuban Revolution, of course, was the world event that most impacted me and every single Cuban in and out of the island. In 1961, I was very close to leaving Boston University to join the Bay of Pigs invasion; God and destiny saved me from possible death or jail, and from having derailed my studies.

For all Cubans, the Castro Revolution was a traumatic life-changing event. Sadly, it ruined my native country and caused great pain to my family; as Cubans would say, *acabó con la quinta y con los mangos*. Castro established a tyrannical regime, abolished freedom of expression, forced around two million Cubans to flee, and assassinated and sent to jail countless others. After 42 years, Libyans finally deposed their mad assassin, while Cubans continue under their madman's yoke after 53. Communism vanished hope of a better future for entire generations and many in Cuba now dream of Miami as a Shangri-La. In the trial for his Moncada attack Castro ironically said:

"History will absolve me." I am certain that history will condemn harshly the nefarious regime that has divided countless families and brought so much suffering to Cubans. It will also record that Fidel amazingly turned two million Cubans from *gusanos* to *mariposas*— from worms to butterflies.

ᴊᴊᴊ

During my 70 years, I have enjoyed excellent health. In Miami Beach I walk for miles looking at the ocean; three years ago, I started to cramp after walking just a few blocks and discovered I suffered from peripheral artery disease, commonly called intermittent claudication as the pain stops when you rest. As plaque builds up, it causes your arteries to narrow; the process is called atherosclerosis, an illness that also affected my father and grandfather. The plaque buildup interferes with blood flow in the iliac arteries, and the legs do not receive the blood and oxygen they need.

When we returned to New Hampshire, I went to see Dr. Thomas Decker, my Lebanese-American internist who has been our family doctor for many years. Tom is in his 50s, and years ago he had a triple bypass operation; he referred me to the Iranian born interventionist cardiologist that attended him, Dr. Heidar Arjomand. Dr. Arjomand decided to place stents in arteries of my left leg. The right leg iliac was so clogged that I needed an endarterectomy where an incision is made in the affected artery to remove the plaque. He referred me to Dr. Victor Kim, a young Korean-American vascular surgeon who performed the operation. I believe only in America I would receive the best possible cardiac treatment from a Lebanese-American, an Iranian-American, and a Korean-American. The surgical procedures that restored my blood flow, the critical electronic diagnostic equipment, and the preventive medicines were all newly developed. I again walk miles every day without pain, and I am training to enter the Miami marathon in the over-seventy category. Cardio vascular disease runs in my paternal ancestry, and this is an area where medicine has made great improvements.

❧❧❧❧

I have benefited from countless inventions, and I will comment on just a few that enhance my daily life:

- This book would have not seen the light without many revolutionary changes in self-publishing, including personal computers, high tech Just-in-Time techniques, internet data transmission, and others. I have gained appreciation for the amazing work done by writers in the past.
- Electronics and telecommunications impact many other aspects of my life. We helped Zuni, in her 90s, cope with these challenges; fortunately, now our grandchildren are helping us.
- The chemical industry's discovery of fiberglass enabled the construction of my boats; wooden boats have existed for millennia, are wonderful, but require extraordinary maintenance work and high carpentry skills I lack—or have very deep pockets.
- We drive many miles each year; our new car has numerous features to make our ride more comfortable, including argonomically designed seats to support my lower back, heated seats to enhance our butts' comfort, an I-Pod and remote cell phone connections, and other marvels I have yet to discover by reading the owner's manual.

❧❧❧❧

The many health related improvements I discussed earlier multiplied by a few million give you the picture: old people are living a lot longer and centenarians are no longer exceptional. This trend presents serious problems, as relatively fewer working folks must support an ever increasing number of seniors. Bismark set the retirement age at 65 when the average German moved to a cemetery at 58.

In addition to the alarming increase in older folks, the new technological wonders are already reducing the amount of personal communications and human contact around the world. Loneliness is epidemic. You now go to the internet to meet new mates; we are at the threshold of uncharted territory. From a personal viewpoint, I never felt lonely after finding my soul mate. I also enjoy interacting with other humans; I try to laugh a lot and make other people laugh with me. I now ask for the Spanish operator at Ortbitz or Travelocity; besides giving me good service, I talk to smart youngsters in Mexico, Guatemala, or other Central American nations. When I tell them how much I admire the Mayas, they cannot stop talking; I worry about getting them in trouble at work, when they talk too much.

David Brooks, the distinguished journalist, wrote a column on the October 28, 2011 New York Times asking a gift from his readers over 70: a brief report on their life and a self-evaluation and grade on five life categories—career, family, faith, community, and self-knowledge. Here is a brief version of the report and self-assessment I sent; I also revised one of my grades.

Career: B

I arrived in America as a young adult to study at B.U. In contrast, approximately 14,000 Cuban children were separated from their families from 1960 to 1962 as part of Operation Peter Pan; their families feared actions that the Communist regime might take against them. Many of these refugee children had to live with foster families and some never saw their parents again; amazingly, many have achieved great success in America. My professional accomplishments also pale in comparison with the improbable success stories of a few Cuban-Americans who rose to the top in business, politics, education, sports, entertainment, the arts and many other fields of endeavor.

America is a meritocracy, and always required hard work to earn promotions on the fast track; I was rewarded for my efforts. I came at a propitious time when a college education and hard work guaranteed a good life with unlimited opportunities. Compensation and benefits rose regularly, and each generation expected to have a better life than their parents. Life was easier, jobs more secure and less competitive, the pace of change slower: conditions that in today's world have disappeared for many. I have always worked to live and not lived to work, a philosophy at odds with America's Calvinist backbone.

For a first generation refugee, I believe I did a creditable job in my professional career, and rose to the top 1 or 2 percent of G.E.'s 400,000 employees. More importantly, my jobs enabled my family to benefit greatly by going around the world. On balance, I believe a B is a reasonable grade for my professional accomplishments.

Family: A-

As I said earlier, our family is our pride and joy. Our children have surpassed our high expectations which we believe reflects a mix of good luck and parenting skills. My family would hopefully give me a straight A in this critically important category, but I marked myself down as I believe there is always room for improvement.

Faith: Preliminary grade C+ — Final grade B

The older I get, the more I envy the deep faith of my wife Lucky, mother Esther, and mother-in-law Zuni. We have visited many of the Catholic Church's sacred sites, witnessed the fervor of the faithful, and seen the remembrances of the Virgin's countless miracles; I have good reason to hope for an afterlife. I am not a regular churchgoer, but have always tried to help others; for years I have been a volunteer driver with the American Cancer Society's Road to Recovery Program.

I was born an optimist, and believe my devout family, modest good deeds, and lack of capital sins hopefully will help me eventually join other cherubs and angels in heaven after atoning for my *peccadillos*; hopefully, I will not be kept in purgatory too long. This is an area where I could certainly use divine inspiration to improve my grade, and I wrote that I hoped to eventually earn a B.

I am delighted to report that I have raised my grade to a B. Although I, thankfully, did not get a religious or saintly calling, I have always acted with integrity and honesty, and tried to help others whenever possible. While nobody should be proud of his sins, I suspect sainthood is a rather boring profession—at least it is not for me. I am certain I have friends in heaven, and they will put a good word on my behalf. Hopefully, the God I believe in will overlook my poor church attendance record, and will look at my behavior.

Community: C+

My mobility has negatively affected my community involvement. I served on the board of our condominium association before we started spending winters in Miami. I also help with church activities. We vote in all elections: it is a privilege and obligation we never had in our native country. Additional volunteer work may help me pull this grade to a B.

Self-Knowledge: A

I credit my father for my high grade in this category. He went through a lot, was a modest man with a great sense of humor, and had an encyclopedic knowledge. He only needed a book to be happy, had an ascetic life philosophy, and accepted his fate without bitterness. I am fortunate to have inherited some of his wisdom which has helped me live more fully. I hope I have passed some of these traits and life attitudes to my family.

TODAY

IN LOOKING BACK, I like to put my identity in perspective; Lucky and I are fortunate to share the same background. A well-known Cuban-American professor, Gustavo Pérez Firmat, has studied extensively the Cuban condition in general and factors affecting Cuba-Americans' identity in particular; I suspect he is related to a close friend of my family in Cuba, Ricardo Firmat. He offers insights on the "1.5 genera-tion," representing children born in Cuba but educated and coming of age in the United States. He notes: "The 1.5 individual is unique in that, unlike younger or older compatriots, he or she may actually find it impossible to circulate within and through both the old and the new cultures. While one and a halfers may never feel entirely at ease in either one, they are capable of availing themselves of the resources—linguistic, artistic, and commercial—that both cultures have to offer." I applied Dr. Pérez Firmat's analysis to our experience:

- Lucky and I lived an unusually full life during our years in Cuba, graduated from high school, maintained close rela-tionships with our parents, speak with a distinctive Cuban accent, and are actively involved in Miami's Cuban life. We have emphasized the importance of Spanish to our children and grandchildren, and our family continues to follow Cuban traditions. Our *Cubanía* was well established when we came to America, we continue to be proud of our roots, and our Americanization never required us to forsake our heritage as many earlier immigrants had to do. We obtained high marks in an anonymous *Prueba de Cubanidad* exam of 397 ques-tions to determine how legitimate your claims to Cuban roots are.

- The United States has been our main residence for over 50 years. We appreciate our adoptive country's culture, and have been citizens for half a century. Our love of history has helped us admire the wisdom of our founding fathers, the American Constitution, and American institutions, which set the fun-damental structure for the world's longest living democracy. We first came to America involuntarily, but our return from Switzerland to California was voluntary; we decided to sac-rifice our quality of life to ensure our children grew up as American as apple pie. America has historically been a country of immigrants, and we would not have been able to fully integrate in the other countries where we lived or visited.

- Our years in Europe, travel opportunities, Cuban roots, and language skills helped us develop a greater appreciation of other cultures.

As a result of our experiences, Lucky and I are three dimensional individuals: one part Cuban, one part American, and one part multicultural; we move comfortably among different cultures, and we have been blessed to be very compatible and adaptable.

Ironically, we have repeatedly gone around the world, but never returned to our homeland as many Cuban-Americans are now doing. Remittances from Cuban-Americans are the Castro's second source of income; your maternal grandmother Zuni went to Cuba to visit ailing siblings and had to pay exorbitant fees for the necessary permits. She also sent them subsistence money from her meager Social Security income. For us, the Cuba of our dreams is like *Camelot*:

> *"It's true! It's true! The crown has made it clear*
> *the climate must be perfect all year.*
> *July and August cannot be too hot*
> *and there's a legal limit to the snow here*
> *in Camelot."*

Such an ideal place, of course, never existed; why spoil my dream by seeing a Cuba where July and August are oppressively hot, air conditioners don't work, and the King will have you beat up or killed at the slightest expression of dissent? My native country and I have changed so much in half a century. Regrettably, I am afraid that the Castros' long reign and misgovernment have inexorably condemned the people of Cuba to continue *resolviendo* until hell freezes over.

TOMORROW

MOM DIED AT 93, which gives me a reasonable genetic claim at longevity; dad died at 69, but he had to fight health problems all his life. I quit smoking years ago, go to the gym five days a week, and staples in my diet now include spinach, broccoli, and carrots. Yvonne and Alina constantly remind us to eat more proteins and vegetables, and fewer carbohydrates. I also learned from one of my bosses the need to do "mental calisthenics," a practice I adopted long ago.

The past two decades have witnessed significant extensions in the sex lives of senior citizens. Old folks are partying more than ever before. I believe in progress, and I expect even better things will come in my lifetime. Most seniors are better off today than at any time in history and hope new advances will allow me to embark on many exciting adventures.

We pray we will never use the long-term care insurance we bought many years ago. We may have to eventually buy a battery operated senior vehicle to cruise down Lincoln Road. The rest of the year, we will live in New Hampshire, hopefully in our Epping home, and may have to install an electric chair to climb up the stairs. Minerva will by then have earned her Masters degree in Nursing, and be highly qualified to keep an eye on us. I recognize we will have to adjust as we graduate from our current status of seniors-in-training; we may even have to limit our travel to cruises and organized tours.

❧❧❧❧

As the popular 2007 film "The Bucket List" with Morgan Freeman and Jack Nicholson shows, everybody who wants to live life abundantly has a list of dreams and wishes to accomplish before leaving this earth. Dreamers are central characters in Spanish literature. For example, Cervantes' Don Quixote insisted in dreaming that *Dulcinea* was a lady and not the wench she really was. We named our sailboat *Dulcinea* for our "possible dream." Daydreaming has been one of my follies, and I pinch myself every day that my life turned out better than my wildest fantasy.

I occasionally buy a Power Ball ticket— particularly when there are no winners for weeks and the main prize reaches astronomical levels. I will tell you a secret: Lucky prays we never win the lottery as she doubts my ability to resist the multiple temptations that accompany great wealth. I believe she should have move faith in me, as I have already won many priceless jackpots that have not even required paying a penny of taxes.

Here are four items in **our** bucket list:

1. Health and independence with family love until we move to our final residence at the Assumption Cemetery in Westport.
2. Travel, occassionally with our grandchildren; I would like to take my grandsons Andrew and Lucas to Paris, where we will visit the Louvre during the day—and the Follies Bergère in the evening.
3. Publish the sequel to my memoir, with the title *Our Octogenarian Adventures: The Last Twenty Years Around the World* on our seventieth wedding anniversary in 2032.
4. Visit a free Cuba with our family; look for my grandparents' grave at *Cementerio de Colón* and for Lucky's at the Matanzas Cemetery.

According to an old Spanish proverb, *no hay mal que por bien no venga;* or, you will ultimately benefit from adverse events. In my case, my unhappiest days occurred when my family and I had to leave Cuba. We absorbed these shocks in my journey, and we went on to have fulfilling lives.

According to an article in *The Economist*, recently published research shows that beyond middle age, people get happier as they grow older. Our Cuban-American journey supports these conclusions— we are still healthy, happily married, and have no financial worries. We are enjoying the fruits of our parenting job, and you are applying the lessons learned from us to raise our six grandchildren. We also cherish the many old and new friends we have made in our journey, and enjoy our calendar: winter in Miami, summer and fall in New Hampshire, and, in between, a few weeks of adventures around the globe.

Experts predict that in the new America work will be a forever endeavor for most, and the number of working Americans over 65 in the labor market is increasing dramatically. It is extraordinary that I arrived as a refugee at 18, retired at 55, and have enjoyed an enviable life for a very long time. In reality, only the first item in our Bucket List is truly important: health, idependence, and love.

Every day when we wake up, we thank God to be alive and for all the blessings He bestowed on Lucky and Paco. As an addict to the New York Times Sunday obituaries, where an interesting life is a requirement, I see many meet their creator at a young age while others enjoy vital lives into their 90s. We are each given a finite number of days. Hopefully, our destiny is to enjoy family and friends for years to come. GOD KNOWS, THE BEST IS YET TO COME!

Colorín colorado,
Este cuento se ha acabado

GLOSSARY

I have used some Spanish words and *cubanismos* to spice up my memoir; only Cubans know this colorful folklore which, I believe, enriches the Spanish language. Two of my favorite sources are Antonio Carbajo's *"El Millón Catorce de Dicharachos Cubanos,"* and an anonymous *Prueba de Cubanidad* with 397 questions to determine how legitimate your claims to Cuban roots are. Below is a glossary of selected Spanish words and *Cubanismos,* referencing where they appear in my memoir.

LETTER TO MY CHILDREN

en la Cuba de ayer	in yesteryear Cuba

MY BIRTH AND FAMILY

consentido, el hijo de la vejez	parents dotted on child of old age
bodeguero	owner or worker in a grocery store
nació con una cuchara de plata en la nuca	born with a silver spoon in the neck
vidriera	glass stand to sell goods

MEMORIES OF MY HOMES

HAVANA, CUBA—GOLDEN CHILDHOOD YEARS

17 ENTRE 14 Y 16 VEDADO: 1940-1947

afilador de tijeras	a sharpener of scissors and knives, usually a Chinese
en las nalgas	in the butt
música sacra	glass stand to sell goods

F Y 15, VEDADO: 1947-1949

mosquitero	mosquito net
bohío	country hut where country folk live
teatrico	small theater
palmiche	palm tree leaves
guajiritos	young country folk; anybody outside Havana
Habaneros	Havana residents

F ENTRE 13 Y 15, VEDADO: 1949-1951

barrio de Llega y Pón Possession	slum called Arrive and Take
policía, nos matan; auxilio, socorro	police, they are killing us, help
Remanganagua	fictional town in the bunnies
pelota	base-ball, a national obsession

88 ENTRE 9 Y 11, AMPLIACIÓN DE ALMENDARES: 1952-1955

Cabrón	*My* goat's name; swear word; S.O.B.
lavandera	woman who washes clothing
Feria Ganadera	agricultural fair, which included animals and horse shows
cola de pato	1950s tailfin Cadillac, the ultimate luxury symbol
señoritas	young virgins, frequently desirable
Jutías	muskrats

POTÍN, PASEO Y LINEA, VEDADO: 1956-1959

el bajito	sandbar
el cayito	very small key
marineros	sailors
pesca del alto	deep water fishing
chambel	wire with fishing hooks attached
plomada	sink
pargo	red snapper
cherna	grouper
bichero	fish hook
pico	beak
barbudos	bearded revolutionaries, Fidel's followers
fusilamiento	shooting, execution
esbirros	Batista followers
gusanos	worms; name given to Castro's opponents
nos dejaron como al gallo de Morón, sin plumas y cacareando	left penniless

WILMINGTON, DELAWARE—START PROFESSION AND FAMILY: 1962-1969

un pollo	a beautiful "chick"
Paco, te llevas la crema; espera a que conozcas a tu suegra, Zunilda	Paco you are getting the best; and wait until you meet your mother-in-law, Zunilda

SANTO DOMINGO, DOMINICAN REPUBLIC, LA TALANQUERA: 1984-1986

bohío	country hut
negrita con trencitas	little black girl with braids

MIAMI FLORIDA: CUBAN-AMERICAN SNOW BIRDS: 1995-PRESENT

el negrito del batey	poor black farm boy
por amor al arte	work for free
maricones	homosexuals
culos	butts
tetas	breasts
tarros	infidelity
chusmería	low class behavior

PEARLS OF WISDOM

que me quiten lo bailao	nobody can take away what you have done
la dolce far niente	Italian expression: the sweetness of doing nothing
la joi de vivre	French expression: the joy of living

YESTERDAY, TODAY, TOMORROW

Media naranja	endearing term for wife
Colorín, colorado, este cuento se ha acabado	Expression that Cuban parents tell their little children after reading them a book, when its time to go to sleep—the end of a story

CPSIA information can be obtained at www.ICGtesting.com
Printed in the USA
BVOW011320180412

288007BV00004B/1/P

9 781432 781774